Previous page: Off-the-grid house on the Oregon coast where rainwater is collected in a scupper. The timber posts on the right provide structural bracing.

This page: The 'm-house' (pronounced 'mouse') is a movable home that leaves the site as it was found. Designed by British architect Tim Pyne, it is fully fitted, highly insulated and incorporates high-specification Scandinavian windows.

IMPRINT

First published in 2009 by Conran Octopus Ltd,
a part of Octopus Publishing Group,
2–4 Heron Quays, London E14 4JP
www.octopusbooks.co.uk

An Hachette Livre UK Company
www.hachettelivre.co.uk

Distributed in the United States and Canada
by Hachette Book Group USA,
237 Park Avenue, New York, NY 10017

British Library Cataloguing-in-Publication Data. A catalogue
record for this book is available from the British Library.

Consultant Editor: Elizabeth Wilhide

Publisher: Lorraine Dickey
Managing Editor: Sybella Marlow
Editor: Zia Mattocks

Art Direction & Design: Jonathan Christie
Colour Illustrations: Colin Wilkin
Picture Researcher: Nadine Bazar

Production Manager: Katherine Hockley

ISBN: 978 1 84091 522 8
Printed in China

DEDICATION

To Barack and Michelle Obama, Gordon and Sarah Brown,
Nicolas and Carla Sarkozy and their friends in China, Russia
and India, and to Green parties throughout the world. Please
read this book and help to make the world a safer and better
place for our children and us.

To Liz Wilhide, my co-author, for the major contribution you
have made to this important book. I would be lost without you.

Thanks also to Matt Wood at Conran & Partners for his
invaluable green building advice.

Terence Conran

ECO
HOUSE BOOK

TERENCE CONRAN

conran
OCTOPUS

This page: Turbulence House, designed by Steven Holl, is situated on top of a windy desert mesa in New Mexico. Composed of 32 prefabricated parts, its form is designed to allow turbulent local winds to blow through its centre.

Below: Photovoltaic panels on the roof of the Papal Audience Hall in Vatican City, Rome. Some 2,400 panels are being installed on the roof of Paul VI Hall to generate clean electricity. St Peter's Basilica is in the background.

Next page: A large opening leading to a sunny deck provides natural ventilation for an eco-friendly house in Napa Valley, California.

INTRODUCTION

This is my fifth *House Book*. Although I have touched on environmental issues before, here I will be looking at everything to do with the home – design, servicing, decoration and furnishing – from the eco point of view. Until relatively recently, green issues were seen as an alternative, a sideline from the mainstream. Now sustainability is the 'new normal', part and parcel of what it means to design and live responsibly and well.

Buildings are the biggest polluters on the planet, responsible for a far greater proportion of the carbon dioxide emissions that get pumped into the atmosphere every year than cars, planes or factories. I was surprised to learn that in the UK, for example, domestic households account for roughly between one-quarter and one-third of total emissions. The statistics will vary from country to country but the potential for change on the home front is obvious. Just as we are urged to change our lifestyles to reduce our carbon footprint and consumption of water, there is a great deal we can do to convert our existing homes into greener, healthier places to live…

Left: Designed by Bruno Pantz, this Swiss eco house has a timber structure and red cedar cladding. The house is oriented to benefit from passive solar gain and is highly insulated.

Most homes, even those built relatively recently, are not decorated, designed, constructed or serviced with eco-friendliness in mind. But you don't have to start again from scratch to make a huge difference to the impact your home has on the environment. From relatively small and economic changes to more dramatic overhauls, there has never been a better time to green your home.

Home improvement has a wider remit these days than simply changing the way your home looks or functions. Environmental issues should be part of every decision you make on the home front – from selecting fabric for soft furnishings to designing and siting a home extension. The purpose of this book is to provide all the information you need to enable you to reduce your home's carbon footprint and in the process directly improve the quality of your life.

In ancient Greek the closest word for 'home' or 'house' is ecos. 'Ecology', the study of the interrelationships between living individuals and their environment, was first used in its modern sense by a Danish botanist, the wonderfully named Eugenius Warming, in the late nineteenth century. Around the same time an Austrian geologist, Eduard Suess, coined the term 'biosphere'. But it was in the 1970s that ecology emerged as a distinct discipline that investigated, in particular, the impact of human activity on the environment. The slogan 'think globally, act locally' came out of a United Nations conference in Stockholm in 1972. Later in the same decade James Lovelock published his *Gaia* hypothesis, which controversially proposed that the earth is a single living macro-organism. *Gaia* is the Greek word for 'land'.

My first *House Book* was published in 1974, when the world was in the grips of an energy crisis. In response to renewed conflict in the Middle East, OPEC raised the price of oil and placed an embargo on shipping it to Japan and the West, allies of Israel in the Yom Kippur War. That embargo lasted from autumn 1973 to spring 1974. As fuel shortages began to bite and petrol stations across the United States ran dry, rationing was introduced and gas-guzzlers sat unsold on dealers' lots. In Britain, the winter of 1973–4 saw the 'three-day week', when high oil prices, coinciding with a miners' strike, resulted in nationwide power cuts and shops and workplaces lit by candlelight. Western economies suffered. Stock exchanges fell sharply, while the deadly

combination of slow growth and high inflation resulted in 'stagflation', an economist's worst nightmare.

For the first time, serious consideration was given to alternative sources of energy – harnessing the renewable power of wind, waves, sun and tide. The aftereffects of this shift in thinking soon trickled down to popular culture. In 1975 the BBC aired the first series of *The Good Life*, a popular and long-lasting sitcom that contrasted, to comic effect, one couple's attempt to live self-sufficiently with the materialistic lifestyle of their neighbours.

That was then. This is now. In the present economic climate, and with every day bringing new evidence of the harm our dependency on fossil fuels has done and is doing to the planet, sustainable, self-sufficient living looks less and less eccentric and more like common sense.

At the beginning of the twentieth-first century it is undeniable that climate change brought about by global warming poses a serious threat to life on earth. Faced with the scale of the problem and the apparent inability of the international community to set and enforce targets to reduce carbon emissions on a global scale, it is understandable that many people have felt that their own efforts to live a greener lifestyle amount to little more than a drop in a leaky bucket. But I think there are signs that this attitude is changing.

On 1 May 2007 a small town in south Devon, UK, became the first in Europe to go plastic-bag-free. Modbury is the home of documentary filmmaker Rebecca Hosking. It was when working on *Message in the Waves*, a documentary shot in Hawaii for the BBC, that Rebecca became aware of the severe impact plastic pollution was having on marine wildlife. A telling sequence in the film shows a Hawaiian green turtle swallowing a plastic bag, which can prove lethal – it is estimated that 100,000 marine creatures are killed by ingesting plastic every year. To her horror, she discovered that the world consumes one million plastic bags per minute, each person using a plastic bag for an average of 12 minutes before discarding it. A huge proportion of those bags, along with other plastic rubbish, finds its way into the sea. When she returned home to Modbury, she was determined to do something about it. After an innovative and spirited campaign, she managed to persuade Modbury's traders to switch from plastic bags to cloth bags, paper bags, cardboard boxes and

Right: Living or green roofs replace land lost to construction, help to insulate houses and create habitats for local wildlife. In addition to the green roof, this productive London garden includes a wormery, compost bins, rainwater harvesting, a bird sanctuary and hawthorn trees planted to attract wildlife.

other recyclable carriers. The result was a huge success and gained widespread media coverage.

I don't think there is any coincidence in the fact that shortly after many of Britain's leading supermarkets began actively discouraging the use of plastic bags much more and promoting reusable alternatives. Walk down the average high street today and you see more and more people toting their groceries in cloth or jute bags. In fact, I have just opened a little food shop in Shoreditch, London, where customers can take away their purchases in a rather chic cloth bag. Soon asking for a plastic bag at the checkout will be to invite acute social embarrassment. In Delhi it could even result in a hefty fine or possible prison sentence. Faced with a mounting waste problem – an estimated ten million plastic bags are used in the city every day – officials have decided to ban them and put draconian penalties in place.

Giving up plastic bags is not going to save the planet on its own, but what the Modbury campaign demonstrates is that people can change their habits once they are made aware of the link between what they are doing, almost unthinkingly, and the possible harm it poses for the environment. Multiply that one change by many others, equally simple – turning the thermostat down a couple of degrees or switching off the television, for example – and there is real potential for improvement.

Dramatic change can be provoked by natural disaster. In May 2007 Greensburg in southern Kansas was devastated by a huge tornado over 2.5 km (1.5 miles) wide with winds measuring over 325 km (200 miles) per hour. Almost nothing was left standing. In the wake of the tornado, city officials decided to take the bold step to rebuild Greensburg as 'the greenest town in America'. The city council passed a resolution that all major municipal buildings were to be built to the highest standard of efficiency and sustainability and a number of developing green technologies are currently being implemented to transform the town into a prototype of sustainable development. Many of the 1,500 local residents have decided independently to reconstruct their homes with green building materials and to high standards of energy efficiency and insulation.

Communities working together at the grassroots level can play a key role in reducing carbon emissions, applying pressure from the ground up. President Bush may have been reluctant to sign up to the Kyoto Protocol on global warming, but that did not prevent Al Gore's film *An Inconvenient Truth* from reaching a wide audience. Mayors of more than 740 American cities, representing a quarter of the country's population, have independently pledged to meet the Kyoto agreement, despite the previous lack of enthusiasm in Washington, while California's governor, Arnold Schwarzenegger, has put environmental issues centre stage in that state. The Eco Mom Alliance, founded in the United States, has had a significant impact raising awareness through campaigns such as 'One Night Off', where households were encouraged to do without energy for an evening. On an even smaller scale, in a number of communities throughout Britain, local groups ('Crags' or carbon rationing action groups) have come together to set themselves personal targets for carbon reduction. The support and encouragement such groups provide is similar to that offered by websites such as the Guardian newspaper's *Tread Lightly*, which encourages users to make their own green pledges. For eco-minded Americans and everyone else who is concerned about climate change, President Obama brings hope at last.

Germany is a country with a good environmental record and currently has 200 times the installed solar capacity of the UK. One reason for this is the fact that the government allows surplus energy generated domestically to be sold back to the grid at a premium price, which makes switching to renewable sources of energy more cost-effective and attractive for the average consumer. Even so, there has still been the need for individual campaigns and local action. When one such campaigner, Ulla Gahn, decided to switch to a green power supplier, she found it difficult to weigh up the alternatives. After she had done her research, friends asked for her advice to do the same, so she started organizing parties where information could be exchanged. These were so successful that they have now spread nationwide.

Many of the most successful environmental schemes are community based, with green awareness spreading like a 'good virus' from house to house, or perhaps like a green version of keeping up with the Joneses. To give the British government its due, its commitment that all new homes built in Britain by 2016 will be zero-carbon is far-sighted and bold. But that leaves the vast proportion of the country's existing housing stock in serious need of eco-upgrading.

Left: Timber is a popular green choice for structural systems, cladding and internal finishes. Care must be taken to source the material from sustainable, managed plantations and to avoid any species that is endangered. The covered first-floor deck at Boundary House, Kent, designed by Michael Winter, shows the timber structure made of glulam beams.

In one sense, living an eco-friendly life means returning to simpler ways. What one leading retailer is currently marketing as 'turtle-friendly' carriers, people of my generation recognize as the humble string bag. I grew up during the Second World War, a time of 'make do and mend', when every family was encouraged to 'dig for victory', to grow their own vegetables, keep a pig and a few chickens, and make their own compost. Petrol rationing meant that if you wanted to go somewhere, you got on your bike. Those years, and the postwar period of austerity that followed, have given me a lifelong hatred of waste, a strong inclination to repair rather than discard, and a preference for quality products and materials that stand the test of time.

Today, at Barton Court, my house in the country, we could do better, but we do grow our own vegetables for the table, make our own compost and collect rainwater, gardening organically as far as possible. Benchmark, my furniture business, which is based in outbuildings near the house, recently won a Queen's Award for Sustainability. The factory uses only FSC-certified wood, never endangered or exotic hardwoods such as rosewood or teak, and generates its own heat by burning chewed-up off-cuts, which produce a more intense heat than logs. My firm of architects, Conran & Partners, is currently working on an eco development that will be powered by biomass.

What I find interesting, in these days of fast food, online shopping and computer games, is that there is clearly an appetite for a return to a slower and more satisfying way of living. You can see this in the resurgence of interest in knitting, for example, and in making one's own clothes, and in the huge demand for allotments. More and more people are growing beautiful vegetables, not flowers, in their back gardens, getting on their bikes to go to work and buying local produce in farmers' markets. They're doing this not because government legislation tells them to, but because they find it enjoyable and more fulfilling, just as I grow my own vegetables because I prefer the way they taste.

In many ways, reducing consumption is the key to sustainable living. It's not simply a case of reducing consumption of energy or of water. It also means buying less, but buying better things – as the saying goes, 'you buy cheap, you buy twice'.

But low-tech is not the only route to a greener lifestyle. Technology can also deliver benefits. To take one small example, we are constantly being urged to turn off the red buttons on our electronic equipment. Sleeping computers and televisions on standby consume 85 per cent of the energy that they use in an active mode. For many people, however, old habits die hard. Now, with 'kill switches' available, which will do the legwork for you and turn off all those red buttons with a single zap, even the laziest couch potato has no excuse.

More than anything else, however, what people really need is information so that they can make effective choices that will cut their carbon footprints and water consumption along with their bills. How much carbon will you save if you insulate your home properly? What is more effective, a rooftop wind turbine or solar panels? What type of water-saving fixtures and fittings are available and how efficient are they? This book is designed to provide those answers.

What you won't find here are guilt-inducing doomsday scenarios. There are enough of them in the papers and I believe they can be counterproductive. I have always been optimistic about the role design can play in improving the quality of people's lives. Today, more than ever before, intelligent design and green design are one and the same.

Terence Conran

Right: Wooden buildings have always been very common in Nordic countries, where timber is plentiful. This vacation house in the Stockholm archipelago is made entirely of wood sourced from managed Swedish forests. No sealants or paints were applied to the exterior. The house is highly insulated and the only heat source is a fireplace, fuelled by dead wood collected from fallen trees.

SERVICING

Left: The Lighthouse, designed by British architects Sheppard Robson, is the UK's first net zero-carbon house. A combined windcatcher/ light tunnel encourages passive ventilation and draws natural light down into the interior.

Over the years we have grown used to flicking on a light switch when it gets dark, turning up the thermostat when we feel cold, and running the tap as and when we feel like it. But the days of cheap energy are gone, and so are the days of treating water as if it was a virtually free and limitless resource. To live within our means, we need to reduce consumption and look for alternative means of supply.

ECO AUDIT

Before you can make effective changes, you need to audit your lifestyle to identify areas that need improvement. The first step is to calculate how much water and carbon you use. There are several ways you can do this. One is to call in an independent assessor, who will work out your individual energy and water consumption and make recommendations about how you can reduce them. Another is to use online calculators – there are many sites on the Internet and the best and most reliable are listed at the back of this book. Either way, you will need to equip yourself with a year's worth of utility bills, work out your annual mileage both by car and by other forms of transport, and think about your patterns of shopping and the associated waste entailed.

COUNTING THE CARBON COST

Global warming, which is responsible for climate change, is caused by the huge increase of greenhouse gases that have been pumped into the atmosphere over the last century or so. There are many greenhouse gases, including methane, nitrous oxide and CFCs (chlorofluorocarbons), but the most serious in its impact is carbon dioxide (CO_2), which is produced by burning fossil fuels, such as coal, oil and gas, and through deforestation – trees remove CO_2 from the atmosphere, so fewer trees means more CO_2.

One of the current problems associated with persuading people to change their habits is that there is no agreed way of measuring the effect we are having on the environment. At present, the most workable model is the carbon footprint, which expresses what each individual contributes to greenhouse gas emissions in terms of tonnes of CO_2. To give some points of comparison: the average US carbon footprint is about 20 tonnes, with the Australians not far behind, whereas in Britain that figure is around 11 tonnes. The average Ethiopian, however, is responsible for a mere 0.01 tonne. For the world to live sustainably, each person would have to be responsible for only 1 tonne's worth of emissions.

A carbon footprint looks at three principal areas: energy consumed in the home for heating, cooling and electricity; energy consumed in travel; and other forms of indirect consumption – in other words, what you buy and the services you use. It is relatively straightforward to calculate direct energy consumption, but indirect consumption is harder to quantify.

Every single product you buy costs energy, from the energy that goes into the raw materials of which it is made, to the processing entailed in its manufacture, and its subsequent transportation, packaging and marketing. Most carbon footprint calculators look at household income, lifestyle and shopping habits to come up with an estimated figure for indirect consumption. Obviously, someone who buys a good deal of convenience food, spends a lot of money on new clothes and is the first to have the latest electronic gadget is going to have a bigger footprint than someone who is thrifty, grows their own vegetables and is a dedicated recycler.

SMART METERS

Quarterly bills mean that people are always making decisions about energy use in retrospect. A large bill may make you wince and think about turning off the lights more often, but in practice such resolutions tend to last about as long as the ones you make at New Year. Smart meters, which give accurate real-time information about energy consumption, provide a much more powerful incentive. Two types are available. The wireless version shows you how much electricity your home is consuming at any given time and how much this is costing you.

Left: Smart meters allow people to see at a glance how much energy they are consuming at any given time and make economies on the spot. They have been shown to act as a powerful incentive for cutting energy wastage.

Above: Conserving water is another key part of the eco lifestyle, and not simply for those who live in hot climates where droughts are common. Collecting rainwater is one strategy.

The plug-in version identifies which appliances are using the most electricity. Recent trials have shown that once people saw how much power they were wasting it became much easier to change ingrained habits. The huge spikes that occurred when the kettle, toaster or tumble dryer were used provided a graphic demonstration of where the energy – and money – was being spent. Seeing the levels plummet when electronic equipment was switched off rather than left on standby was equally persuasive.

What smart meters graphically reveal is that the highest consumers of energy are appliances that generate heat or remove it. This means appliances such as ovens, electric or tumble dryers, air conditioners, electric fans, toasters, coffee makers and kettles are high up on the list. Standard tungsten bulbs, which emit 95 per cent of their energy as heat, also consume a lot of power.

Perhaps surprisingly, about a third of household electricity consumption is accounted for by electronic equipment. That figure, on current estimates, looks set to rise. Large plasma-screen TVs devour energy. Listening to the radio through a digital TV consumes 50 times more energy than listening to an analogue radio.

WATER

Why worry about water, especially if you live in a country such as Britain, where rain often stops play? The answer is that climate change, which has brought severe floods to some areas that have never experienced them before and severe drought to others, affects everyone on the planet. A flood in a wheat-growing region halfway across the world, which ruins the crop, will drive up the price of bread in your shopping basket. A drought in an arable area will increase the demand for expensive imported foodstuffs.

When we think about our water consumption, we only tend to consider what we use directly – the water we drink and the water we use in cooking, washing and gardening. With water metering on the increase, more of us are becoming aware of our levels of consumption and perhaps taking steps to reduce them. What we don't think about very often is what environmentalists call 'virtual' water, which is the water that is consumed to produce food, cotton and paper, among other products. In countries that rely heavily on imports, a high proportion of the national water footprint may be generated abroad. The United States has the biggest water footprint in the world. Other countries that have high water consumption are Greece, Italy and Spain. Britain has a water footprint about half that of the United States, but a greater proportion of it is generated externally.

Calculating your water footprint, which can be done online in the same way as calculating your carbon footprint, takes into account both direct uses of water and indirect or 'virtual' uses. As with carbon, direct uses are easy to measure. Do you take showers or baths? Do you have a swimming pool? How often do you wash the car or water the garden? Indirect uses are more bound up with the way you shop and the type of lifestyle you have. If your diet includes a high proportion of meat, for example, your water footprint will be bigger – it takes 16,000 litres (4,228 gallons) of water to produce 1 kg (2¼ lb) of beef and 2,400 litres (634 gallons) to produce a hamburger. If you prefer coffee to tea, your water footprint will be bigger – it takes 140 litres (37 gallons) of water to produce a single cup of coffee, compared to the 35 litres (9 gallons) it takes to produce a cup of tea. Clothing also has associated water costs – 2,000 litres (528 gallons) goes into a cotton T-shirt, 8,000 litres (2,114 gallons) into a pair of leather shoes.

ENERGY

Below: Large-scale solar power installations are an increasingly common sight in some parts of the world.

Right: Wind turbines are a form of renewable energy that generate considerable controversy. Critics point to their high embodied energy.

We use energy in the home in many ways, both directly and indirectly. In developed countries, a high proportion of energy is used to moderate the climate indoors and bring it to within a comfortable range, either by heating or by cooling. Another significant use is to power appliances, electronic equipment and artificial lighting. Then there are the indirect costs that are implicated in what we buy and how much waste we produce.

In many countries the energy infrastructure is well out of date. Typically a small number of large power stations, either ageing nuclear plants or generators that burn fossil fuels, deliver electricity to individual homes via a national grid. Other lines of supply transport oil or gas over thousands of miles, from where the fuel is extracted and processed, to domestic households where it is burned in furnaces or boilers to provide heat. Organizations such as Greenpeace have pointed out the inherent waste in this type of system. The average UK power plant loses two-thirds of the energy it produces before it ever reaches our homes, a great proportion of it disappearing up into the atmosphere via the cooling towers.

In some parts of the world significant attempts have been made to move away from these wasteful centralized sources of power, with their unsustainable dependence on finite and harmful fossil fuels. A number of cities in Sweden, Denmark, Holland and Germany, for example, have invested in what is known as 'combined heat and power', or CHP, building small generating plants capable of supplying both heat and electricity to local areas and communities. Many of these are powered by biomass, generally waste wood and straw; others produce biogas from waste, which minimizes emissions. Because CHP plants are on a small scale and sit among the communities they serve, there is also less energy wastage associated with transporting power over long distances.

Here, it is important to make the distinction between biomass and biofuels, although the terms are often used interchangeably. Biomass is waste material. Biofuels, which have been promoted as an alternative to oil, particularly for transport purposes, are extracted from crops grown on land that would otherwise be producing food. The rising investment in biofuels has been identified as contributing significantly to current world food shortages.

In the future, it is possible that CHP generators, supplemented both by renewable energy from the sun, wind, waves and tides, and domestic power generation of various kinds, will replace those centralized dinosaurs. Right now, it might surprise many people to know that it is *energy efficiency* that is our single greatest source of power. Taking steps to save energy is what every individual can do.

SAVING ENERGY

Saving energy should be just as instinctive as putting on your seat belt when you get into the car. Turning off lights, turning the TV off standby mode, unplugging equipment and turning down the thermostat cost nothing and will save you money into the bargain. For slightly more effort and expense, simple changes like improvements to insulation will bring big energy-saving benefits and quickly recoup their cost. In some cases, when you save energy you save water, too (see page 58). Cutting down on waste (see page 172) also reduces indirect consumption.

HEATING

- Lower your thermostat by one degree C and save 240 kg (529 lb) of CO_2 per year. If you feel cold, put on another layer. A cooler temperature is healthier and makes you more active.
- Turn the heat right down at night. Warm beds with hot-water bottles not electric blankets.
- Turn off your heating when you are not at home. Don't heat an empty house.
- Keep furniture and curtains away from radiators to prevent them from blocking heat.
- Draw curtains at night to keep heat in rooms. Lined or interlined curtains are more insulating.
- Place foil panels behind radiators to reflect heat into the room.
- Fit radiators with thermostatic controls so that you can control heat levels in each room.
- Fit hot water cylinders or tanks with thermostats and make sure the temperature is no higher than 60ºC (140ºF).
- If you have gas central heating and your boiler is coming to the end of its life, install a new condensing boiler, which is highly efficient.
- Take short showers instead of baths to save the energy that goes into heating water.
- Sign up to a green energy provider that invests in renewable schemes. There is no proof that 'green tariffs' offered by standard power companies are actually invested in renewables.
- Have your boiler regularly serviced so that it operates as efficiently as possible. If your home is heated with a forced-air system, change the filters regularly.

INSULATION

- Insulate your hot water tank or cylinder and lag hot water pipes.
- Install cavity wall insulation.
- Install or upgrade loft insulation.
- Insulate under floors if possible.
- Draught-proof windows and doors and cover letterboxes and keyholes.
- Double- and triple-glazed windows keep in the heat. Fit low-E glass in areas where you have extensive glazing, such as in a conservatory (see page 136).

APPLIANCES

- If you are replacing an old appliance, opt for the most energy efficient, which will typically consume a third less energy. In Britain, the most efficient appliances are graded A**. In the United States, look for Energy Guide or Energy Star labels. A number of websites also allow you to compare the energy consumption of different brands – there can be a great variation in power consumption between one model and another.
- Defrost your fridge and clean dust off the coils at the rear on a regular basis so that it runs more efficiently. Site it away from ovens or boilers so that it doesn't have to work too hard. Don't leave the door open for the same reason. Check the seals to make sure that the doors to the fridge and freezer compartments close properly. Don't put hot or warm food straight into the fridge – let it cool first.
- Defrost your freezer regularly. If you have a chest freezer, put it in a cool environment, such as a basement or garage, where it won't have to work so hard.
- Freezers work best when they are stocked to near capacity. Refrigerators, on the other hand, are most efficient when they are no more than three-quarters full.
- Make sure that you run full loads in the washing machine and dishwasher, and wash at lower temperatures or on eco settings – 30ºC.
- Some dishwashers and washing machines have a 'hot fill' feature that allows them to be connected directly to your home's hot water supply. This means that the hot water can be heated without using electricity, for example by a solar thermal panel.
- Only boil as much water in a kettle as you need. If you are only making one cup of tea, only boil a cup of water. A new 'eco' kettle features a central reservoir and a measuring button that releases the required amount of water for boiling into a separate chamber.
- When you are cooking on a hob or stove, use the right size ring for the size of the pan. If you put a small pan on a large ring, 40 per cent of energy you are consuming will be wasted heating the air. Unless the recipe states otherwise, cover pans so that the contents heat more quickly.
- Turn off your oven five minutes before the recommended cooking time. It will maintain sufficient heat to cook the food.
- Energy-efficient ways of cooking include using pressure cookers, steamers and microwaves. Toasters use less energy than grills. Convection ovens use less energy than standard ones.
- Try to avoid using the dryer. In warm or dry weather, dry clothes outside on a line. Alternatively, you can use a ceiling-mounted wooden clothes rack on pulleys or a similar kind of airer. If you must have a dryer, choose a model that has a fast spin cycle, which dries clothes more quickly, and remember to clean the lint filter regularly to ensure that it works most efficiently.
- Relax your standards a little. Sweep or mop instead of frequent vacuuming. Reuse towels rather than washing them straight away.
- Give up the hairdryer and towel your hair dry instead.

LIGHTING

– Get into the habit of switching off lights when you leave a room.
– Switch to energy-saving bulbs, particularly for those lights you use most in your home.
– Make the most of natural light to avoid unnecessary use of artificial lighting (see page 54).
– If you keep the lights burning when you are away from home as a security precaution, put them on a timer so they aren't left on all the time.
– Use solar-powered lights in the garden.

ELECTRONIC EQUIPMENT

– Switch it off! Don't leave TVs, DVDs, set-top boxes, stereos, amplifiers, printers and other electronic equipment on standby. A DVD player on standby is still using 85 per cent of the energy that it uses when you are actually watching it.
– Turn off your computer when you are not using it. Computers in sleeping mode use almost as much energy as they do when they are being used.
– Laptops are more energy-efficient than desktop computers.
– Unplug chargers, for example mobile phone chargers, after you have finished charging. A charger that is warm to the touch is still drawing energy, even if you have taken away the charged device.
– Resist the temptation to upgrade to energy-hungry equipment, such as plasma TVs.
– Only switch on the television when there is something you want to watch. Don't leave it on in the background all the time.

USEFUL GADGETS

I am the last person to advise anyone to buy a gadget on the basis that it will make life easier. So many of those household contraptions that people are tempted into buying end up languishing in the back of cupboards or taking up valuable space on the countertop. And if they are in regular use, they are often performing tasks that could easily be accomplished with a minimum of effort. Who really needs an electric tin opener? When it comes to saving energy, however, there are a few devices that really do help.

– The first are smart meters, which give you the information you need about your patterns of energy consumption (see page 24). These don't cost much and some electricity companies are considering providing them free to their customers in the near future.

– Standby savers or kill switches, which enable you to switch off all those devices that are normally left on standby at the press of a button, are another good idea. One type of standby saver looks like a standard extension cable. You plug all the equipment you would normally leave on standby into the sockets and then when you use the remote control to switch off the TV, power is cut to the other devices, too.
– If your home is being fully rewired, or if you are building from scratch, kill switching can also be achieved by doubling up the power circuits. One circuit supplies power to appliances that need to stay on all the time, such as fridges, as well as appliances that we are accustomed to switching off, such as lights and irons. The other circuit supplies power to appliances that are often left on standby. These can then be centrally switched off after use or at night.

Left: Save energy by using appliances such as dishwashers and washing machines on cool cycles.

Right: Energy-efficient light bulbs use considerably less power than standard tungsten bulbs. Tungsten bulbs are now being phased out in many countries.

Far right: Choose appliances that have the highest ratings for energy efficiency and water consumption.

HEATING

If you live in a temperate part of the world, keeping your home warm will account for well over half of the energy you use. Significant carbon savings can be made by improving insulation, upgrading existing boilers or furnaces, or switching to alternative and renewable sources of supply.

PASSIVE STRATEGIES

Nowadays we tend to view our homes in a rather mechanistic way, as containers that we heat up or cool down depending on what the weather's like at any given time. This hasn't always been the case. Traditional or vernacular dwellings, from the yurt to the igloo, have long displayed a more holistic design approach based on accommodating both prevailing conditions and site specifics. In cool climates, that often meant orienting a building towards the south to benefit from passive solar gain, sheltering it with earth and arranging living spaces in a tight plan around a central heat-producing core. The Chinese construct brick sleeping platforms that incorporate a small fireplace – the mattress goes on top, providing a nice warm bed for the night.

Most of us do not have the opportunity to build a new home from scratch. We can't change the orientation of our house, raise it up if it sits in a cool hollow or turn it around so that it is not exposed to prevailing winds. Nevertheless, there are a number of passive strategies that can be employed to reduce dependence on supplementary heating.

Perhaps the single most effective passive strategy is improving insulation to keep the heat in (see page 32). Other approaches make use of solar gain – the warming power of the sun's rays. These include:
– Making the most of south-facing elevations by enlarging windows or openings so that the greatest advantage can be taken of the sun's energy.
– Building in flexibility with respect to living arrangements. If you have enough space, it can be a good idea to replan the layout on a seasonal basis, so that in the winter you sleep at the top of the house where warm air accumulates and in the summer you sleep downstairs where it is cooler.
– Using massive materials, such as brick, stone and concrete, which warm up slowly and release heat slowly. During the day, these materials will store the heat of the sun, and then release it gradually overnight – the same principle as putting a brick inside a storage heater.

Right: Large openings allow heat from the sun to penetrate into the interior and reduce the need for supplementary heating.

Far right: This zero-carbon house is so well insulated and has such a high degree of airtightness that very little additional heating is required.

INSULATION

Improving insulation is one of the cheapest and most cost-effective ways of saving energy. In Britain, some local councils now publish aerial thermal surveys that identify to what degree a home is leaking energy. You could also pay to have a pressure test carried out, which locates where air is escaping. Doors are sealed and then air is pumped inside until the air pressure increases and leaks can be detected.

The insulating performance of a structural element, such as a roof or a wall, is expressed as a U-value (or heat transmission coefficient). The lower the U-value, the higher the insulation. The calculations that go into determining a U-value take into account the thermal conductivity of each component of that element – outer skin, underlying structure, insulating material, inner skin and applied decoration.

Building regulations set very high standards for insulation in new homes, which also apply to extensions of existing properties. In the future, it is likely that new homes will be so highly insulated that requirements for space heating will be minimal. Grants are available in some areas for making improvements to insulation.

PREVENTING CONDENSATION & COLD BRIDGES

In temperate parts of the world there is the need to strike the right balance between air movement, or ventilation, and insulation, which is one of the most critical of all energy-conservation strategies. This is generally expressed as the principle: 'build tight, ventilate right'.

One of the risks associated with sealing buildings too hermetically is condensation, especially in areas that are naturally more humid, such as kitchens, bathrooms and utility rooms. Cold bridges, where heat readily travels from a warm interior surface to a cold external one, often via a good heat-conducting material such as metal, also cause condensation. Metal window frames, solid masonry walls and single glazing are common types of cold bridge.

Condensation promotes fungal growth and is bad for your health and the structural integrity of your home. Strategies for avoiding it include the following:

– Fitting mechanical extract in bathrooms and kitchens.
– Ensuring insulated windows have frame or trickle vents.

– Fitting a heat exchanger or heat-recovery ventilator. These recover heat from vented warm air and transfer it to cool air coming in.
– Passive stack ventilation using thermal chimneys or flues, or high-level windows. Warm air rises, drawing in cool fresh air and promoting healthy ventilation.
– Breathing wall construction, making use of semi-permeable materials, for example recycled paper insulation.
– Avoiding the use of non-porous paints, wall coverings and flooring.
– Preventing cold bridges by detailing frames and lintels in separate sections, increasing external insulation and installing double or triple glazing.
– Ensuring that insulation is properly installed, with no gaps or interruptions in the material.

INSULATING MATERIAL

Insulating materials vary widely, both in their performance and composition. The 'inconvenient truth' for the eco designer is that synthetics such as polyurethane are more efficient insulators than natural materials. However, the fact that many synthetic insulating materials have been shown to have an adverse effect on indoor air quality and health, and the fact that their production is environmentally damaging, can be a persuasive argument in favour of natural products. On the other hand, some forms of natural insulation need to be used in greater thicknesses to provide an appropriate level of thermal performance, which means that they will not be suitable if a cavity wall, for example, has insufficient depth.

Insulating materials also vary in their means of installation. In some cases, fitting is most definitely the job of a professional. Poor fitting can compromise thermal performance – unusual or awkwardly shaped spaces and obstacles such as electrical meters pose challenges for the installer. Another factor to consider is durability. Certain materials are prone to settlement, sagging and physical degradation through exposure to humidity. It is also worth bearing in mind that very few insulating materials are suitable for every context – choice has to be based on the type of construction and the specific location. You may need to use two or more types.

COMMON TYPES OF INSULATING MATERIAL:

- *Expanded polystyrene.* Highly efficient, durable and resistant to moisture, movement, rot and compression. Available in boards or beads. Synthetic petrochemical product that is non-biodegradable and emits toxic fumes when burned.
- *Extruded polystyrene board.* Similar qualities to expanded polystyrene, but performs slightly less well.
- *Polyurethane board and foam.* Highly efficient, water-resistant and durable. Foam requires professional installation. Synthetic petrochemical product that emits toxic fumes when burned.
- *Glass mineral wool.* Highly efficient, durable and rot-resistant. Available in rolls or batts. Derived from natural abundant minerals and may have some recycled content, but has high embodied energy. Fibres can irritate skin, nose and eyes. Performance affected by damp.
- *Mineral wool.* Highly efficient, durable, rot-resistant. Made of recycled steel slag. Non-biodegradable. Fibres can cause irritation to skin, nose and eyes.
- *Cellulose.* Highly efficient. Made of recycled newspaper with simple inorganic salts added for fire protection. Available in batts or as loose fill. Loose fill is easy for the amateur to install – the material must be 'fluffed up' to break up the chunks for maximum efficiency. Cellulose can also be sprayed onto walls in a slightly dampened state for a tighter fit, which is a professional job. Ideal for breathing wall construction and in lofts. Biodegradable and recyclable. Can be compromised by damp.

- *Sheep's wool.* Supplied in batts that are easy to cut and shape. Recyclable, renewable and biodegradable. Low embodied energy. Naturally resistant to decay and rot. Retains insulating properties when slightly damp. Not advisable for unventilated wall cavities. Good acoustic and thermal performance; keeps homes warm in winter and cool in summer.
- *Hemp.* Natural product that is recyclable, renewable and biodegradable. Suitable for breathing wall construction, floors, ceilings, walls and roofs. Low embodied energy. Densest form of natural insulation. Durable and with excellent thermal and acoustic performance. Safe and easy to install.
- *Flax.* One of cheapest plant-based insulation products. Good for breathing wall construction. Good thermal performance. Available in batts that are easy to cut and shape. Recyclable, renewable and biodegradable.

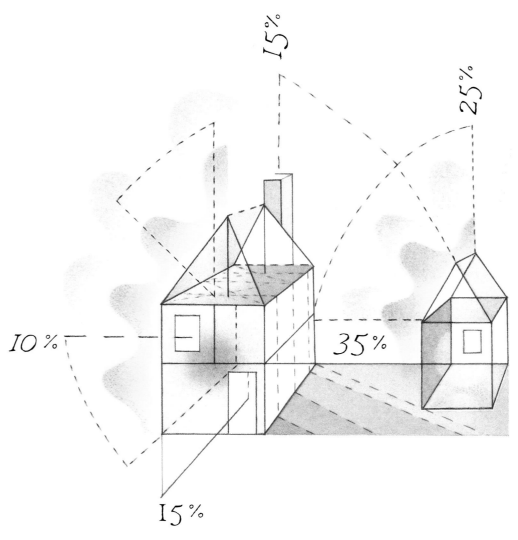

WHERE HEAT IS LOST

- Up to 35 per cent of heat lost in a home that is not insulated is lost through external walls. If your home has cavity walls, insulation added between the outer and inner skins will cut heat loss dramatically and save you money on your fuel bills. In many areas, cavity wall insulation is subsidized and will pay for itself in less than two years. For older properties, which tend to have solid walls, you can add insulation either externally or internally. Internal insulation is generally easier to fit yourself. It comes in a variety of forms, including solid urethane panels and thick foam faced in paper.

- Up to 25 per cent of heat lost is through the roof. Energy advisors recommend adding loft insulation to a minimum depth of 30 cm (11¾ inches).
- Between 15 and 20 per cent of heat lost is through draughts – poorly fitting window frames, doors, letterboxes, attic hatches, chimneys and the like. One way of testing where draughts are coming from is to hold a feather in front of obvious gaps. The main remedies include door brushes and rubber draught strips. A sausage-shaped draught-excluder can also be highly effective.
- Another 15 per cent of heat lost is accounted for by gaps in flooring,

either between the floor and skirting boards or between individual floorboards. Seal gaps with a proprietary sealant. Thick rugs can also provide an insulating layer.
- Single-glazed windows contribute up to 10 per cent of total heat loss. Double or triple glazing is the recommended solution. There are new types of glass on the market that make double glazing twice as efficient (see page 70). Curtains and blinds also keep heat in.
- Don't forget to lag hot water pipes, and hot water tanks and cylinders. The recommended thickness for a cylinder jacket is no less than 75 mm (3 inches).

CONVENTIONAL HEATING SYSTEMS

How is your home heated? In Britain and Europe the most common form of central heating is a wet system, where water is heated by a boiler and distributed to individual radiators by a network of pipes. In the United States, most homes have furnaces that pull in air, heat it and then blow it out again. Other types of system include radiant ones, where heating elements are buried in ceilings, walls or under floors. Stoves or fireplaces may supply ambient heating, along with individual space heaters such as electric heaters, gas fires and the like.

In the vast majority of cases, these conventional heating systems rely on burning some kind of fuel. With the possible exception of wood, such fuels carry a high environmental cost. The worst offender is coal, which generates pure carbon dioxide when it is burned. Oil is also carbon-intensive. Gas has a slightly lower carbon footprint because it produces a lot of water vapour when it is burned.

If you can't switch to a green alternative, for whatever reason, the next best thing to do, after making improvements to insulation, is to upgrade your heating system. Both boilers and furnaces are generally coming to the end of their lives after 10 to 15 years. If your appliance also breaks down frequently and needs costly repair, it is also worth thinking about getting a replacement sooner rather than later.

Before you go ahead with the installation, it can be beneficial to get advice on what size of boiler or furnace is required. If you have invested in double glazing or other forms of insulated glazing, and if you have increased other forms of insulation as well, you won't need such a big heating appliance. Many people install boilers and furnaces that are much too large for their needs.

In some countries, such as Britain, by law all replacement boilers must be the highly efficient condensing type. Modern condensing boilers are more compact than older models and reclaim heat from exhaust gases, which cuts down on the amount of fuel required to produce the same degree of heat. Combination or 'combi' boilers are a type of condensing boiler that supplies instant hot water without the need for a separate tank or cylinder. The most efficient boilers in the world are manufactured in Germany – these can achieve energy-efficiency ratings of up to 98 per cent.

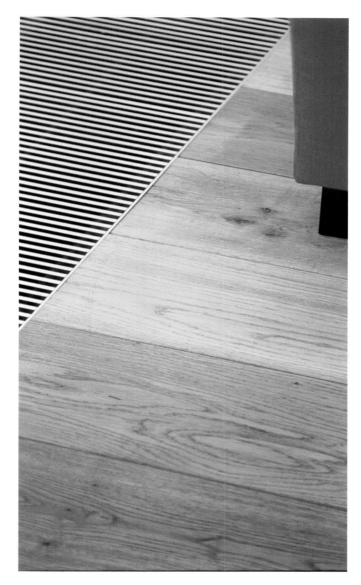

Left: The traditional European tiled or masonry stove, sometimes known as the kachelofen, employs the principles of thermal mass. Heat from burning fuel is stored in the brickwork, tile or masonry and then radiates out slowly.

Right: The most common form of radiant heating is underfloor heating. It can be installed under solid wood, stone, concrete and other massive materials.

In the United States, many states offer tax credits if you upgrade to a more efficient furnace. The degree of efficiency required will depend in part on whether you live in a region that has severe winters or not. If you do, an energy-efficiency rating of 90 per cent is recommended. Some new types of furnace have two-stage burners. When the weather is mild, the burner runs at a slower speed and generates a lower level of heat. This reduces temperature swings, which in turn prevents wear and tear because the furnace is not continually cycling between 'on' and 'off'.

Boiler efficiency is further enhanced by modern electronic controls, time switches, room thermostats and individual thermostatic valves on radiators (also mandatory in Britain). Digital thermostats can help to reduce your energy bills by up to 10 per cent. Intelligent controls, which learn your patterns of use, fine-tune a system even further. Avoid controls that operate at set times of the day. In a house that has been designed to benefit from passive solar gain, the main thermostat should be located in the warmest room, which is generally the south-facing living area.

RADIANT HEATING

Because radiant heating warms through conduction, not convection, it produces a more natural and comfortable interior climate than a heating system that warms the air. It is also good for asthma sufferers, as dust mites and other allergens are less likely to be stirred up by rising warm air. The most common form is underfloor heating, but radiant heating systems can also be installed in walls and ceilings.

The two most common forms of underfloor heating are electric and hot water. Electrical systems can be powered by alternative sources of energy, but most commonly use mains electricity. Hot-water underfloor heating is more disruptive to install, but can be very energy efficient. There are many highly efficient condensing boilers developed specifically for use with hot-water underfloor heating; most of these are manufactured in Europe. Conventional boilers should be avoided, as these will run inefficiently for much of the time – in underfloor heating, the water is heated to a lower temperature than water circulated to radiators. Underfloor heating can also be linked to solar thermal systems. However, underfloor heating is not very efficient in areas when you have a rapidly changing environment: that is, hot one moment and cold the next.

Because a radiant system heats the entire plane of a floor (or wall), the choice of materials plays an important part in overall efficiency. Materials with high thermal mass, such as concrete, stone and tile, will warm up slowly and retain heat for longer, which will reduce temperature swings. Underfloor heating can also be used successfully under wooden flooring. Avoid carpeting the floor – you will literally be adding a layer of insulation that will prevent some of the heat from being radiated into the room.

ALTERNATIVE SOURCES OF ENERGY

Concern for the environment, combined with rising fuel costs, means that more and more people are looking to alternative sources of energy to power and heat their homes – 'microgeneration', in the current buzz term. While solar thermal, photovoltaics, heat pumps and other forms of green energy (see pages 38–47) are still far from mainstream in some parts of the world, they are no longer seen as solutions for only a handful of dedicated eco-pioneers. The UK's Energy Saving Trust has reported that enquiries into renewables are up by a fifth over the past year. There is still a long way to go. In Germany a million roofs are fitted with solar panels of some sort. In the UK that figure is 90,000.

A number of factors can hold people back from taking the plunge. One is cost. Photovoltaics, in particular, are very expensive and the payback period is measured over the long term. However, the recent sharp rise in energy costs has shortened the payback period significantly; the bigger fuel bills get, the faster you will recoup the initial outlay. Many people spend a great deal of money putting in new kitchens and bathrooms in the expectation that they will add value to their homes. There's every reason to think of investment in carbon-saving technologies in the same light.

In some parts of the world financial incentives and packages to encourage investment in renewable energy have been put in place. As mentioned previously, Germany's exceptional record when it comes to installed solar capacity owes a good deal to the fact that domestic producers can sell their surplus back to the grid at a premium rate, an initiative that has since been adopted by 15 other countries. Other types of assistance include solar mortgages, which allow householders to spread payments over time, just as they do for house purchases, and government grants. In one particular scheme, which has been piloted in Berkeley, California, the city lends the householder the upfront cost of solar installation, which is then paid back via a property tax. The assessment remains with the property, so that if the original owner moves, the new owner takes on the tariff.

Lack of familiarity can also be a stumbling block. Most of us can get our heads around the ins and outs of a conventional heating system, but what does a heat-recovery pump actually do? Installation of an alternative system can also be a cause for concern, particularly in areas where there simply aren't the professionals out there who have the relevant experience. As in other types of home improvement, there are a number of unscrupulous operators touting their services; the sums of money involved mean that you have to be particularly cautious. Bodies such as the Low Carbon Building Programme in Britain have a register of recommended suppliers and installers.

Finally, there are the controversial claims and counter-claims that cloud the issue. Is there any benefit to a rooftop wind turbine, or is it just a green accessory? One minute a particular form of renewable technology looks like it provides the answers, and the next a report is published setting out the reasons why it doesn't.

Weighing up the pros and cons of various forms of renewable energy means that you have to do your research. It can also be well worth calling in a professional independent energy consultant to identify which system will work best for you and be most cost- and energy-efficient. It may well be the case that you will need a combination of different technologies to meet your needs most effectively. Most importantly, make sure your that home is insulated to the highest possible standard first – there's no point investing in alternative sources of energy if you are going to waste what you produce.

Below: Straw and wood waste can be used as fuel for biomass boilers. Most of the material would otherwise be incinerated or disposed of in landfill.

Right: An array of photovoltaic panels on the roof supply electricity for this zero carbon house. Water is heated by solar thermal panels, supplemented by a biomass boiler.

SOLAR THERMAL

Solar thermal is a tried and tested technology that uses the sun's energy to heat water. It's a rapidly expanding area of renewables, growing at an estimated rate of 50 per cent per year. For some years rooftop solar panels have been a common sight in sunny Mediterranean countries. In 2006 Spain passed a law that states that all new housing must have solar thermal collectors. But even in more northerly regions solar thermal can be very effective. Marstal, in Denmark, gains all of its hot water in summer and a third of its overall heating requirements per year from a solar thermal plant on the outskirts of the town. In the UK a solar thermal system is capable of meeting 60–70 per cent of domestic hot water needs per year. Although solar thermal systems are most economic when they are installed in new houses, especially as integral building elements, they are also highly suitable for retro-fitting.

HOW DOES IT WORK?

The main element of a solar thermal system is a collector that captures the sun's energy and heats liquid piped through it. There are three types of collector: the flat-plate collector, which is the most familiar, the excavated-tube collector, which is more expensive and more efficient but can be slightly problematic, and the unglazed-plastic collector, which is principally used to heat swimming pools.

There are two types of heat distribution. Direct circuits heat water from household taps. These are more common in warm climates where there is little risk of temperatures dropping below freezing. Indirect circuits, which are more typical in the UK and other temperate regions, use a separate circuit to transfer heat from the collectors to the water cylinder. Most of these are pump-assisted. The pump and controls ensure that the system only operates when the solar panels have generated enough energy to heat the water in the cylinder.

Solar thermal systems either require a separate pre-heat cylinder positioned between the cold water feed and the existing cylinder, or the replacement of the existing cylinder by a large cylinder with two heat exchangers or coils, one connected to the solar panel and one to the conventional boiler. Size of the pipework is also critical. If pipes are too wide, heat can be lost in transfer.

POSITIONING THE COLLECTORS

The siting and angling of solar collectors is critical for efficiency. Panels can be fitted to roofs, on adjacent buildings or in the garden. They must face within 90 degrees of south (in the northern hemisphere), which basically means any position from southeast through to southwest. Tilt angles vary according to latitude. In the UK, the optimum tilt angle is 35 degrees to the horizontal. It is also essential that the collectors are not overshadowed by trees or existing buildings.

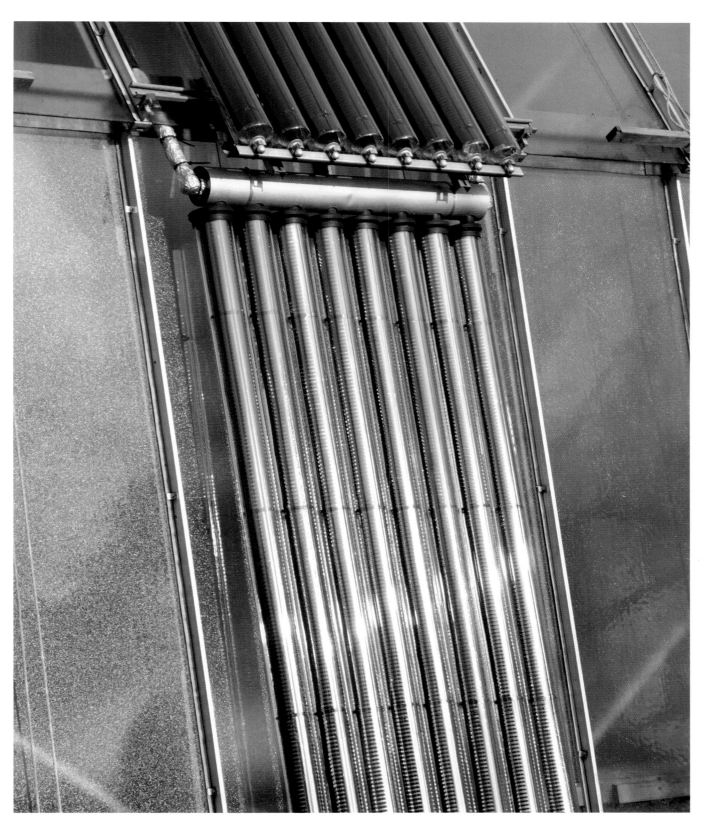

Pros

- Energy for free; solar thermal panels work even on cloudy days because they operate on the principle of light absorption.
- Established technology.
- Can be installed alongside an existing hot water system or used in combination with underfloor heating. Installation is relatively quick, with a minimum of disruption.
- Low running costs – a small amount of electricity is required to power the pump.
- Low maintenance.
- The most affordable form of solar heating; grants available in some areas.
- Small-scale installations are ideal for swimming pools.

Cons

- Produces most energy when demand is lowest.
- Cylinder may need to be replaced with a much larger version, which means you need enough space to accommodate it.
- Must be correctly designed and installed by accredited professionals.
- You may require planning permission if your house is listed or in a conservation area or if the panels sit more than 200 mm (8 inches) above the roof tiles.

Left: Solar thermal uses the sun's energy to heat water. It is a tried and tested alternative technology that can be very effective, even in northern countries.

PHOTOVOLTAICS

Another type of solar generator is the photovoltaic cell or PV, which, as the name suggests, converts the sun's energy into electricity. PV cells, made from silicon, are grouped to form modules, which are then arranged in panels or arrays of panels. Solar tiles and slates are also available in a range of colours, along with transparent cells or film that can be installed on glazed roofs or within windows.

Huge advances have been taking place in this area of technology over recent years. One new development is a complete roofing system that integrates solar thermal and PV. The tiles are installed in the same fashion as ordinary tiles. Another potential breakthrough, which could see windows functioning as powerful solar panels in the near future, has emerged from research carried out at the Massachusetts Institute of Technology. Transparent dyes in the glass capture and redirect light to PV cells in the window frame where it is converted into electricity. Because far fewer cells are required, the price of the technology could plummet.

HOW DOES IT WORK?

Sunlight falling on PV panels is converted into electricity. Because there are no moving parts, the generation is entirely silent. The electricity produced is direct current (DC), which then has to be converted to alternating current (AC) in an inverter. The PV system must be connected to the mains supply via a fuse box for safety.

During the day, the PV system generates electricity continuously, with the surplus or spare capacity flowing into the grid. At night, when electricity is not being generated, or at times of exceptional demand, power can be imported back from the grid. Even in countries where households receive only a relatively small amount of money for the surplus electricity they produce, it is possible to make net savings. Where the 'feed-in tariff' is higher, the financial incentives are even greater.

PV systems can also be run off the grid, in which case surplus electricity is stored in a battery that acts as the main power supply. An inverter is still required to convert the DC electricity to AC.

POSITIONING THE PANELS

Like solar thermal panels, PV panels can be installed on the roof, on the ground and also on south-facing walls. Maximum output (in the northern hemisphere) is achieved with a south-facing orientation. Optimum tilt angles vary according to latitude. In southern England, for example, a 30-degree tilt is best, whereas in Scotland the angle increases to 40 degrees. Obstacles such as high surrounding buildings, chimneys and trees that shade the panels will reduce efficiency. PV tiles or slates that are integral to the roof structure are much less intrusive.

Systems must be sized, designed, detailed and installed by accredited professionals. Issues include: where to run electrical wiring, placement of junction boxes and detailing of supporting frameworks.

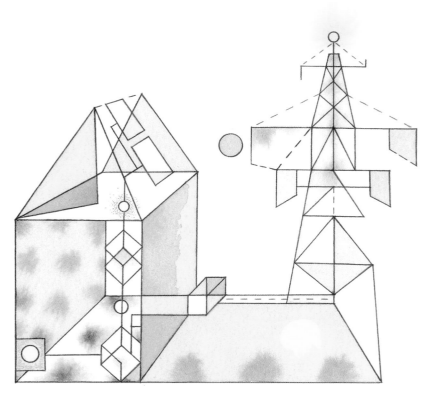

Pros
- Clean, free electricity that is entirely silent.
- Generates power even on cloudy days.
- Very low maintenance because there are no moving parts.
- PV panels have a long lifespan of up to 30 years.
- Grants and other forms of financing available.
- Surplus power can be fed back into the grid.

Cons
- High cost. However, this looks likely to come down in future and payback periods will continue to shorten as fuel costs rise.
- Must be installed by an accredited professional.
- Planning permission may be required if your house is listed or if you live in a conservation area.

Left: An array of photovoltaic panels generates clean electricity. Siting and angle of panels is critical.

HEAT PUMPS

Like solar thermal, heat pumps have been around for some time and are particularly popular in Sweden. The technology involves moving heat from where it is plentiful – from the ground, air or water – to where it can be used for space or water heating, with the assistance of an electric-powered pump. The basic principle is similar to vapour compression used in refrigeration, but it makes use of the heat-producing end of the thermodynamic cycle. Some systems provide heat only, while others can also be used for cooling.

Heat pump systems are most efficient when they are powered by renewable electricity and are serving underfloor heating or low temperature radiators in a well-insulated home. When they are powered by conventional electricity,

the efficiency is about the same as a condensing gas boiler and low temperature system. This means heat pumps are more attractive substitutes for households that otherwise would have to rely on a fuel such as oil. A separate system is usually required to meet hot water needs.

HOW DO THEY WORK?

Heat can be recovered from the air, water or ground. The most common forms of system are 'air to air' and ground source heat pumps (GSHP). Air to air systems, which are more popular in commercial buildings, collect the heat in the outside air and deliver it via fans to the indoors. They can also operate in reverse to cool the air. Ground source heat pumps transfer heat from the earth either to air or water. These can also be used for cooling.

Ground source heat pumps extract low grade heat from the ground using closed pipe loops buried in trenches or sunk into boreholes. The fluid in the loop is usually a refrigerant or antifreeze. The heat is then upgraded to a higher temperature and distributed to a water heating system, such as underfloor heating, or to an air distribution system. You will either need a big enough garden to lay the piping horizontally or in a more compact overlapping 'slinky' fashion, or you will need to sink a very deep borehole. A survey will be required to identify the position of existing buried services – such as septic tanks, for example. You will also need to determine the soil type, as different soils have different rates of transferring heat.

Pros

- Renewable source of free energy.
- Well established.
- Supplementary energy is only required to circulate the refrigerant, not to upgrade the heat.
- Carbon savings increase if a renewable form of electricity is used to power the pump.
- Ideal for heating underfloor systems, particularly if the flooring material has good thermal properties.
- Cheaper than oil, LPG and electric heaters.
- Grants available.
- Lifespan of over 40 years.

Cons

- Expensive to very expensive. Can approach the cost of photovoltaics.
- Less efficient when powered by conventional electricity.
- Does not produce high enough temperatures to heat hot water directly.
- GSHP requires disruptive installation to dig trenches or boreholes and enough ground space to run the pipework.

Left: Ground source heat pumps can be used in tandem with underfloor heating. Flooring materials that have high thermal mass, such as concrete or stone, increase the efficiency of such radiant systems.

ROOFTOP TURBINE

For many, the only acceptable wind turbine is the traditional windmill, whose sails, incidentally, rotate counter-clockwise, instead of clockwise like modern wind turbines. The Dutch government is investing significant sums in restoring the remaining windmills dotted around the countryside and similar projects are in operation elsewhere. In Britain old watermills are also being revisited with a view to bringing them back into use in the form of micro hydro schemes.

The rooftop turbine is almost as controversial as large-scale on-shore or off-shore wind farms. In theory it is supposed to generate a significant degree of a household's electricity needs from free wind power. In practice, results have been disappointing. It could be argued that the biggest contribution made by the rooftop turbine has been to bring environmental issues into greater prominence. Studies suggest that more development is needed before this type of technology can deliver the benefits its proponents claim for it.

HOW DOES IT WORK?

Small-scale domestic wind turbines produce free power from the wind, which is converted from rotational energy into electricity via a generator. Initially they seemed attractive because of their low cost and became widely available in DIY stores. The difficulty is that in many urban locations they often do not generate much power, because wind speeds fail to reach what is recommended. Where small-scale turbines have been more successful are in exposed, windy rural areas.

Manufacturers' claims are often based on optimum conditions, which are unlikely to exist in densely populated areas, where wind-shadowing from surrounding buildings is common. A rooftop turbine needs to extends a minimum of 9 m (30 ft) above the highest point of the roof and face in the direction of the prevailing wind. They don't perform well in turbulence, caused by obstacles such as high buildings, and sudden gusts, which don't turn the turbine but shake it on its axis, can cause mechanical failure. Power can also be lost in the process of converting rotational energy into electricity, through cabling and by connecting turbines to the grid. To connect a turbine into the grid, you need a grid controller, an isolator and an inverter. Turbines connected to batteries need a voltage regulator.

Pros
– Low cost for small turbines, rising in price according to size.
– Can be effective in isolated, rural locations, especially in very windy areas. Coastal locations can be ideal.
– Free energy.

Cons
– Under-performs in most urban locations due to wind-shadowing from surrounding buildings.
– Needs to be mounted so that it extends at least 9 m (30 ft) over the highest point of the roof.
– Planning permission is generally required.
– Wind turbines have high embodied energy due to their means of production, which must be set against whatever carbon savings they provide.
– Noisy.
– Can affect the structural integrity of your house. Most experts recommend siting a turbine well away from buildings.
– Energy loss associated with generation, cabling and grid connection.

MICRO COMBINED HEAT & POWER (MICROCHP)

Like the larger versions of CHP, which are used to provide heat and power for local communities, microCHP combines a boiler to heat water with a generator to provide electricity. The technology is relatively well established and has been used in Europe for some time, but it is much less common in Britain.

Unlike CHP-generating plants, however, microCHP systems run on fossil fuels, typically either diesel, gas or LPG (liquefied petroleum gas). Where such systems score highest for efficiency is in the generation of electricity right where it is needed. This is much less wasteful than relying on electricity generated in a remote power station and transported long distances to your home.

Pros
– Efficient production of electricity.
– Compact and quiet.
– Proven technology.
– Good for remote locations.

Cons
– Reliance on fossil fuel.
– Relatively expensive to install.

HOW DOES IT WORK?

There are different types of microCHP systems, but in general fuel is burned in a boiler to provide hot water for space heating as well as energy to drive a generator to provide electricity. Systems can be connected to the grid so that surplus electricity can be sold back. They can also be off-grid, which is ideal for houses in remote locations. In this case, electricity is stored in a battery, either directly or via an inverter.

Left: Rooftop wind turbines often under-perform in urban areas, where wind-shadowing from surrounding buildings can pose a problem.

Right: Micro combined heat and power systems run on fossil fuels, but they do generate electricity right where it is needed, which is less wasteful than transporting power over long distances. They are often used to provide heat and electricity for homes in remote locations.

BIOMASS

Biomass is defined as energy produced from organic matter. In practice it tends to be wood waste of various kinds, of which there is a considerable supply. In the UK it is estimated that six million tonnes of wood is disposed of in landfill annually. Many of the small CHP plants that power local communities are fuelled by biomass. Types of biomass include logs, wood chips and pellets made of reconstituted sawdust.

Burning wood is generally considered to be carbon-neutral, because the carbon released by combustion is taken in by growing trees that release oxygen as a by-product. However, some experts disagree, pointing out that there are energy costs associated with processing and transporting timber, and that wood smoke contains a variety of noxious substances.

HOW DOES IT WORK?

You can burn biomass in stoves, open fires and wood-fired boilers. In theory a wood-fired boiler can be directly substituted for a conventional boiler and will work alongside an existing heating system. In practice it can be more complicated than that. Siting the flue can be a critical issue. You will also need a considerable amount of space to store the fuel and keep it dry. Some wood-fired boilers can take biomass in a range of forms; others are specifically for solid fuel or pellets. You can feed the boiler directly or via a hopper, which cuts down on the effort required.

Burning wood in open fires is the least efficient use of the fuel, as a considerable proportion of the heat produced, along with the emissions, goes straight up the chimney. In a well-insulated house a wood-burning stove can be a much better option and is much less complicated to install than a biomass boiler. Modern wood-burning stoves are very efficient and recirculate the air to reduce emissions. Installing floor vents above the stove will warm upstairs rooms. Leaving internal doors open will also spread the heat around. Where very high levels of insulation have been achieved, a wood-burning stove can supply almost all the supplementary space heating required – you can also cook on them. European tiled stoves store heat for a very long time – the tiling gives them a high thermal mass and makes them function like storage heaters, which results in a more even distribution of heat. An added advantage of any kind of stove is that it provides a cosy focus for the home.

While wood-burning stoves have become a popular eco option, there can be drawbacks. In suburban areas, smoke can be a nuisance for neighbours. And although the more expensive modern stoves burn quite cleanly, and some are even approved for use in smoke-free zones, they have to be performing at peak efficiency for emissions to be low. Using poorly seasoned or damp wood can increase the smoke output, as well as run a stove below its optimum operating temperature. A choked fire burns dirty, releasing a lot of smoke and tar that can clog up the chimney. It is important that stoves are not over-sized, particularly in highly insulated homes. Running a large stove with the vents closed because it is producing too much heat will result in an increase of smoke – the alternative, to open doors and windows to let the heat out, is clearly nonsense.

Pros
- Carbon-neutral, with certain reservations.
- Reduces wood waste.
- Biomass boilers produce space heating and hot water much more cheaply than conventional fuels.
- Efficient wood-burning stoves can supply all supplementary space heating in well-insulated homes.

Cons
- Biomass boilers are much more expensive than conventional boilers and can be complicated to install.
- Fuel needs to be stored in a dry place and may take up a lot of room.
- Wood-burning stoves are not generally efficient at heating water.
- High on maintenance – requires regular feeding and cleaning.
- Obtaining fuel can be difficult in urban areas.

Far left: There are different types of biomass boiler. Some burn logs, others burn chips or pellets made of reconstituted sawdust.

Left: Modern wood-burning stoves can be very energy efficient, but they have to be performing at peak efficiency for emissions to be low.

COOLING

Warmer summers, due to climate change, have put an additional burden on our energy resources in the form of the power required to run air conditioning. In Britain sales of domestic air-conditioning systems are up by about a third since the mid-1990s. In the United States cooling the home during the summer has accounted for a significant proportion of energy use for some time. With temperatures likely to continue rising, it is important to look for alternative means of keeping cool. At the very least, set your air conditioner to a higher temperature – there's no need to chill your home excessively.

Mechanical cooling, achieved by fans and air conditioners, is not regarded as environmentally friendly. Even if you are generating your own electricity from some form of alternative supply, such power-hungry appliances do not represent the best use of it. Fans, which circulate air rather than cool it, produce heat during operation. Some types of air conditioner can be efficient, removing more heat than the energy required to operate them, but from a green point of view they are far from an ideal solution. While heat pumps can provide an element of cooling, this might not be enough in really hot weather to make interiors comfortable. The answer instead lies in adopting one or more traditional passive design solutions, such as exploiting thermal mass, ventilation and shading.

THERMAL MASS

Materials that have a high thermal mass, such as stone, masonry and concrete, absorb heat slowly throughout the day and release it during the night. As a result, they can play an important role in reducing the amount of energy required for heating. Insulating the home to a high standard and keeping the windows shut during cold weather will trap this warmth inside.

In the summer, the same principle operates. During the day, the thermal mass built into the house absorbs the heat and gradually warms up. Windows should be kept shut to keep hot air out and shaded to prevent excessive solar gain. Then at night, windows should be opened to discharge the heat that has built up in the fabric of the house.

Making the most of thermal mass entails a high degree of insulation and airtightness. Orientation is also critical. In the northern hemisphere, south-facing facades with large expanses of glazing will allow heat to penetrate into the interior during the winter. In the summer, these windows will require extensive shading to reduce heat gain. Arranging the layout of your home accordingly – with living areas to the south and bedrooms and utility areas to the north – will also help to make the most of these passive strategies. By contrast, in climates that are warm all year round, windows should be kept small on the side of the house that faces the sun, with screens, verandas, porches and similar features keeping the sun off external walls and windows.

Above: A deep overhanging awning keeps the heat of the sun off windows and walls, and provides shading for an outdoor terrace.

Right: Slatted or louvred screens break the strength of sunlight and create evocative patterns of light and shade.

VENTILATION

Air moves naturally according to differences in pressure and temperature, and air on the move, which lowers levels of humidity, is cooling. Passive ventilation strategies can go a long way to promoting a comfortable temperature indoors during the warmer months.

Cross-ventilation, which makes use of differences in air pressure, is one such strategy. Opening doors and windows on opposite sides of the house creates a through-draught that cools the interior. If these openings are sited in line with prevailing winds, the flow rate will be highest and hence most cooling, with air blowing from the side of the house that faces into the wind through to the opposite or 'wind-shadowed' side. Single-sided ventilation can be adequate for small rooms, if the window is large enough. Cross-ventilation can be blocked by even the lightest of curtains – Venetian blinds offer a degree of privacy with much lower air-resistance.

Warm air rises and cool air falls. This 'stack effect' can also be exploited to cool the interior by allowing air to rise unimpeded to open windows and skylights at the top of the house. Central atria, vents or open stairwells draw warm air upwards, pulling fresh air in down below. Traditional sash windows, which can be opened at the top and bottom, can drive a good stack effect within a single hot room. In theory, the whole house stack effect will work even on still nights, whereas cross-ventilation does need air movement outside to create a pressure difference across the house. At night you can get cross-ventilation working in tandem with the stack effect if you open downstairs windows – provided that you can resolve obvious security issues.

In hot climates, many vernacular housing types feature an internal courtyard. This maximizes the surface area available for heat loss and sets up invigorating patterns of cross-ventilation. Damping down courtyards or outdoor terraces also promotes fresh cooling breezes. Another traditional cooling feature is the windscoop or windcatcher. Mounted on the roof, it directs air down through the building in a masonry channel, cooling it along the way.

Right: Adjustable vents allow you to promote cross-ventilation and cool the interior.

Next page: A south-facing room in a New York penthouse features louvres to reduce solar gain. Top-opening windows encourage passive ventilation.

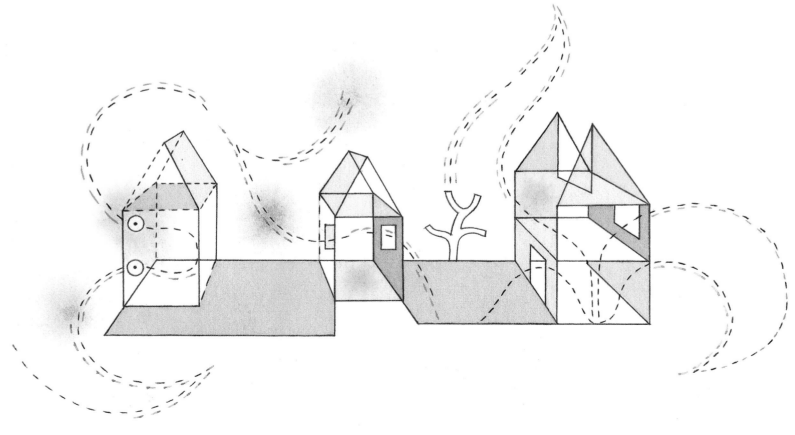

SHADING

Shading windows is an obvious way of reducing heat gain in the interior and is most critical for those openings on a south-facing elevation (north-facing in the southern hemisphere). Most people think of shading in terms of curtains and blinds, but there are many more types. Adjustable slatted or louvred shades allow you to vary the angle according the height of the sun in the sky. Types of shading include:

– *Slatted or Venetian blinds.* These are cheap, easy to use and good at controlling glare, but heat can be transferred from the blinds into the interior.
– *Mid-pane blinds.* These blinds are sandwiched between panes of glass in double- or triple-glazed units. Such units are expensive, but the blinds never need cleaning and do not impede windows from opening fully.
– *External blinds and awnings.* Effective at shading south-facing windows from the sun.
– *Shutters.* Louvred shutters are a traditional way of ventilating houses in warm countries. Internal shutters can be used with outward-opening windows. For sash windows and inward-opening windows, external shutters are required. Shutters can provide extra insulation during the winter.
– *Fixed overhangs.* Most effective with high-angle sun on south-facing facades.
– *Covered porches and verandas.* A hot-country solution to shading external walls and windows at ground-floor level.
– *Planting.* In temperate regions deciduous trees shade windows and walls in the summer, but allow winter sun through.

LIGHTING

Above left: Stairs with open treads make the most of available light.

Above right: Solar tubes can bring daylight down into internal areas that lack windows.

The incandescent light bulb, Thomas Edison's quintessential 'bright idea', is well over a century old. The first electrical product that everyone wanted, arguably it created a demand for electricity itself, where none had previously existed. Now its days are most definitely numbered.

The reason for this will be obvious to anyone who has ever burnt their fingers on a lit bulb. Ordinary incandescent bulbs – cheap, disposable and until now widely available – are incredibly inefficient. They convert only 5 per cent of the energy they use into light; the rest is converted into heat. It has been estimated that lighting creates as much carbon emissions as 70 per cent of the world's passenger cars. A number of countries have already passed legislation to 'ban the bulb' – Australia was first, pledging to replace incandescent bulbs by 2009–10; in Britain the switch-off is scheduled for 2012; in the United States by 2014. During the phased withdrawal of these bulbs, the higher wattages are already becoming unavailable in many areas.

Switching to more energy-efficient light bulbs is high up on the eco to-do list. A related strategy, which can also be very effective, is to look for ways to improve the quality of natural light in your home.

ENHANCING NATURAL LIGHT

The more daylight the interior of your home receives, the less you will have to rely on artificial light sources to provide illumination during the day, which means lower energy consumption. At the same time, expansive areas of glass that flood the interior with natural light can also lead to unwanted heat gain or heat loss. The position of windows and the type of glazing used has to be considered within the overall context of passive solar design (see page 30).

One strategy to enhance natural light is to plan the layout of your home so that hard-working areas such as kitchens, where a higher degree of light is required, are

Above left: A remodelled cottage in New South Wales has an airy, expansive quality due to the large openings that let daylight flood in.

Above right: Planning restrictions meant that this new eco house in west London, designed by Alex Michaelis, could not be any higher than the wall surrounding the site. The solution was to sink a large proportion of the accommodation underground. A glazed panel allows natural light to spill down into the levels below.

located where daylight is at an optimum level. Upside-down layouts, where bedrooms are situated on the ground floor with living areas above, make sense because most of the time we use our bedrooms we are asleep.

Making new openings or enlarging existing ones are direct ways of bringing more daylight into the home. Particularly valuable in this respect are high-level windows and toplighting. The amount of light a window admits into the interior has to do with the 'sky factor'. Windows at lower levels, where clear sky is only a small proportion of the view they frame, admit less light than those higher up. This means that enlarging windows by raising their height will result in brighter conditions than widening them will. High-level windows also allow light to penetrate further into the interior. Rooflights, positioned over stairwells or other strategic spots, spill light down into the interior and generate an expansive feeling of well-being. Another option is to install solar tubes.

Many older properties, such as terraced houses, tend have windows only at the front and rear. Apartments, too, may have rooms that are single-aspect only. 'Borrowing' light from spaces that have a better quality of natural light can help to boost levels in dark areas. One way of borrowing light is to open up the layout by removing partition walls. Another is to keep partitions as transparent and minimal as possible. Internal glazing, either in the form of doors or screens, can help to spread available light around. Internal openings, from thin vertical slivers to round portholes, will do the same, and help with natural ventilation. Glass floors or panels of glass set in upper floors will draw light down through a space, as will open or cantilevered stairs.

And don't forget the impact of decoration. White, reflective surfaces and finishes are naturally light-enhancing. Window treatments that expose as much of the window as possible or that are adjustable, such as blinds, allow the light to stream in (see page 76).

ENERGY-EFFICIENT LIGHT SOURCES

One area where my aesthetic preferences struggle with my eco intentions is lighting. For all its faults, the incandescent bulb has survived for so long because people like the light it emits. Tungsten bulbs are quite close in colour temperature to candlelight – you can see this in photographs of interiors taken at night, where the light shows up in the warm end of the spectrum. Warm light is relaxing, flattering and hospitable.

The same, unfortunately, cannot be said of energy-efficient compact fluorescents. Although great strides have been made in improving the quality of light they produce, they still fall short of tungsten's rather comforting light.

Fluorescent light sources produce light with a greenish tinge, which can be a little too clinical for the home. One simple remedy and a traditional one, is to use the bulbs in tinted shades. Lampshades lined in a warm rosy colour can help to soften the light and make it more welcoming.

Like them or not, the incandescent bulb won't be with us much longer. The average home has 25 light bulbs, which account for roughly 10 per cent of a household's energy consumption. Low-energy bulbs consume only a fifth of the energy of incandescent bulbs. LEDs are even more efficient. Sooner or later, we are all going to have to make the switch.

Above: The average home has 25 light bulbs. If these are the incandescent type, you can end up wasting a good deal of energy. Compact fluorescents come in a wide range of fittings and shapes, which makes replacement straightforward.

Right: Size and placement of openings will dictate how much natural light your home receives. Brighter conditions mean less reliance on artificial light sources during the day.

Compact fluorescents (CFLs)

These are the bulbs that are poised to replace incandescent bulbs in the near future. Nowadays, CFLs are available in a wide range of sizes and shapes, including the classic bulb shape, and fit every conceivable form of light fixture, which makes replacement extremely simple. They are relatively more expensive, but much longer lasting, with a lifespan up to fifteen times longer than a tungsten bulb. As previously mentioned, the colour cast is not ideal, but this may well improve in future. Unlike old fluorescents, modern versions light up much more quickly. One cause for concern, however, is that CFLs contain mercury, which is a hazardous pollutant. Disposing of CFLs remains problematic and if one breaks in the home, there may be the risk of contamination.

Energy-efficient halogen

Some manufacturers produce energy-saving halogen bulbs, which use 30 per cent less energy than tungsten bulbs and mains- and low-voltage halogen. These can be directly substituted for either tungsten or halogen bulbs, and have the additional advantage of being fully dimmable.

LEDs

LEDs or 'light-emitting diodes' are considered by many experts to be the future of lighting. These tiny bulbs, familiar in display panels and in electronic equipment such as computers and televisions, fit directly into an electrical circuit and are lit by the movement of electrons in semiconductor material. They are increasingly being used in domestic lighting and are becoming much less expensive. LEDs give off hardly any heat, consume a mere 3 watts to produce as much light as an incandescent bulb, and last for incredible periods of time – between 50,000 and 100,000 hours.

Don't forget

– Switch off the lights when you leave the room.
– Keep the curtains or blinds open on long light evenings to reduce dependence on artificial lighting.
– Sadly, dimmer switches do not save electricity, but they do improve the quality of light and therefore of life!

WATER

SAVING WATER

Water-saving is going to become more and more critical in the future and there is a great deal every household can do to reduce consumption. As with energy, simple changes of habit and lifestyle can amount to considerable savings.

Before indoor plumbing, water was husbanded like the precious resource that it is. After decades of treating water almost as if it were free, we need to change our bad habits to use water more wisely. Think before you leave a tap running for any period of time – whether you are brushing your teeth, filling a glass, shaving or waiting for the tap to run hot. Over the last half-century water consumption has trebled, the greater proportion of that increase being used for washing and for flushing toilets. In certain dry areas of the United States a staggering 80 per cent of the average household's water consumption is used to water lawns, hose down patios and driveways, and clean cars. That's clean drinking water going right down the drain.

Right: Changes to lifestyle can go a long way to minimizing water consumption. Showers, provided that they aren't power showers, use less water than baths.

Far right: Collecting rainwater from the roof provides a supply of water for a number of uses, including garden irrigation.

WASHING

- Modern dishwashers use less water than washing dishes by hand. If you are in the market for a new model, choose one that is the most efficient. In the UK, those will be rated A**; in the United States, look for Energy Star labels. Always run full loads at low-temperature or eco settings. A full load uses less water than two half loads.
- If you don't have a dishwasher, fill one sink with washing water and the other sink with rinsing water. Don't let the water run while rinsing. Don't scrub pans under a running tap. Leave them to soak.
- Wash vegetables in a bowl or partially filled sink, not under a running tap, then reuse the water on indoor plants or the garden.
- Run full loads in washing machines and always use the low-temperature or eco setting. When buying new, choose energy-efficient appliances.
- Wash clothes, towels and linen less frequently.
- Turn off the water when you are brushing your teeth. Brushing your teeth with the water running wastes 6 litres (1½ gallons) a minute.
- Turn off the tap or shower when you are shampooing your hair or shaving.

- Take short showers instead of baths. A bath uses 80 litres (21gallons) of water; an average shower uses 6 litres (1½ gallons) per minute. Power showers, however, use 15 litres (4 gallons) per minute. You can invest in a shower timer to make sure that you don't take too long and use too much water – about five minutes is plenty.
- Put a bucket in the shower while you are waiting for the water to heat up and use the cold water in the garden, to water houseplants or to flush the toilet.
- If you don't have a shower, put the plug in before you run a bath and adjust the temperature as the tub fills.
- Bathe young children together.
- Install low-flow showerheads and put aerators on all of your taps.
- Separate temperature and flow controls on a shower allow you to turn off the water briefly while you shampoo your hair, for example, without losing the temperature setting.
- Fill a bucket to wash the car instead of using a hose. Or take the car to a commercial car wash that recycles water.
- Turn the thermostat on your hot water tank down to 60°C (140°F).

DRINKING & COOKING

- Fill a jug with water and put it in the fridge to use as drinking water. Don't run the taps waiting for the water to get cold.
- Don't buy bottled water. If you need to take water with you when you are away from home, reuse a plastic bottle or water flask and fill it up at the tap.
- Only fill the kettle with as much water as you need. If you're making one cup of coffee or tea, only boil one cup of water. If you live in an area that has hard water, make sure you remove limescale from your kettle regularly to keep it working efficiently. An eco-friendly way of removing limescale is to soak the element overnight in vinegar.
- Think about cutting down on the amount of meat you eat. Meat production requires a high consumption of water. Tea uses less water to produce than coffee.
- Cooking methods such as steaming are more energy-efficient and water-saving. Using a multi-level steamer to cook vegetables is less wasteful than boiling them separately. Don't fill a pan with water just to boil a few vegetables. Cooking food in a minimum of water preserves nutrients. Choose an appropriately sized pan.
- Compost peelings (see page 166) instead of using a waste- or garbage-disposal unit.

TOILETS

- Install low-or dual-flush toilets.
- Flush less often.
- If you have a bidet, both sexes can use it as a low-flush urinal.
- Displace water in your toilet cistern using one of the many water-saving products on the market. They're cheap and you will save up to 1 litre (1¾ pints) per flush. Or you can fill a plastic bottle with water or pebbles and use that instead. The Duke of Edinburgh uses a brick.
- To check if your toilet is leaking, put food colouring in the cistern, wait half an hour and see if there is any colour in the toilet bowl.

GARDENING

- Choice of plants can go a long way to reducing water consumption for garden irrigation (see page158).
- Recycle greywater from sinks, bathtubs and showers to use in the garden.
- Collect rainwater in a water butt or underground tank.
- Sweep terraces and hard landscaped areas rather than washing them down.

MAINTENANCE

- Fix dripping taps and leaks. A dripping tap can waste up to 140 litres (37 gallons) a week.
- Have a water meter fitted so you can monitor your consumption.
- If you have a water meter, you can tell if there is a leak in your system by turning off the water and taking two readings a short while apart. If they are different, you might have a leak.
- Make sure you know where the mains cut-off or stopcock is located.

WATER-SAVING FIXTURES AND FITTINGS

A stage further on from making changes to lifestyle and patterns of consumption is to invest in water-saving fixtures and fittings. Many of these are not expensive and they can help you make further cuts in your consumption.

Taps and showerheads: Water-saving taps and showerheads are either aerated or flow-restricted. Some can be retro-fitted to existing taps with a minimum of fuss.

Aerated taps and showerheads force air through the water, cutting consumption by half. The flow is soft and bubbly with no reduction of pressure.

In flow-restrictor taps and showerheads, the water is forced through smaller holes. This results in a fine, firm spray and a significant reduction in water consumption.

Left: Greywater, which is water recycled from showers and basins, and which is only marginally dirty, can be recycled and used to flush toilets, wash the car or water plants.

Above: There are a number of different fittings you can apply to taps and showerheads to reduce water consumption. These either restrict or aerate the flow.

Water-saving toilets: When low-flush toilets were first introduced some while ago, they were not very efficient and as a consequence people were flushing them twice, which increased water consumption. Designs have improved a great deal since then. Modern low- or dual-flush toilets use much less water than old-style toilets and are mandatory in some countries for all new installations. Normally these allow for both half-flushing and full-flushing. Most countries insist on no more than 6 litres (12 pints) for a full flush and 3 litres (6 pints) for a half-flush.

A new type of toilet that has recently become available has an integrated hand basin and tap. When you wash your hands or run water into the basin, the water is diverted into the toilet's cistern and is used for flushing. This design is about 20 per cent more water-saving than a dual-flush toilet.

There are also a number of devices on the market that allow you to retro-fit a standard toilet and reduce water consumption. Some designs fit into the cistern and turn the toilet into a dual-flush; others allow you to control the duration of the flush. Toilets with front-mounted handles can also be converted into dual-flush toilets.

Composting toilets: It is estimated that flushing toilets account for about a third of a household's water consumption. One way of cutting water use considerably is to install a composting toilet. This type of waterless toilet, which turns human waste into organic compost, connects directly to a large sealed container in a basement or lower level. From time to time, other organic matter, such as garden clippings or vegetable peelings, must be added to the container to assist the breakdown of the human waste, which is otherwise chiefly carried out by air circulating in the container. An exhaust vent extracts smells and emits them above the roofline. Although these toilets require no energy input, a small fan is usually recommended.

One disadvantage of a composting toilet is that it can be difficult to install in a standard house. In some parts of the world, for example, urban areas in the United States, they are prohibited. However, for new houses, particularly those in remote areas where drainage is problematic, they can be a good solution. (Colette, the French novelist, was a great believer in the outdoor privy!)

COLLECTING RAINWATER

A very simple way of reducing water consumption is to collect rainwater and use it to water the garden or wash the car. Set-ups are quick and economical and generally involve connecting a water butt or barrel to a downpipe leading from the roof gutter. There is usually some form of filter to strain out debris. However, it is important to bear in mind that some composite roof coverings, such as asphalt, will taint the water and make it unacceptable even for garden irrigation. Lead, commonly used for flashings, is another toxic pollutant. Rainwater collected in butts must not be allowed to stand for long periods or it can become septic.

Larger, more sophisticated systems involve burying a tank or cistern underground where rainwater is collected and stored. These systems have integrated pumps and filters and produce water that is clean enough for non-potable uses, but they can be disruptive to install and are also expensive.

Where filtered rainwater is used in the home, there must be no connection between rainwater pipes and drinking-water pipes because of the risk of contamination.

USING GREYWATER

Water that has already been used once and is only mildly dirty – for example, in showers and baths – is greywater. This is distinct from 'blackwater', which is water flushed from toilets, and water from kitchen sinks, which contains a high proportion of grease, detergent and organic matter.

In some circumstances, where the water has been used for rinsing and is not overly soapy, greywater can be directly used in the garden or for washing the car. One gadget that facilitates this consists of a 3.5 m (11½ ft) hose with an in-line bulb hand-pump. You hang one end outside the window and put the other into a watering can or butt. Squeezing the hand-pump gets the siphon effect going and then gravity takes over. The advantage of this device is that you can choose which to recycle. Interceptor kits that connect to the outflow pipe from the bath and sink collect all greywater indiscriminately, which is not always advisable.

For other non-potable applications, greywater needs to be filtered and treated first. One environmentally friendly method of doing this is first to filter the water through crushed gravel and then run it through reed beds where micro-organisms feeding among the plant roots act as biological purifiers. As well as being land-hungry, there are risks associated with this type of recycling, in particular the risk of groundwater contamination. Many experts believe that at present water-saving measures are more effective at reducing consumption than recycling.

Far left: Large-scale rainwater collection in Australia. Water drains from the roof directly into large corrugated cisterns.

Left: On a smaller scale, even the humble garden butt, connected to the downpipe, can provide water for plants and washing down outdoor surfaces.

Next page: Designed by Bark architects, Tinbeerwah House is sited on an east-facing escarpment in the Noosa hinterland of Queensland, Australia. Deep overhangs provide shade from hot summer sun and openings are arranged to give cooling through breezes.

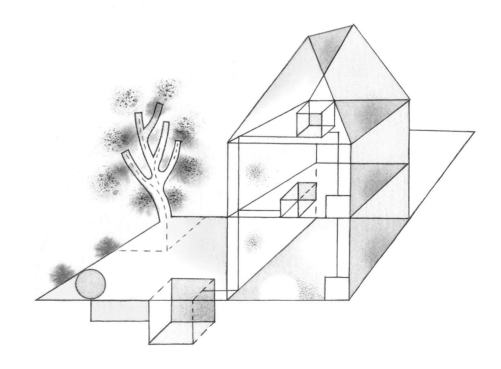

BASIC FABRIC

Many different materials go into the construction and decoration of our homes and some are greener than others. Most of us are not in the position to tear down the basic structure of the places we live in and build them again from scratch, but there is still a great deal we can do when it comes to choosing surfaces and finishes, furniture and furnishings. Natural, eco-friendly materials have the additional advantage of creating healthier, more comfortable surroundings in which to live.

In many cases, it is a question of straightforward substitution. Flooring made of bamboo or palmwood, both of which come from plentiful and renewable resources, make highly practical alternatives to hardwood and are surprisingly close in appearance. Modern organic paint ranges are now available in a variety of intense shades, which means you do not have to abandon your aesthetic principles to do your bit for the environment. Reclaimed or recycled materials, such as salvaged stone, lend depth of character and reduce wastage.

Left: Timber is an incredibly versatile material, as well as an environmentally friendly one. Depending on the type, it can be used for structural purposes, as cladding, or for interior joinery and final finishes.

In other respects, it can be more difficult to define whether a particular material is environmentally friendly or not. One key consideration is 'embodied energy'. Embodied energy is the sum total of all the energy that goes into the production of a particular material: the energy used to harvest or extract the raw material, to transport it to a factory or mill where it will be refined, processed or dimensioned, to transport that processed material or product to the construction site or supplier, and the subsequent energy required to install it. By this token, a material such as steel is very high in embodied energy, while a material such as hardwood imported from halfway across the globe is higher in embodied energy than timber sourced from local trees.

Another factor to consider are the fixings, adhesives and dressings that are required to make a particular material perform well and to prolong its life, or the binders that may be used in its composition. Many of the most common of these are products of the petrochemical industry, and as such are derived from the world's diminishing supply of fossil fuels. Synthetic glues, binders, seals and varnishes can be highly toxic and have been shown to 'offgas', or release dangerous compounds into the air, which can have a deleterious effect on human health. This means that it is not enough simply to choose a green material – you have to make sure that the way it is installed and maintained does not compromise its credentials.

In the commercial sector, environmental awareness is growing at an exponential rate. On the one hand, this is good news for the average person, as more green products and materials are coming onto the market all the time. On the other hand, it means that consumers must be even more wary. Many manufacturers, producers and retailers go to great lengths to persuade their customers that their products are environmentally friendly, sometimes on the flimsiest of pretexts. Independent certification is ultimately a more reliable guide to choice.

RECYCLED ELEMENTS

Reclaimed or recycled materials or building elements – such as windows, doors, flooring and so on – can be an excellent eco option. They are not, however, always the cheapest. Good-quality reclaimed materials, particularly those with an appealing patina of age, are often more expensive than new. Reclaimed bricks and roof tiles, for example, often command a premium, although they offer much more character. It's always worth buying from a reputable dealer or supplier and inspecting carefully before you make a purchase. Materials that haven't been carefully salvaged can be a liability. Floorboards, for example, should be denailed, parquet must be cleaned of any traces of bitumen and bricks should be free from old mortar.

Below: Japanese tatami mats, made from natural materials, provide a low cushioned platform for floor-level sleeping.

Right: Corrugated-iron roofing is a feature of Australian vernacular building that also often crops up as a feature of eco design. The corrugations promote water run-off.

WINDOWS

Windows are a key element in eco design. Depending on where they are positioned, how large they are and how they are shaded, they play an important role in passive solar strategies, in natural ventilation and in natural daylighting (see pages 30, 50 and 54). Another crucial factor is how they are constructed and of what materials they are composed.

Ordinary single-paned windows are responsible for up to 10 per cent of the heat lost from the interior. In older properties, where windows may fit poorly, warm air escaping through the gaps around the frame can account for much of that heat loss. Standard single-glazed windows also serve as cold bridges. Ideally, a window should have the same thermal performance as the adjacent wall. When it doesn't, heat takes the path of least resistance, travelling through materials with the highest conductivity, and a cold bridge occurs. Materials with high conductivity include glass and metal – which means metal-framed single-glazed windows are particular offenders in this respect.

INSULATED WINDOWS

You can improve the energy efficiency of your home to a significant degree by replacing existing windows with highly insulated varieties. Most people are familiar with the principle of double glazing, where an insulating layer of air is trapped between paired panes of glass. The most common double-glazed units are framed in PVC and such products have been heavily sold over the past few decades, often unscrupulously, making 'double-glazing salesman' a byword for sharp trader. On aesthetic grounds, they can also be something of an eyesore, especially where they have been substituted for original sash windows in a period house.

Modern insulated windows are much more sophisticated and much better looking, too. Those with the highest green credentials are framed in wood or in composite frames made of wood clad in aluminium. Double glazing is better than single glazing, but falls short of the efficiency of triple-glazed units. In Germany, double glazing has recently been banned in new construction.

Very high-performance insulated windows are triple-paned, with the gaps between filled with argon or krypton gas. Some of these units incorporate integral blinds sandwiched between the panes, which can be controlled from the inside of the window to regulate heat gain and

cut down on maintenance. They may also include frame or trickle vents to prevent condensation. Others are lockable in an open position for secure ventilation at night-time.

Many of the windows with the highest specification and best thermal performance are manufactured in Sweden. Some are available off the shelf in standard sizes and shapes, but bespoke designs are also possible. Larger panes are more efficient than windows composed of multiple small panes because perimeter length is minimized and there are fewer places where a cold bridge can occur.

UPGRADING TRADITIONAL WINDOWS

In some cases it is possible to upgrade traditional windows, such as sash windows and other period designs, by retro-fitting them with double glazing. There are a number of companies which specialize in this work and which are able to advise in individual cases. However, a sash window retro-fitted with double glazing will not be as efficient as a new insulated unit. This is particularly true if the window is subdivided into multiple panes. If your windows can't be fitted with double glazing, fitting brushes and other types of draught-proofing can help to cut heat loss.

Left: Windows set into the plane of the roof are good for toplighting or for introducing daylight to attic conversions. The greater proportion of sky that is visible, the brighter the light in the room will be.

Below left: Highly insulated triple-glazed windows provide optimum energy efficiency.

Above: High-specification windows can be ordered in many different shapes and sizes. This long horizontal opening is fitted with low-E glass.

Left: Windows composed of large panes are more efficient than those composed of multiple small panes, because there are fewer places where a cold bridge can occur.

WINDOW FRAMES

Choice of material for window frames has a direct bearing on thermal performance. At the same time, there are other factors to consider, such as durability and maintenance, as well as the environmental impact of sourcing and production. Common materials used for window frames include hardwood, softwood, aluminium, steel and PVC.

Because the heat lost through a window frame over the lifetime of its use is likely to have a greater impact than the energy consumed to produce it, the general advice is to opt for a material that has least conductivity, which means wood. The second least conductive material is PVC and the most conductive is metal.

WOOD

Wooden window frames may have the highest thermal performance, but they are not trouble-free. The greenest choice is hardwood grown in temperate regions, such as oak, chestnut and larch. These woods do not require subsequent finishing with paints or preservatives and are very low in maintenance. They are also long-lasting, recyclable and come from a renewable resource. Windows with hardwood frames are among the most expensive.

Softwood shares many of the advantages of hardwood, with a key difference. This is the fact that it requires sealing with either varnish or paint to keep out moisture, which would otherwise warp and rot the timber. Treated with paints or seals, frames will need recoating every five years or so. Using synthetic paints compromises green credentials, as these products are derived from petrochemicals, are toxic during manufacture and application, and are non-biodegradable. Synthetic paint also has a high level of VOCs (volatile organic compounds), which can offgas into the air and pose risks for human health.

In the case of either softwood or hardwood, it is important to ensure that it comes from an FSC-certified source (Forestry Stewardship Council). Wood grown in local plantations has lower embodied energy than imported wood. Softwood species are faster growing than hardwood.

ALUMINIUM

Strong and lightweight, aluminium is a popular choice for window frames, not least because it is very durable and requires very little maintenance once coated or anodized. Many types of metal – and aluminium is no exception – are recyclable with no loss of quality, and most aluminium windows contain a recycled element. However, on its own aluminium is not a green choice because it has high embodied energy, derives from non-renewable resources and has poor thermal performance.

STEEL

Steel-framed windows were popular between the wars and were a common feature of mass housing in the 1920s and 1930s. On the plus side, steel is easy to recycle and most steel windows have a significant recycled content. On the down side is the material's high embodied energy, poor thermal performance and the fact that it derives from non-renewable resources. Steel needs to be coated or painted regularly to prevent corrosion.

PVC

In the UK, PVC windows have accounted for a significant part of the market in recent years. In other parts of the world, where timber is more abundant, this has not been the case. PVC has been popular, particularly for double-glazed units, because it is cheap, virtually maintenance-free, and can be shaped into a wide range of different profiles and designs. It comes second to wood in terms of thermal performance, although it is slightly less durable.

However, PVC (polyvinylchloride) is one of the most problematic of plastics. Like all plastics it is a product of the petrochemical industry, with the environmental damage that entails. It is non-biodegradable and highly toxic when burnt. PVC can be recycled, but currently most is discarded to landfill.

Aesthetically, PVC windows are also highly displeasing. Because PVC is not as strong as wood or metal, sections are thicker, which gives windows a clumsy, inelegant appearance. PVC can also be prone to discoloration.

COMPOSITE

Composite windows, made of softwood clad with aluminium, have the potential to offer the best of both worlds. Softwood performs just as well thermally as hardwood, but is cheaper and faster growing. The thin aluminium cladding reduces maintenance to zero and results in the windows achieving lifespans of up to 50 years. Framing can be very elegant and minimal. The principal eco disadvantage is the high embodied energy of the metal, although this can be somewhat reduced if there is a recycled content.

Far left: The material used to frame windows has a critical bearing on thermal performance. Hardwood has the highest thermal performance.

Left: Traditional sash windows can sometimes be retro-fitted with double glazing to improve their efficiency.

Top: High-specification Scandinavian timber-framed windows have good eco credentials.

Above: These window are fitted with low-E glazing and are operable to promote natural ventilation.

Next page: A conversion of an old cottage in Australia involved building a new raised pavilion. Closed on two sides for privacy and acoustic separation, it opens onto a veranda on the other two sides, accessed by sliding doors.

LOW-EMISSIVITY

The most common way of improving a window's energy efficiency is by doubling or tripling the panes. Recently, however, new types of glass have come onto the market, which can dramatically cut heat loss.

Standard glass radiates heat on the colder side. In the winter months, that equates to the external face of the glass or the external pane in a double-glazed unit. Low-E glass (low-emissivity) glass has a thin near-invisible coating of metallic oxide on one side, which reflects heat back into the interior. There's little visual difference between low-E glass and standard glass, and both are cleaned the same way.

Low-E glass is designed to be used in double- or triple-glazed units. A double-glazed unit that incorporates low-E glass has a similar U-value to a triple-glazed unit. Low-E glass installed in a triple-glazed unit results in a U-value that approaches nil. In a multiple-glazed unit, the low-E glass is installed as the inner pane, with the coated side facing into the gap between the layers of glass.

Low-E glass comes in a range of coatings, suitable for different climatic conditions. In addition to those that promote high solar gain, there are also those that promote low solar gain, which can help to keep interiors cool in warm regions of the world.

One manufacturer produces windows that combine low-E glass with an 'extra clear' outer pane. The extra clear pane increases the amount of heat from the sun that reaches the interior and the low-E glass keeps it from escaping. Such windows are said to be twice as energy efficient as double glazing.

WINDOW TREATMENTS

A low-tech way of preventing excessive heat gain in the summer and heat loss in the winter is to choose the right type of window treatment. Window treatments fulfil a range of other practical functions, too – from providing privacy to light control – which means there may have to be an element of compromise between competing needs.

Curtains. Particularly when they are lined, curtains make good insulators. Interlining with 'bump', a soft wadding, will increase their insulating properties further. Curtaining glazed doors, or doors that lead onto porches and other intermediate areas, can also help to prevent draughts.

Make sure that curtains draw back well clear of the window frame, so that you make the most of natural light during the day. Similarly, avoid any window treatment that overhangs the top of the glass – the upper portion of the window is where the greatest proportion of natural light comes in. Curtains should stop well above radiators, so you don't block heat from reaching the rest of the room.

In the summer months, when cooling is important, you can swap heavy winter curtains for lightweight, semi-transparent drapery. Unless privacy or security is a real issue, keep the curtains open on long summer evenings to reduce your reliance on artificial lighting.

In all cases, natural fabrics are best. Avoid synthetic materials or those that require dry-cleaning.

Blinds and shutters. With rare exceptions, blinds generally do not offer much in the way of insulation, but they do stop draughts from badly fitted windows and they are far more effective than curtains at light control, which means

Right: Curtains suspended from a rail placed well above the glazed door allow maximum light to come into the interior during the daytime.

Far right: Roman blinds, which lift up into pleats, are an elegant way of screening a window. Venetian blinds offer more flexible light control.

Opposite, left: Louvred glass that can be adjusted according to need promote natural ventilation.

Opposite, right: Panels of fabric act as a spatial divider without blocking too much light.

that they can help to keep the interior cool in summer by controlling the amount of sun that comes in.

Least flexible are fabric blinds, such as roller or Roman blinds. Most of these either pull down or are lowered down, which tends to block light. An alternative is blinds that pull up from the lower sill, leaving the upper portion of the window clear, which gives privacy without too much loss of light. Sail-like fabric blinds or awnings can be a good way of shading areas such as conservatories that have glazed roofs.

Other types of window coverings include Venetian blinds (in metal or wood), louvred shutters and plantation shutters (see page 51). These can be adjusted according to the time of day or strength of the sun, which helps to strike the balance between the need to optimize natural lighting and the need to keep interiors cool.

FLOORS

After walls and ceilings, floors represent the largest surface area in the home, which means that your choice of flooring material can have a critical bearing on the impact your home has on the environment. In general, the best advice is to select a floor or floor covering that is natural rather than synthetic, and one that is locally sourced rather than imported or transported long distances. But there are also a number of other factors to consider, including whether or not the material is recyclable and comes from a renewable source, what impact it has on indoor air quality and human health, and what contribution it can make to passive solar strategies. Means of fixing or installing, such as the use of adhesives or cements, as well as seals and dressings such as varnishes, can also affect the overall eco-worthiness of a flooring material.

Below: Reclaimed hardwood parquet flooring makes an attractive and durable floor, although it can be expensive. Provided that the top layer is thick enough, parquet can be sanded and refinished.

Right: Bamboo flooring is a good eco alternative to hardwood. It is very stable and resilient.

WOOD

One of the most versatile of all building materials, wood has a long history of use in the building industry, both in construction and in the form of final finishes. Even so, it is a material – or family of materials – of which we never seem to tire.

Wood occupies the middle ground between hard, heavy massive materials such as concrete, stone and tile, and carpets, rugs and natural-fibre coverings at the softer end of the range. As a flooring material it is resilient, comfortable, relatively warm and durable (in solid form rather than veneer or manufactured varieties). It is suitable for use over underfloor or radiant heating systems. Environmentally, wood has a good deal going for it, too. Wood is a natural renewable resource that can be reused and recycled and is biodegradable.

Flooring woods include various species of hardwood, which is dense, strong and often attractively patterned, softwood, which is more prone to moisture penetration and pest attack, along with various types of manufactured composites, such as plywood and wood laminate. Many types of composite wood flooring contain synthetic binders and resins, which tends to rule them out on eco grounds.

Points to consider:
– Always choose FSC-certified wood that comes from a sustainably managed plantation.
– Choose local wood wherever possible. Wood sourced locally has lower embodied energy than wood that has been transported over long distances or imported.
– Avoid endangered species, particularly tropical hardwoods and wood from old-growth temperate forests.
– Choosing salvaged or reclaimed boards cuts down on waste. Reclaim existing wooden floorboards by sanding and sealing them rather than laying a new wood floor. Parquet and other veneered formats can be reclaimed and sanded, as long as the top layer is thick enough.
– Avoid wood-laminate products that contain synthetic binders and resins such as formaldehyde. Plywood contains formaldehyde in lower and less harmful concentrations than other types of laminated products.

WOOD FINISHES

Many of the most common types of wood finish are either solvent- or plastic-based, and should be avoided on environmental grounds. Solvents contain high levels of VOCs (volatile organic compounds). Seals and varnishes, such as polyurethane, effectively coat the wood with an impenetrable skin of plastic. There are many alternatives that perform just as well or better. Deep-penetrating natural oils, such as linseed oil and tung oil, provide good water-resistance and serve to harden the wood, making it less vulnerable to damage and abrasion. Beeswax, applied in successive layers, enhances the colour of the wood and smells pleasant. Natural water-based stains can be chosen if you want to colour the floor.

BAMBOO

Incredibly fast growing, renewable and plentiful, bamboo makes an environmentally friendly alternative to wood. Bamboo reaches full maturity in about five to six years and its cultivation requires little in the way of human intervention. It is naturally pest-resistant and requires no fertilizer; in fact, it actually improves poor soil. The principal drawback, ecologically speaking, is that most of the bamboo used in the production of flooring, panelling and worktops is grown in China and Indonesia, and the associated transport costs raise its embodied energy. Another is the fact that some formaldehyde is used in the laminating process. The best sources of bamboo are those manufacturers which control the entire process from harvest to finished product and can guarantee that a minimum of formaldehyde has been used.

Bamboo flooring comes in laminated boards or planks made of strands or strips of bamboo fibre. It is very stable and resilient. The hardest grades are stronger and more durable than maple or oak. The material has a lively surface grain and comes in a range of woody colours. It can be installed by nailing or stapling; alternatively, it is fixed with a water-based adhesive.

Other bamboo products include panels for wall cladding, counters and worktops, textiles and papers.

Linda Garland, founder of the Environmental Bamboo Foundation, believes that bamboo has great potential as a structural element in eco-friendly construction as well as its more familiar use as cladding and flooring. Just as bamboo floors resemble hardwood floors, bamboo houses need not resemble beach huts — the material is strong and adaptable enough to be used in frame or panel structures.

PALMWOOD

Palmwood is derived from coconut palms that grow in abundance in plantations around the world, and is a natural, renewable resource. Coconut palms are grown for their nuts; after about a century, the palm will have become too tall for nutrients to reach the top and it will stop producing nuts. At this point it is cut down and replaced with a shorter, younger palm.

Palmwood comes from cut palms that would otherwise go to waste. The wood is produced by cutting, slicing and kiln-drying the raw material and then laminating the strands and bonding them with a non-toxic adhesive. Palmwood flooring comes in tongue-and-groove planks, which are nailed or glued in place. Stable and very durable, it comes in characteristically rich, dark woody colours, with an overt graining pattern.

Other palmwood products include panels, which can be used for cladding, and plywood.

CORK

Cork comes from the bark of the evergreen cork oak (*Quercus suber*), a tree native to Mediterranean regions. Cork oaks naturally shed their bark every ten years or so, which means the bark can be harvested without damaging the trees. Most of the cork that is harvested goes to make bottle-stoppers. The waste product of bottle-stopper production is used to make tiles and sheets for flooring and other internal finishes.

Cork's unique cellular structure, which traps air, makes it light, cushioned and springy. It is also naturally fire-resistant. In the past, most cork tiles were composed of cork granules bound with adhesives containing formaldehyde. Now many manufacturers have switched to environmentally friendly water-based pigments and solvents.

The biggest producer of cork is Portugal, which means that transport costs can increase embodied energy. However, as well as being renewable, recyclable and recycled, cork also has good thermal- and sound-insulating properties. It is also antibacterial and hypoallergenic. Sealing is required; waxes make an environmentally friendly alternative to synthetic seals.

Left: Used wholeheartedly, cork can make a surprisingly attractive and comfortable floor. Cork flooring is made from the waste of bottle-stopper production.

LINOLEUM

Contrary to popular belief, linoleum is a wholly natural product, with the principal ingredient being *oleum lini* or linseed oil. Other ingredients include pine resin, powdered cork, wood flour, powdered limestone, pigment and hessian, which is used for backing. The mixture is pressed onto the hessian backing, dried and then baked at high temperatures. From an eco point of view, the main drawback is that fertilizers are used in linseed production.

Lino comes in a wide range of colours and patterns and has a host of practical advantages. It's warm, resilient, antibacterial, antistatic and hypoallergenic, which makes it an excellent choice if there are asthma sufferers in the household. It is also naturally fire- and burn-resistant. Biodegradable and recyclable, it is very durable and actually becomes harder as it matures over time. No sealing is required. Formats include sheet, which requires professional installation, and tiles, which are easier to lay.

RUBBER

Rubber flooring came into fashion as a domestic floor covering during the vogue for high-tech, and has seen a revival as the colour range has widened extensively. Up until now, however, most rubber flooring, has been entirely synthetic.

A new type of rubber flooring has recently come on the market, which is 90 per cent natural in composition. Natural rubber comes from rubber trees, which are particularly efficient at absorbing carbon dioxide from the atmosphere. Natural rubber flooring comes in a similar range of colours and patterns to the synthetic variety. Some types, however, do include a proportion of PVC or other plasticizers and it is important to check the contents. Recycled rubber, principally made of recycled car tyres, is another eco option.

All types of rubber flooring are warm, antistatic and antibacterial. Flooring is available in tiles or sheets. Rubber is very durable, can be recycled or down-cycled, and has good sound-insulating properties. However, it does offgas to a degree and rooms must be adequately ventilated as a result.

Above: Linoleum is composed entirely of natural ingredients and scores highly for hygiene. The material is also hypoallergenic, biodegradable, recyclable and naturally fire-resistant.

Right: In the past most rubber flooring was synthetic. Recently, new types have come on the market, which are 90 per cent natural in composition. A similar vibrant colour range is available.

CERAMIC TILES

Ceramic tiles come in a huge range of colours, sizes and textures, which broadens the decorative scope. Flooring-grade tiles are very durable and suited to wet locations, such as bathrooms and kitchens; they can also be installed over underfloor heating. They are easy to maintain and require no further dressing or sealing. Fully vitrified tiles can be used outdoors.

Clay, the main ingredient of ceramic tiles, is an abundant natural resource. Common tile adhesives have a high VOC content, but water-based alternatives are available. The greatest drawback of ceramic tiles, however, is their high embodied energy, which comes both from the way they are made and processed and the fact that many tiles are imported.

TERRACOTTA TILES

Terracotta tiles share many of the same attributes as ceramic tiles. Most are manufactured, although some are hand-produced in areas such as Mexico, Provence and Tuscany. Even handmade tiles have a relatively high embodied energy due to the energy costs of transportation. Like their mass-market alternative, quarry tiles, terracotta tiles work well over underfloor heating.

Left: Terracotta tiles, like other ceramic products, have high embodied energy because of the way they are produced. However, they can contribute thermal mass and work well over underfloor heating.

Left: Irregular stone flags have a countrified appeal. Reclaimed or salvaged stone is the greenest option.

Below: Stone and ceramic tile, which have high thermal mass, can contribute to passive heating and cooling strategies. These dense materials warm up slowly and release heat slowly.

STONE

One of the most beautiful of all natural materials, stone makes an extremely durable and attractive floor. Types vary widely in colour, patterning and texture, from the smooth opulence of marble to dark, sleek slate or the cool, contemporary elegance of limestone. The high thermal mass of stone, particularly in thicker slabs, means that it is a good choice for homes designed for passive solar gain and it is also very effective installed over underfloor heating. Similarly, in warm climates, stone contributes to natural cooling.

While stone is generally viewed as an abundant natural resource, it is not strictly speaking renewable. Some types that have been particularly prized are becoming rare – Yorkstone, a type of exceptionally weather-resistant sandstone in high demand for garden paving, is a case in point. Quarrying can have a degrading effect on natural habitats and landscapes. A further drawback, from an eco point of view, is that many types of stone are transported over long distances, in some cases thousands of miles. Together with the weight of the raw material, this increases embodied energy. Dressings and seals, applied to reduce staining in the case of more porous types of stone such as limestone, can further compromise the material's eco friendliness.

The greenest option is to use reclaimed or salvaged stone, or, failing that, stone sourced locally. Heavier, thicker slabs, which need to be bedded in sand and mortar, are more environmentally friendly than thinner tiles, which are stuck in place with adhesive.

BRICK

Natural in origin, brick is a standard construction material in many areas of the world. As a flooring material, brick contributes to passive solar strategies due to its high thermal mass and can be used over underfloor heating. Because of the high heat required for the firing process, however, brick has relatively high embodied energy.

CONCRETE

Despite its image as the brutal material of the housing block and multi-storey car park, concrete has many green credentials. The principal ingredients are Portland cement and aggregate (sand, gravel and crushed rock), all abundant and often locally available, which reduces energy costs associated with transportation. In recent years, great efforts have been made by the concrete industry to reduce the energy required to make Portland cement. In some cases, this has meant using alternative fuels; in others, a proportion of fly ash, waste from coal-fired power stations, has been added to the mix to reduce the amount of cement required. Concrete is 100 per cent recyclable and crushed concrete can be used instead of aggregate, easing pressure on these resources.

Like brick, stone and other dense materials, concrete has high thermal mass, which makes it a good choice for a house designed to benefit from passive solar strategies. When exposed, it reflects heat further into the interior. It's naturally fire-resistant and does not require further coatings. Concrete is an ideal material to use over underfloor heating. In warm climates, it significantly aids natural cooling.

CARPETS AND RUGS

While not the universal flooring solution it once was, carpeting remains popular because of its softness, warmth and sound-insulating properties. Cosy and comfortable underfoot, carpet encourages floor-level living and can provide a unifying element in open-plan layouts. Although in recent years it has given ground to smooth floors, particularly those made of wood, it still retains a significant part of the market. However, carpeting can harbour dust mites and is not advisable for households that include sufferers of asthma or allergic reactions.

For the green consumer, key issues associated with carpet include the fibres of which it is composed, the type of backing and underlay, and its eventual disposal. By far the greatest proportion of carpet that is installed in homes contains a synthetic component, generally to reduce cost and improve stain-resistance and wear. Backings and underlay are often synthetic, too. By and large, carpet does not last as long as other types of flooring and most used carpet is disposed directly to landfill. Carpet is not suitable for use over underfloor heating, as it provides an insulating layer that prevents some of the heat from being radiated into the room. Always check the label before making your selection. A recycled logo does not necessary mean that the carpet has been made of recycled materials – it may simply indicate that the carpet can be recycled.

Rugs can be more versatile. In the days before fitted carpets, many households rotated rugs on a seasonal basis, storing them away in the summer to allow a stone or timber floor (with its cool undercroft) to have a maximum 'thermal flywheel' effect and replacing them in winter to increase insulation and prevent draughts.

Types of fibre include:

– *Wool.* All-wool carpets and rugs are the most eco-friendly choice, particularly if they are backed with hessian and laid over felt underlays. Wool is a great sound and thermal insulator; it's recyclable, renewable and biodegradable and relatively long-lasting. However, it is fairly demanding to maintain and expensive. Where it is imported, embodied energy costs increase.
– *Cotton.* Cotton shares many of the same eco advantages as wool, although it is not a good insulator. It's unsuitable for areas of heavy traffic and requires frequent cleaning. In many parts of the world, cotton is imported; pesticides are also heavily used in cotton growing. The most common form of cotton floor coverings are rugs.
– *Synthetic fibres.* Polyester, polypropylene and nylon are the most common synthetic fibres used in carpet manufacture. They may be used in wool blends to increase durability, or on their own. All of these fibres are products of the petrochemical industry, have high embodied energy and are non-biodegradable. Green consumers should also avoid carpeting backed in synthetic foam.
– *Recycled fibres.* Recycled carpet can be made of textile fibres or from recycled PET (polyethylene terephthalate), the type of plastic that is found in plastic bottles. A method of recycling nylon is also being developed. Some manufacturers also operate a number of schemes that either recycle used carpet into new carpet, restore and clean used carpet or down-cycle its components.

Natural-fibre coverings

The family of natural fibres includes fibres derived from plants, such as sisal, seagrass, coir and jute. These generally grow in tropical areas, which gives the products a higher embodied energy due to associated transport costs. With the exception of jute, natural-fibre floor coverings are coarse and generally withstand heavy traffic fairly well. Seagrass, which is naturally water-resistant, cannot be dyed. Staining, however, is an issue with other natural fibres: even water will stain sisal.

For best results, natural-fibre floor coverings should be laid over underlay. They can be fitted wall-to-wall like carpet, or used as area rugs, runners and mats. Unlike carpet, natural-fibre coverings are hypoallergenic.

Far left: Concrete, especially types that incorporate a proportion of fly ash, can be viewed as a green choice. It's naturally fire-resistant and does not require further coatings.

Above and below: Rugs made of natural fibres, such as wool, cotton, sisal and seagrass, provide extra warmth and comfort underfoot during the winter. In summer, when cooling is what you want, they can be rolled up and stored.

WALLS AND CEILINGS

Walls and ceilings collectively constitute the largest surface area in the home. The materials of which they are constructed inevitably have an impact on passive solar strategies and related issues. How they are decorated also has implications for health and natural ventilation.

Walls made of heavy materials, such as concrete or masonry blockwork, absorb heat during the day and gradually release it overnight, helping to keep the interior warm in winter and cool in summer. Infilling a timber-framed structure with masonry can help to prevent excessive heat gain or loss and reduce temperature swings, thus reducing the need for supplementary heating or cooling.

Beyond the cosmetic, there is no need for walls to be subsequently finished at all. Exposed stone or brickwork can be full of character. Even polished concrete and plaster have their charms. Whatever else goes on top should ideally enhance the ability of the structure to 'breathe' and regulate humidity levels naturally. Covering a wall with an impermeable render or a plastics-based paint can lead to a build-up of condensation. Modern commercial paints have been shown to contain a high proportion of VOCs (volatile organic compounds), which have a serious effect on human health. That is to say nothing of the environmental damage caused by their production and subsequent disposal.

Left: Exposed brick, which requires no further treatment or coatings, makes a rugged backdrop in a contemporary setting.

Above: A concrete wall, with exposed marks from shuttering, has a tough industrial aesthetic.

Right: Vernacular buildings tend to make use of local materials, such as stone cleared from fields or quarried nearby.

NATURAL PLASTERS

One of the most common finishes for walls and ceilings is plaster. The basic ingredients of plaster are sand and a binder, which is usually cement, gypsum or lime. Gypsum plaster and plasterboard are the most popular choices for internal finishes.

If you are going to use conventional plaster, gypsum plaster is recommended over cement plaster because it is more permeable. Greener still is plasterboard made of recycled newspaper and gypsum over a recycled gypsum core. From a practical point of view, gypsum plaster is easier to work than other natural alternatives, such as lime-based plaster, and it dries faster. Plastered walls can be left bare and minimally sealed with a coat of wax to prevent dusting.

Alternatives to gypsum include a number of traditional plasters, which have been used for centuries. One type is akin to the classic Moroccan interior finish *tadelakt*. This may be tinted with pigment and is rubbed to a silky, waterproof finish with a slight sheen. Other types include clay plaster, which can also be used as an external stuccoed render, and other lime-based mixtures that have a smooth, chalky finish. These preparations need specialist application and are undoubtedly harder to work, but they bring real aesthetic benefits as well as environmental ones.

Left: Bare plaster has a warm appearance. A light coat of wax will prevent dusting. Choose gypsum plaster and plasterboard over cement plaster.

Right: Alternatives to gypsum plaster are various traditional plasters, some of which are lime-based. These need to be applied by a specialist.

NATURAL PAINTS

Modern commercial paints are the product of the petrochemical industry and the formulations with which we are familiar today have been on the market for a comparatively short time. Before the postwar boom in these industries, most domestic paints were 'natural' to some degree – although they may well have contained harmful ingredients such as lead. Synthetic paints, on the other hand, such as emulsion or latex paint, contain a high proportion of plastic. When you paint a wall with a coat of emulsion, essentially you are sealing it with a thin layer of plastic and compromising the wall's ability to 'breathe'. The plastic content of the paint means that it is static, which in turn means that the surface will attract dust and bacteria.

Despite the heavily promoted practical advantages of conventional paint – ease of application, quick drying times, vast colour range, specialist textures and finishes – increasingly we are counting the environmental cost. There are three serious issues: impact on human health, means of production and waste.

VOCs (volatile organic compounds), which are found in most conventional synthetic paints (as well as seals and varnishes), and which offgas into the atmosphere affecting indoor air quality, have been shown to cause allergies, asthma and skin irritations, as well as more serious disorders.

It is often impossible to tell exactly what chemicals paint contains – formaldehyde, fungicides, bactericides and heavy metals are common additions. Polyurethane is present in most 'non-drip' paints. It is estimated that about 15,000 different chemicals are used during the manufacture of paint, varnish and cleaning products. The sheer surface area involved means that the effect of such ingredients is not negligible. Given that we spend a large proportion of our time indoors, that amounts to a significant exposure to pollutants whose long-term effects are not fully understood.

Commercial paint production is extremely wasteful. Like any petrochemical process, it devours fossil fuels. The production of polyurethane, for example, a common type of varnish, involves a process that results in 90 per cent wastage. The waste is stored in tanks because there is no other way of disposing of it. Neither is there a safe or biodegradable way of disposing of old or unused paint, which means that the toxic chemicals used in these formulations represent a significant pollutant.

Until the last decade or so, natural paint ranges were rather limited in colour and texture. This is no longer the case. Natural paint suppliers now offer a range of beautiful vibrant colours, either pre-mixed or made up using natural pigments. Different textures are also available and application has markedly improved. Best of all, natural paints are biodegradable and can be disposed of safely without causing any damage to the environment.

Types of Natural Paint

– *Distemper.* Old-fashioned, traditional, lime-based paint with a soft, chalky appearance. It has to be applied over lime-based plaster, as it won't adhere to gypsum plaster. Distemper is prone to flaking and is not very durable, so it must be regularly renewed.

– *Oil-based paints.* Most natural paints on the market use linseed oil as a binder – one company has its own linseed farm near its factory. Pigments come from a range of natural sources, including madder root, oak bark and crushed minerals. Mineral pigments are generally more durable and more intensely coloured. Solvents include turpentine or citrus-peel oils, which although wholly natural can cause mild irritation.

– *Water-based paints.* Similar to oil-based paints, but the solvent is water. Contain zero VOCs.

– *Clay paint.* Renewable, non-toxic paint, but there is only a limited range of colours.

– *Limewash (whitewash).* Care must be taken during application because of the caustic nature of lime. Several coats are needed for full coverage.

PAPER

Wallpaper has seen a revival of interest in recent years, with large-scale motifs and photo-realist patterns supplanting more conventional geometric and floral designs. Paper comes from a natural renewable resource and is eminently recyclable, which means that wallpaper is an acceptable cover-up for the eco decorator, provided that the adhesives and pastes used are water-based and natural in origin. Avoid papers that are coated with vinyl to make them water-resistant, as well as designs that feature blocked foil.

Greener still are papers woven from a range of natural fibres, including mulberry, hemp, arrowroot, jute, bamboo, seagrass, sisal and wildgrass. Most of these are overtly textured, which adds to their appeal. Colours tend to be muted and neutral, with the exception of bamboo and sisal papers, which are available in stronger shades.

Far left: Choose natural paints or low-VOC paints over commercial varieties, which include many harmful chemicals and cannot be disposed of safely.

Centre: Natural paints have improved dramatically and are now much easier to apply and available in vibrant colours and evocative textures.

Left: Wallpaper has seen a comeback in recent years. Avoid using pastes, such as PVA glue, which are plastics-based. Traditional starch-based adhesives are a greener option and are recommended by quality wallpaper manufacturers.

CLADDING AND PANELLING

Other options for interior decoration include cladding or panelling using solid materials. Wood is the classic example and many different types of format are available, from tongue-and-groove cladding made of softwood to hardwood-faced veneers. Tiles and mosaic – stone, ceramic and glass – are also common choices, particularly for areas in the home, such as kitchens and bathrooms, where ease of cleaning and a high degree of water-resistance is required. For a soft, upholstered look, walls can be lined in fabric, which also has insulating qualities. Natural fabrics, which absorb moisture, are compatible with breathing wall construction.

As with all surfaces and finishes, the eco designer has to take into account whether the material in question comes from a renewable resource, is low in embodied energy and recyclable, and whether the means of application and installation is environmentally friendly (see Floors, page 78). Depending on the material chosen, cladding or panelling walls and ceilings can add an insulating element. Impervious materials, however, such as ceramic tile, may affect moisture regulation and cause a build-up of condensation. Many eco designers recommend that tiling extends only part of the way up the wall for this reason.

Far left: Slotted timber cladding on the walls and units creates a unifying element in a bathroom.

Left: Here the basic timber panels that make up the house's structure have been left exposed on the walls and ceiling.

Right: Tiles have high embodied energy, but they are very durable and water-resistant, which makes them a practical choice for bathrooms and kitchens.

Below right: Exposed corrugated-iron sheeting is a humble material that brings depth of character in its weathered state.

Next page: An eco conversion of an existing building in Switzerland saw the walls lined with 40 cm (15³/4 inches) of insulation made of recycled newspaper. The internal walls are clad with natural wood treated with penetrating oil to increase water-resistance.

FURNITURE AND FITTINGS

Years ago, I was talking to the British interior designer David Hicks about furniture and what to do with pieces that did not merit the status of antiques but which weren't junk either. Somehow we came up with the idea of buying a big warehouse, fitting it out with a conveyor belt, and installing ourselves on viewing platforms where we could make instant decisions about the worn-out sofas, chairs, tables and wardrobes that were presented for our inspection. We imagined ourselves sending scratched tables to be stripped and refinished, rickety chairs to be mended and sofas covered in hideous fabric to be reupholstered in bright modern prints. It was a flight of fancy – with more than a hint of Heath Robinson (I seem to remember punch-cards printed with our instructions came into it somewhere) – but the germ of the idea combined our shared dislike of waste with our aesthetic preferences for clean lines, strong colour and simple pattern.

Nowadays our idea does not seem so far-fetched. In Britain, the financier John Studinski has been involved with a charity that employs homeless people to collect, repair, reupholster and sell secondhand furniture. Similar schemes are thriving in many local communities, training young people in associated skills and providing a source of affordable furniture and fittings for those on low incomes.

For many years, as the fashion industry infected interior design with its own hectic pace, the high street has increasingly encouraged us to view home furnishings almost as disposable items. Bored of your kitchen? Rip it out and put in a new one. Is your sofa tired and sagging? Trade it in for this season's model. The result of this approach has inevitably caused waste and increased consumption of energy and natural resources. 'The type of person who buys his own furniture', might once have been an aristocratic put-down of a self-made person, but in the not-so-distant past most people's homes included pieces that had been in the family and new purchases were always made with the expectation that they would not need replacement.

As a retailer, I cannot pretend that I don't want people to buy things. But I do believe, and have always believed, that quality is important. A well-designed and well-made piece of furniture has the potential to last a lifetime, if not several lifetimes, provided it is looked after. There would not be a thriving market in antique furniture if that were not the case. In fact, good-quality furniture made out of good-quality materials has the potential to improve with age and use, acquiring character, value and patina over time.

Increasing environmental awareness directs us to think just as carefully about how we furnish our homes as how we use energy and water. Unfortunately many manufacturers and retailers are less than transparent about how their products are made and where the raw materials are sourced. As consumers become more aware and demanding, this looks likely to change, but until there is some form of independent certification that applies across the board, there remains the risk that people will be taken in by the kind of vague, feel-good claims that are commonly known as 'greenwashing'. For that reason, it is important to scrutinize labels, ask questions and generally do your research before making a purchase.

ECO DESIGN

On the positive side, from my own involvement in design education (as Provost of the Royal College of Art and Chairman of the Design Museum in London), I see encouraging signs that young design graduates take their environmental responsibilities very seriously indeed. Rather than the self-consciously worthy and, frankly, rather 'twee' products that have been marketed under the general heading of 'eco', the new breed of designer views green issues as part and parcel of the entire process of development and production. One group, [re]design, who exhibited in 2007 at the Bluebird Café in London, has the inspiring slogan: 'For designers who don't want to make landfill'.

Designers who don't want to make landfill have a number of strategies open to them. Furniture and fittings can be made out of recycled elements – hybrid tables and chairs, for example, composed of salvaged bits of other tables and chairs. Or they can make inspired use of what otherwise would be waste material – such as lampshades created out of food packaging or lampbases made out of crushed plastic bottles. Recycled plastic – vivid and graphically patterned – has inspired a host of applications from seat furniture to worktops and cladding. At the very least, materials should be as local and sustainable as possible, be processed in the most energy-efficient way and be recyclable at the end of their (hopefully) long life.

Right: Being eco-minded when it comes to furnishing your home means taking the long view by consuming less, buying better quality furniture and fittings, and ensuring that pieces are made of sustainable materials.

SECONDHAND

From the antique in the auction showroom to the chair missing a leg sitting in the builder's skip, secondhand furniture comes at every price point and level of desirability. But whatever the source or price tag, 'pre-owned' pieces are greener than new. We have always sold flea market furniture in the Conran Shop, much of it sourced in Paris, and I am always happily surprised how well such items do and how quickly they are snapped up.

The Internet has lent a whole new impetus to what has always been a thriving sector of the furniture business. While demand for high-end antiques has tailed off in recent years, sites such as eBay continue to go from strength to strength and attract millions of eagle-eyed bargain-hunters waiting to bid for other people's cast-offs. Greener still are sites like Freecycle, where people offer household items and furniture that they no longer want for free. The basic concept behind freecycling and other exchange sites makes good environmental sense – but participants do have to be wary. Unlike eBay, where a system of feedback helps to keep descriptions of goods as accurate as possible, on free sites you have to take it on trust that 'in good condition' means what it says and is not simply an open invitation for you to collect someone else's rubbish for them. Even so, such sites represent a good way of tackling the problem of waste and easing the pressure on landfill. Unwanted gifts constitute a significant proportion of what is offered both on auction and free sites. A recent survey conducted on behalf of eBay estimated that £4 billion of gifts are not wanted by their recipients.

Back in the real rather than virtual world, shopping in junk shops, charity shops and car boot sales at least offers you the opportunity to try before you buy – to sit in the retro chair and see if it feels comfortable, to examine the chest of drawers for telltale signs of woodworm, to decide whether the table with the water ring is really worth the asking price. As is the case with more expensive antiques, doing your homework pays off. If you are attracted to furniture from a particular period, spending some time researching contemporary designers and manufacturers can help you to spot the genuine article from the lookalike. Modern retro – pieces from the 1950s, 1960s and 1970s – is a particular favourite with young collectors these days.

Above: Many people are attracted to secondhand or vintage furniture not simply because it is often cheaper than new, but because of its quality. Furniture that has stood the test of time is generally robustly made.

Right: An eclectic mix of styles and periods works well in a simple setting. Sourcing furniture from secondhand outlets brings with it the pleasure of discovery as well as the thrill of bargain-hunting.

Architectural salvage provides another twist to the secondhand. Many of the more established architectural salvage companies started out in business several decades ago, when they found a ready clientele among aficionados both of period style and high-tech. A salvage yard was the place to go if you were looking to source a Georgian fireplace, but equally it offered quirky fixtures and fittings such as school lab desks, church pews and shopfront shutters, which lend both depth of character and a shift of scale to domestic interiors. Lots of revolving bank doors are on offer at the moment.

FITTED UNITS

Hard-working areas of the home – kitchens and bathrooms in particular – are often treated as fitted spaces, with built-in storage, appliances and fixtures. In recent years, consumers have spent more and more money improving and upgrading these parts of their homes. It's not surprising. Years ago the kitchen was a workaday place behind closed doors – now it is the heart of the home. Bathrooms were once clinical, faintly punitive places – now they are domestic spas and centres of well-being.

For the green consumer, ripping out old fitted units, worktops and sanitaryware and installing new ones is wasteful of resources. But that does not mean you have to settle for second best. There are a number of ways in which you can revamp fitted areas without breaking the bank or harming the planet. These include:

Above: Architectural salvage is another fruitful source of secondhand fixtures and fittings. These industrial shelves serve as a place to store crockery and glassware.

Right: Small signs of wear and tear add character to vintage pieces. Look out for clean simple lines and pieces made of solid, natural materials. Buying secondhand or freecycling are both green forms of consumption.

– Fitting new cupboard doors, drawer fronts and worktops onto existing carcases. These can be sourced from many retail outlets or custom-made. Avoid MDF (medium-density fibreboard) because it has a high formaldehyde content. ZF MDF is formaldehyde-free.

– Opting for salvaged materials and fixtures. Reclaimed basins and baths often have more character than new models. Old cast-iron bathtubs can easily be refurbished, look as good as new and are a lot more comfortable than many modern fittings. Worktops made of reclaimed wood, stone or recycled material are practical, good-looking and environmentally friendly.

– Using recycled materials. One company makes a fully recycled kitchen, with worktops composed of post-consumer coffee cups and cupboard doors made of recycled yoghurt pots. Many composite worktops on the market have a high recycled content and excellent practical performance.

DESIGN

Design changes, such as reconfiguring layouts, making new openings, or loft and basement conversions, are generally prompted by the need for more space or the desire to improve the quality of the space you already have. But they can also go a long way towards greening your home.

Such alterations, whether or not they have an impact on basic structure or servicing, are generally more complicated and more expensive than the essentially cosmetic changes discussed in the previous chapter. Some people might think that worrying about eco issues, when perhaps all they're after is an extra bedroom or a bigger kitchen, will only add an unnecessary level of confusion and extra cost to a home improvement project. But if you seek out the right professional help – and you will almost certainly need professional help at some stage – building in a green way does not have to be more involved or more difficult. Nor does it have to be more expensive. In fact, you may well save money both up front, in the cost of construction materials, and in the long term, by increasing the energy efficiency of your home.

Left: The m-house is a completely prefabricated house that is designed to be transported directly to the site, rather like an upscale mobile home.

These days intelligent design is green design. In many parts of the world that attitude is increasingly becoming enshrined in building codes and legislation. In Britain, for example, it is already the case that a new extension must meet very high standards of insulation, even if the rest of the house does not. Such standards will only be raised in future, so it's worth being ahead of the game.

BASIC PRINCIPLES

The construction industry has a huge carbon footprint. First there are the materials and the energy costs associated with their production and transportation – construction materials account for 30 per cent of road freight in Britain. Secondly there is the problem of building waste, arising from demolition and from spoiled and surplus materials on site. Thirdly there is the energy consumed during construction.

Eco designers and builders look to reduce the carbon footprint of construction in a number of ways. Most crucially, they seek to design and build so that houses are as energy efficient as possible over the course of their lifetime. The carbon savings that come from insulating to a high degree and using alternative sources of energy will, over a period of decades, more than offset the embodied energy of the materials used in a building's construction.

That is not to say that choice of construction materials is unimportant. Local materials, with low embodied energy, as well as materials that are reclaimed or recycled, are preferable, although not always cheaper. So, too, are specific design and building solutions. Many eco builders use prefabricated structural systems, which tend to be more energy efficient to produce and will also result in less site wastage. Similarly, designing a building or an extension of a building so that it can be dismantled, reused or recycled takes the long view.

GETTING PROFESSIONAL HELP

Unless what you are planning is very straightforward – simple changes to the layout, for example – and does not entail making any alterations to the basic structure of your home, you will need professional advice, certainly at the planning stage, along with a competent contractor or building professional to carry out the work.

The standard advice applies: ask around for personal recommendations, ensure that whomever you employ has the relevant professional accreditations, take up references and put everything in writing. When you are factoring green issues into the design equation, you also need to make sure that individuals have the relevant experience and a track record in this kind of approach. The last person you need is a professional on a learning curve.

ARCHITECTURAL SERVICES

For the more complicated home improvement projects, such as conversions and extensions, it's a good idea to employ an architect, at least for the design stage. A good architect will help you to refine your ideas and will work with you to formulate a brief that delivers what you want. He or she may well come up with ideas that you have not considered yourself – which is not to say that you will find yourself getting talked into something you don't like, merely that people who haven't had design training often find it difficult to anticipate the knock-on effects of spatial change, especially changes to volume.

Once you have agreed on the outline scheme, your architect will go on to draw up the proposals, submit plans for approval and negotiate the various official hurdles on your behalf. After this stage, you can either choose to project manage the job yourself, by hiring builders or contractors directly, or you can retain the services of your architect to oversee the work and ensure that everything runs smoothly and to budget. The latter option is preferable for large-scale projects that entail the coordination of a number of diverse trades with on-site deliveries of materials, fixtures and fittings.

Increasingly, these days, many architectural practices, both large and small, are well up to speed on eco design. They may also have on-going associations with energy consultants and other technical specialists who can advise in specific cases. As ever, it is important to ensure that you are on the same wavelength. Poor communication lies at the heart of many of the difficulties that arise between clients and architects. Before you commit, ask to see examples of previous work – don't expect a practice that favours traditional vernacular buildings to come up with a gleaming modernist design, or vice versa.

SPECIALIST CONSULTANTS

Any kind of home improvements, especially extensions and conversions, inevitably result in a period of domestic upheaval. If you are already planning disruptive building works, you may wish to take the opportunity to upgrade or alter servicing to make your home more energy- and water-efficient at the same time. Independent energy consultants can audit your home and lifestyle and make suggestions about the type of energy-saving environmentally friendly changes you could make that would best suit your requirements (see page 24). If you need a new roof, for example, it might be worth thinking about installing solar thermal panels or solar slates. Other sources of advice include energy suppliers, although these, naturally, tend to promote their own products and services as well as giving more general recommendations.

BUILDERS AND CONTRACTORS

Horror stories about building professionals abound and it might seem that finding a reputable, efficient contractor, who works to schedule and budget and who is *also* eco-aware would be an almost impossible task. That needn't be the case. Although green builders may be in a minority within the profession as a whole, this looks likely to change as demand for their services increases. As is true when you are employing any other type of professional, word-of-mouth recommendation can be a good place to start. Ask to see examples of previous work, get estimates in writing and take up references.

Another way of tracking down the right people for the job is to use a searchable database or green register to find eco-builders in your area or those who specialize in a particular type of work. Some eco-firms have a wide range of expertise, covering the traditional trades of plumbing, carpentry, masonry and decoration, as well as the installation of condensing boilers, solar thermal systems and other more specific alternative technologies. Others are experienced in the eco-refurbishment of old buildings. Then there are specialists, such as plasterers who have experience working with lime plasters and renders, decorators who only work with eco paints and finishes, and carpenters who use only locally sourced sustainable timber.

Top right: A timber structure goes up.

Centre right: Prefabricated elements arrive on site.

Bottom right: Fitting roof glazing.

BUDGETING

A common perception of eco design is that it is more expensive. While some types of alternative technology are undoubtedly costly to install, designing and building in an environmentally friendly way can, in fact, be cheaper than conventional approaches, both in the short and long term. As mentioned before, eco-friendly construction materials, surfaces and finishes are often more economical than standard ones. But the most telling argument, financially speaking, is the savings you will make over time in reduced utility bills. Making your home more eco-friendly should also enhance its market value.

In many parts of the world, grants and tax breaks are available for green home improvements and these can help to offset initial costs. In the United States, federal tax credits are available if you install energy-efficient windows, doors, roofs and heating, among other alterations. Depending on the state, there may be other tax breaks on offer, too. Similarly, in Britain, grants for making energy-efficient improvements, such as installing insulation, come from a number of sources: the government, local authorities and energy suppliers themselves. In certain cases, you may need to meet eligibility criteria.

On the most basic level budgeting means covering your costs, ensuring that you have enough money to carry out the work to a proper standard, including about 5–10 per cent extra as a contingency allowance in case things go wrong or not according to plan. But it can also entail working out your priorities, so that you spend your money on what is most important to you. Think about what you would like in an ideal world, then look for ways to bring your plans within your means.

Once work has started, try to resist the temptation to make radical changes to the brief. Budgets (and schedules) fly out of the window when that happens.

PERMISSIONS

Pioneers of the green movement faced many challenges, not least of which was the need to persuade planning authorities and building inspectors that their designs were safe and viable. Many found that if they wanted to build in a particular way, especially if they were intending to use unconventional materials such as straw bale or rammed earth, they were forced to campaign to change local building codes first and prove that the construction they were proposing would be structurally sound and fire-resistant.

As eco-awareness has grown, official resistance to eco design has dramatically lessened. In fact, in many cases, the shoe is now on the other foot. There have been recent instances of proposals for houses gaining permission in areas where new development would otherwise be frowned upon, simply because those houses have been designed to high eco standards. However, the inclusion of 'green' features in a design are no guarantee of planning approval being granted, particularly in dense urban or conservation areas. Any alterations that affect the external appearance of your home as viewed from the street, changes to the roof and changes to listed properties may all be contentious, no matter how environmentally friendly they are.

It is always a good idea to discuss what is permissible and what is not with your local planning officer before you go ahead and make a submission. It will save time in the long run and hopefully avoid the frustration of having your proposal turned down. One of the benefits of using an architect is that he or she will be able to fight your case for you and make any necessary alterations to bring your scheme in line with local codes.

It is also a good idea to inform neighbours about what you are proposing before the planning process begins. Many of the objections that hold up the process of approval are based on fear of the unknown. The planning process is not known for its speed, but good lines of communication can help to smooth your path.

RENTED PROPERTY

It's often difficult to make any significant changes to rented property, certainly the type of far-reaching changes that would affect energy efficiency on a significant scale. Rental agreements vary, but few tenants are allowed to alter windows, walls or roofs, for example, to improve thermal performance. Weather-stripping windows, doors and letterboxes, and sealing gaps around light fittings can go some way to improving insulation, as can heavy drapery.

This page: Glazed balustrading encloses a metal stairway. Significant changes to existing houses, as well as new buildings, have to meet stringent building regulations designed to ensure that the end result is structurally sound and fire-resistant, among other factors.

CHANGING THE LAYOUT

Older houses are generally not planned to take advantage of passive energy strategies or natural ventilation. Separate rooms, assigned notional functions and connected to each other by hallways and stairs, are still the norm in the majority of new houses, too, despite our growing preference for multipurpose space.

One of the reasons why people make changes to the way their homes are laid out is to make everyday routines easier and more efficient. Another is to enhance spatial quality by creating open-plan free-flowing areas. But making changes to the layout can also help to make a home more environmentally friendly.

CHANGING ROOM USE

One simple way of improving your home's energy efficiency is to change the way you use the rooms at your disposal. Typically, in storied houses, bedrooms will be upstairs and living areas on the ground floor. This convention has a lot to do with notions of privacy, with 'public' areas, such as living rooms, being easily accessible from the front door and 'private' areas being tucked away on the upper levels.

From an eco point of view, there are certain drawbacks to this traditional type of spatial arrangement. Rooms or areas on the upper levels of a house will be naturally better lit than those on the lower levels. This is because windows that are higher up reveal a greater proportion of the sky than windows at ground or semi-basement level, where the sky is likely to occupy only a narrow margin at the top. Since most of the time we spend in bedrooms we spend asleep, it makes better sense to locate these areas on the lower levels of the house, where the quality of natural light is not as good, and devote the lighter upper levels to living areas and kitchens where we spend the majority of the daylight hours.

Even if your home is not arranged over two or more levels, it can also be worth taking a look at the way the principal rooms are orientated. In the northern hemisphere, rooms that are south-facing will be warmer and brighter than those facing north. Allocating room use so that the main living areas have optimum conditions of natural light and passive solar gain can help to reduce your dependence on artificial lighting and heating, cutting down on your household's overall energy consumption.

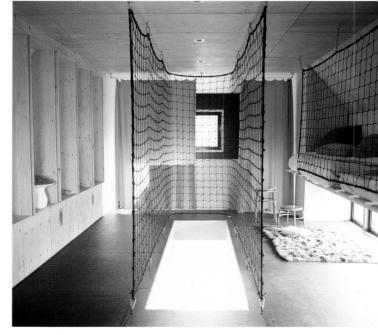

OPENING UP

One of the most popular types of home improvement consists of taking down partition walls to create multipurpose spaces – living/dining areas, kitchen/eating areas and even cooking/eating/living areas. Part of the attraction of this type of layout is the sense of informality and inclusiveness that it promotes. Another benefit is the enhanced sense of space. Knocking down walls doesn't win you much direct floor area, but it does generate a feeling of openness and help to spread available natural light around.

The greatest eco advantage of an open layout is the improvement in natural light and ventilation. In a typical terraced house, removing the central dividing wall results in a space that is lit by windows front and back, and potentially ventilated by through-currents of air. In warm climates, cross-ventilation assumes an even greater importance.

The complexity of the work depends on whether or not the walls you are removing are structural or not. Structural walls play a supporting role; partition walls are simply spatial dividers. If you remove all or a portion of a structural wall, you will need to install a compensating element, such as a beam or lintel, above the opening to take the weight that the wall had previously been supporting. Always seek professional advice about whether a wall is structural or not. If it is, you will also need advice about the right size of beam or lintel to put in its place.

Another way of opening up the interior is to remove walls that separate staircases and hallways from main living areas. This type of alteration can also help to aid ventilation and improve the quality of light. If your home is over two stories, however, fire regulations may prevent you from knocking down the wall that encloses the staircase.

You don't necessarily have to remove entire walls. Internal portholes or windows and narrow horizontal or vertical slivers can enhance the feeling of space, create vistas and views, and spread light around.

On the downside, opening up the layout of your home can make it harder to heat. One answer is to opt for a central source of heat, such as a wood-burning stove, which radiates warmth to the surrounding area. Another is to build in an element of flexibility, such as sliding partitions and screens, so that you can close off areas that are not in use and retain heat where it's needed.

Left: Opening up a stairway and enclosing it minimally with a glass balustrade enhances the sense of volume and spreads available natural light around.

Below left: Minimal screening around an open stairwell is provided by netting secured top and bottom.

Above: A central partition houses a fitted kitchen within an open-plan layout and helps to define distinct areas within the space.

Right: A mezzanine level can provide additional floor area without compromising light or views.

Next page: Extending out into the side return can have a dramatic effect on ground-floor spaces. Here the roof of the extension has been glazed, bringing light down into the new kitchen.

CHANGES TO VOLUME

Below: This wall of double-height glazing has external slatted shutters to provide security and light control.

Below right: One of three separate units designed around a courtyard in north London. The terrace walls are made of polycarbonate cladding and double glazing. The timber frame is made of timber i-beams and paralam. Passive solar gain and natural ventilation comes through the south-facing glazing and rooflights.

When we think about making changes to the way our homes are planned, we tend to focus on the layout of each floor and how the individual spaces or rooms relate to one another. Changes to volume, however, which may entail using the roof space, inserting a mezzanine level or cutting away part of an upper floor to create a double-height area, can offer a great deal of potential, both in terms of spatial quality and practicality.

Opening up from top to bottom, rather than from side to side, allows light to spill down from above. Since toplighting is brighter than natural light admitted by lower or ground-floor windows, you will need to rely less on artificial sources during the day – the intensity and quality of the light is also inherently uplifting. Provided that the windows on the upper level can be opened, stack ventilation, whereby rising warm air escapes at the top of the house, will be encouraged.

These types of changes tend to involve substantial structural work. If you subdivide a double-height space by building a mezzanine across part of it, the new level will need to be supported by the existing load-bearing walls. The only non-structural alternative is to create a raised platform that is self-supporting. Cutting away part of an existing upper floor to create a double-height space generally doesn't affect the basic structure of your home, but you may need to reroute the staircase or install a new means of access.

This page: Opening the space into the roof and exposing the structural elements provides a great sense of volume. Toplighting comes from a pair of rooflights.

BUILDING IN FLEXIBILITY

We expect our homes to fulfil many more functions today than they did in the recent past. Homes have always been places of refuge and shelter; now they are often places of work, places where we entertain family and friends, as well as being repositories for a wide range of different types of household goods and belongings. It's a lot to ask.

No home could ever be entirely future-proof, but one way of staying ahead of the game to a certain degree is by building in as much flexibility as possible to avoid the need for costly and wasteful change further on down the line. In terms of spatial arrangement, this can take the form of movable partitions, screens or dividers, so that you have the option to close off different spaces or open them up as need dictates. Sliding or folding doors or panels that

run from the floor to the ceiling are less intrusive visually because they do not interrupt the ceiling plane.

A flexible, shape-shifting interior is dependent on adequate servicing. This means, for example, making sure that there are enough power points to allow for different spatial arrangements. Underfloor heating also allows more flexibility in terms of furniture configuration than a system that involves fixed radiators.

There is another aspect to flexibility, and that is good organization behind the scenes. People vary widely when it comes to the amount of clutter they can tolerate – some are only comfortable surrounded by possessions, others need the tranquillity of relatively empty space. Whichever camp you fall into, it is essential to organize your belongings in

Above: Doors that run floor to ceiling are more space-enhancing because they do not interrupt the ceiling plane and allow spaces to be read as a whole.

Above right: A considered approach to storage and organization helps to keep spaces flexible.

a workable fashion, whether they are largely out on view, or stowed in fitted cupboards. Waste is endemic in our society and a good deal of waste on the domestic front arises from simple disorganization – things that go missing and need to be replaced, or things stored inappropriately so that they deteriorate or break. Keeping your possessions in good order is one of the ways in which you can cut unnecessary consumption and hence your carbon footprint.

Where space is tight, ingenious fitted solutions, combining storage with pull-down or fold-out tables or screens, can deliver multiple benefits, serving as home offices or even eating areas. To be effective, such fitted elements must work seamlessly, which means constructing them to a high specification.

Left: A sleeping area is screened from the main living space by a pair of partitions that fold back on themselves.

Above: A layout arranged on a long axis has great clarity. Slatted doors provide an element of screening while allowing air to circulate.

MAKING NEW OPENINGS

Above: This eco-friendly house in Napa Valley, California, features large openings that blur the boundaries between indoors and out.

Right: Making a new opening or widening an existing one to improve access to the garden is a popular type of alteration. To avoid compromising the energy efficiency of your house, new openings should be fitted with high-specification glazing.

Far right: The open rear wall of the ground-floor kitchen allows the garden to become part of the living space. The projecting roof creates a sheltered terrace.

Windows and doors – their siting, construction, size and orientation – have a huge impact on the energy efficiency of our homes. They also define how our homes appear, which is why alterations to existing openings or creating new ones are so strictly regulated, particularly on front elevations. While you can put in a new picture window at the rear or side of your house without the need for planning approval, changes that radically affect the way your home appears from the street are often not permitted. This is particularly true in urban areas, especially where much of the existing housing stock consists of visually homogenous terraces.

The complexity and hence expense of the work varies. Enlarging a window by lowering the sill has no structural implications. Widening a window, increasing the height of a window or creating an entirely new opening means that you will need to install a lintel or beam across the top of the new opening to bear the load of the wall.

Our contemporary preference for light, airy surroundings and a desire to bring living spaces closer to outdoor areas has made these types of alterations more popular. But increasing the number of windows, along with their size, has implications for energy efficiency. In temperate climates expanses of standard glazing drain heat from a building during cold weather and raise heat levels uncomfortably during the summer. To avoid compromising the thermal performance of your home, new windows need to be of a high specification, double or triple glazed (see page 70) and preferably fitted with low-E glass. It is also important to think about siting and orientation, too. In the northern hemisphere, new openings on south- or west-facing walls can enhance passive solar strategies.

In warm climates, central open courtyards have long been a feature of vernacular houses. Central courts or atria encourage cross-ventilation and maximize the amount of surface area available for heat loss as well as help with privacy and security.

SOLAR TUBES

One way of introducing natural light into dark internal areas is to install a solar tube. These can also be an effective way of improving light conditions if your home is not oriented in an optimum way. Aside from reducing dependence on artificial light sources, and hence cutting carbon emissions, solar tubes deliver a quality of bright natural light that has been shown to be extremely beneficial to health and well-being.

A solar tube is essentially a form of rooflight. A roof-mounted clear dome, generally made of polycarbonate, directs light down a tube to a ceiling diffuser, which might be directly below, on the other side of a void, such as an attic space, or offset through a void. The interior of the tube is highly reflective to maximize the amount of natural light that is captured.

Solar tubes, or sun scoops as they are sometimes known, are ideal for lighting internal bathrooms, stairs and hallways, or other areas in the home where there are no windows. They come in a range of sizes and can be used on pitched or flat roofs. For best performance, they should be mounted on the south-facing side of the roof and where there are no overshadowing trees or buildings. Adjustable elbow joints allow the tubing to be offset if necessary, for example if there are obstructing beams in a roof space, although straight vertical runs provide maximum light. Some systems come with light and sun deflectors, which capture light at low and high angles, boosting light levels by up to 20 per cent. There are also designs on the market that are flat rather than domed, which makes them more suitable for fitting to houses in conservation areas. Different types of flashing are also available, so that the installation blends as unobtrusively as possible with the existing roof covering.

CONVERTING LOFTS

Loft or attic conversions are one of the most popular and cost-effective ways of gaining more space. Cheaper than moving and relatively hassle-free, converting a loft is a good way of adding value to your home while providing much-needed extra room.

From an eco point of view, loft conversions represent a more efficient use of space than extensions or digging out basements, which necessitate the loss of ground area. Particularly if the roof is in need of renewal, they also offer the opportunity to invest in solar technologies, for example solar thermal panels or photovoltaics, or at the very least to increase the level of insulation. If you are going to use the loft as a bedroom or study, you will need to install one or more rooflights and, depending on positioning, this can have a beneficial effect on natural light levels on the floors below.

HEAD HEIGHT AND OTHER REGULATIONS

Nowadays almost any attic can be converted, even those in newish houses that have preformed roof trusses. The key consideration as to whether a loft is convertible or not is head height. Regulations vary. In Britain, building regulations stipulate that at least half of the converted space must have a head height of 2.3 m (7½ ft).

Many loft conversions do not require planning permission. Since rooflights sit flush with the plane of the roof and do not alter its contour or appearance, these can be installed on the front elevation without the need to seek official approval – unless you live in a conservation area or your home is listed. Similarly, dormer windows installed at the rear of a property are also exempt, provided that they are no bigger than a specified size. Dormers at the front or side, and those that look over parks or other public spaces, do require planning approval. You will also need to submit your plans to the planners if the conversion will increase the volume of your home by 15 per cent or more, which could well be the case if you live in a flat on the top floor. In terraced properties, converting an attic may entail building onto party walls of neighbouring houses, in which case you will need to seek a party-wall award (or two). Your neighbours will have the right to appoint a surveyor at your expense to inspect the works and determine that there is no adverse effect on the structure of their own home.

Even if your conversion does not need planning permission, it must still conform to local building codes and regulations. Structural work to the roof and floor will need to be inspected before final finishes are installed. Fire regulations must also be met. If your home is over two stories, excluding the attic, you may need to install a fire door or closed fire-protected stair between the loft and the rest of the house. The design and position of access stairs is also subject to control.

FUNCTION

Before you go ahead with the work, think about how you are going to use the space. This is a decision that needs to be made within the context of your home as a whole and how it functions. Options include:

Storage space. A dry, well-insulated loft can serve as a repository for a wide range of belongings, relieving pressure on living areas and bedrooms. Basic conversion is straightforward and involves strengthening floor joists to take the weight of what you put up there and boarding out the floor. Built-in shelves, racks and cupboards allow you to make the most efficient use of the space. You will also need artificial lighting.

Extra bedroom. Most people convert their lofts to provide an extra bedroom. All habitable rooms, which include bedrooms, must have a window, so the conversion work is necessarily more involved. Finishes and fittings need to be of a higher standard, too. If there is enough space, you may be able to include a shower, skin and/or toilet.

Study. If you earn your living at home and you don't have clients turning up on a regular basis, or deliveries to manage, a converted loft can provide the psychological separation from the rest of the household that is conducive to productive work. An added bonus is that the quality of natural light and air will be good.

Spatial enhancement. Installing rooflights and cutting away part of the loft floor can improve the quality of space on lower levels by introducing natural light to otherwise dark areas and increasing volume.

Roof garden. Loft conversions can offer the opportunity to devote part of the space to a roof garden, or to extend outwards to create a balcony or terrace.

Left: An attic conversion extends out onto a small balcony. Loft conversions win you more living space without any loss of ground area.

WHAT'S INVOLVED

Loft conversions are such a standard home improvement project that many building companies specializing exclusively in this type of work have sprung into being. If you go this route, the company will design the conversion for you, obtain the necessary permissions, if required, and carry out the work. A reputable general contractor should also be able to handle the construction side more than adequately, although you might have to negotiate any bureaucratic hurdles yourself and possibly seek advice from an architect or surveyor regarding structural issues. For a more original conversion, especially if you are intending to install a bathroom or shower, or if there are difficulties with access, it can be well worth employing an architect.

The main structural work entailed in loft conversions consists of strengthening up the joists and, if you are going to install a rooflight, strengthening up the roof rafters. Roof joists are not designed to take the weight of flooring, furniture and people. Strengthening is carried out by bolting on additional joists alongside the existing ones. Similarly, roof rafters are not strong enough to bear the weight of windows and will need to be doubled up in the same way. If you add a dormer window, you will also have to provide additional support for the roof structure above the new opening.

How much extra work is involved will depend on how you intend to use the space and the standard of fittings and fixtures you require. You may need to widen the access hatch or build a new staircase if you are going to be using the new area on a regular basis, rather than just as a storage repository.

You may decide to live somewhere else whilst the work is going on as it can be pretty disruptive to family life.

Above: A glazed gable end flanked by two rooflights brings plenty of natural light into a converted loft. Low shelving is ranged under the eaves and heat is supplied by a wood-burning stove.

Right: Due to developments in technology, almost any type of attic can be converted these days, including those with preformed roof trusses. Head height is the critical issue.

Right: A half-glazed roof and end wall creates a soaring light-filled space on the top level.

Below: A bathtub under the eaves in a converted attic, with openable rooflights to promote natural ventilation.

Right: In some cases, it may be possible to build an entire structure on top of a roof. Here a sleeping area has direct access to a decked roof terrace.

WINDOWS

Roof windows come in a wide range of sizes and specification and are available either off-the-shelf or in custom, made-to-measure designs. Broadly speaking, there are three basic options – the rooflight, which sits flush with the plane of the roof and is openable; the skylight, which also sits flush with the roof plane but is generally not openable; and the dormer, which is a vertical window that projects from the roofline. You can also fit solar tubes (see page 117). Installing any roof window, with the exception of solar tubes, entails structural work. To some extent, choice of rooflight will be determined by the size and nature of the area you are converting. From an eco standpoint, rooflights should be of a high specification, fitted with high-performance glazing and openable to encourage natural ventilation.

Other factors to consider include:
Cleaning and maintenance. Grimy windows block natural light and are an eyesore. Rooflights that pivot centrally facilitate cleaning.
Means of operation. Ideally, at least one roof window in a loft should be openable. There is a wide range of options, including handles, push bars, winders, pole winders and electrical control.
Light control. To prevent an excessive build-up of heat in the warm months, roof windows need to be shaded, either by blinds fitted to the inner side of the glass or incorporated within the glazing unit.
Architectural character. Conversions of lofts in period properties or in buildings in conservation areas may require special windows that are designed to be in keeping with the period or style of the property.

Above: In a compact spatial arrangement, stairs leading to a converted attic space/mezzanine have been fitted out underneath as storage space. Natural paint has been used on the walls.

Right: A stairway to a converted attic is lit by four roof windows that spill light down into the level below.

Far right: There are many different types of space-saving stairs. These open treads are supported centrally.

STAIRS AND OTHER MEANS OF ACCESS

A key consideration in the design of any loft conversion is the means of access. In many homes, attic spaces are accessed via a hatch cut into the ceiling, which may be fitted with a retractable or sliding ladder of some kind. This may be adequate if you are simply intending to convert your loft as a dedicated storage area, but in all other cases you will need to install a more secure means of access. If you intend to move large pieces of furniture into the new space, you will probably have to increase the size of the opening.

Building regulations are specific about certain aspects of stair design – the steepness of pitch, for example, and the height of risers. Handrails are also mandatory. It is important to remember that not all commercially available stairs or ladders meet these regulations. If the converted loft will be used on a daily basis, and if there are children or elderly and infirm people in the household, safety assumes an even greater importance. Be aware that stairs may have to be enclosed and separated by a fire door if your home is over two stories high.

How you access the loft can have a significant impact on spatial design. A proper staircase can be very desirable, especially if the loft is in regular daily use, and will integrate the new space with the rest of your home in a much more natural way. However, conventional stairs take up the most room and you may have to sacrifice more floor area on the level below than you wish. Other options include:

Spiral stairs. Stairs that turn around a central support take up relatively little room and are secure enough for regular, daily use. Because there are no risers, they don't block natural light and they can make an attractive feature in their own right. There are many designs on the market in a range of materials.

Open stairs. Stairs with open treads or those that are cantilevered from the wall are visually light and less intrusive than a closed staircase.

Fixed ladders. For occasional use, fixed ladders can provide a more stable means of access than a sliding or retractable loft ladder. Variations include 'paddle' steps, where the treads are alternated.

CONVERTING BASEMENTS

Right: Basement conversions are much more feasible than they used to be, due to improvements in damp-proofing. They remain an expensive option, however.

Basement conversions used to be something of a rarity, particularly in Britain where much of the existing housing stock lacks full basements. In countries like the United States, where basements are a more common feature, these have tended to be used as utility areas, recreation rooms and home workshops or hobby areas. Cellars also make good wine cellars and are ideal for swimming pools.

In recent years, basement conversions have become more popular. New techniques and materials mean underground excavation is easier to achieve than ever before and damp can be more effectively controlled. At the same time, planning authorities have begun to look more favourably on this type of conversion because it is so environmentally friendly.

An obvious eco advantage of a basement conversion is that it provides extra space – in many cases, quite substantial amounts of space – without the loss of land or garden area. Basements can even be extended out under a garden, with the soil and planting replaced on top. But there are energy savings too. A house with a basement is about 10 per cent more energy efficient than a house without one. This is down to the earth-sheltering effect. Basements, surrounded by the thermal mass of the earth, warm up slowly during the day and release heat slowly during the night. You can make the most of this effect by installing underfloor heating in your basement and choosing some kind of dense material, such as stone, as the final floor finish.

In comparison to other types of home improvement, basement conversions are undoubtedly expensive. The more your home is worth, the more cost-effective the conversion will be. At a time of great house-price volatility, this is an investment to make for the longer term. In many cases, however, a basement conversion will still be cheaper per square metre than moving to a house of equivalent size once moving costs, taxes and other expenses are also taken into the equation. Compared to attic conversions, where much usable floor area is lost under the eaves, there are no issues with head height – a converted basement can provide a whole additional level rather than just a single extra room.

PERMISSIONS AND REGULATIONS

For obvious reasons, a basement conversion is not going to attract objections from neighbours on the grounds of loss of light or overlooking, two standard complaints about new extensions that often arise during the planning process. However, there are other potential areas of contention. In dense urban areas, particularly if your home forms part of a terrace or is semi-detached, excavation work may affect neighbouring foundations, which may need to be underpinned. Your neighbours will be entitled to the services of a surveyor (at your expense), who will inspect the work at agreed stages to ensure there is no risk of subsidence. Where work has an impact on the foundations of adjacent buildings, you will need a party-wall agreement.

Planning permission is also often required. This will almost certainly be the case where lightwells need to be sunk at the front of the house, or if your home is listed or in a conservation area. Converting a basement to form a separate office or self-contained flat, which counts as change of use, will also require permission.

Unsurprisingly, a wide range of building regulations will also need to be met. Means of escape, drainage, foundation design, structural work and fire protection are some of the issues addressed by such legislation. Bear in mind that work must be inspected and passed in stages – if you proceed past a given stage without gaining approval, an inspector can insist that you uncover or dig up what you have done, which will cost you time and money.

IS IT FEASIBLE?

The feasibility of a basement conversion depends to a large extent on existing conditions. If the level of the water table is very high, it may well prove much too expensive and complicated to damp-proof the new area. If you live in an area that is prone to flooding, converting a basement could well be money down the drain. Tree roots can cause an obstruction, and many trees in urban areas are protected. Excavating under concrete slab foundations, which are common in newish houses, will add to the difficulty and cost of the work. Another factor is the siting of drainage. Houses where drains are built to the side are easier to convert than those with drains that run underneath.

Preliminary tests need to be carried out before work starts to determine if there are any such problems. Holes dug to a certain depth near your house or around its perimeter will reveal exactly what conditions you have and what type of foundations will be required for the new space.

TYPES OF CONVERSION

The simplest type of basement conversion, which may entail little or no structural work at all, is to tidy up an existing basement that has been under-used or used as a repository for junk. The introduction of natural light via ground-level lightwells, improved surfaces and finishes, and better servicing and access can win you extra living space. You may also need to make improvements to existing damp-proofing, tanking walls and floors before final finishes are installed.

Much more complicated is to enlarge a small cellar or excavate a whole new basement, either directly under the existing ground floor or part of the way into the front or rear garden. Houses rest on their foundations, which carry the load of the walls, floors and roof. Excavating beneath those foundations means underpinning. This used to be a difficult and messy business but new techniques are much less disruptive, so much so that it can be possible to remain in your home while the work is underway. The usual method is to sink new concrete foundations around the perimeter of your home before the basement is excavated and then to dig out the new area through what will be the front lightwell. Because the work is carried out at the front, this also avoids the difficulty of getting plant and digging equipment into the rear gardens of terraced or semi-detached properties.

An alternative is to excavate under your garden, either to the side or the rear, and replace soil and planting once the basement is finished. Some form of access will need to be provided from ground level, but otherwise there is little disruption to the structure of your existing house.

Most basement conversions are single level. Given the right conditions, you can achieve full head height, which effectively adds another storey to your home. At the very least the new area should have a head height of 2.4 m (8 ft). Basements that are converted to provide facilities such as indoor swimming pools can be much deeper.

GETTING THE WORK DONE

Basement conversion is specialist work, which generally falls outside the expertise of the average contractor or building firm. As this type of home improvement has become more popular, more companies dealing exclusively with basement conversions and excavations have sprung up. As with loft conversion companies, these outfits provide a full service, including surveying ground conditions, designing the new area and specifying its foundations, obtaining the necessary permissions and carrying out the construction work. Many people who convert their basements choose this package route.

The other main option is to employ an architect to design and draw up the scheme, and then employ a specialist basement conversion firm to carry out the work. An architect may be able to suggest ways of reorganizing your house as a whole so that the new basement is better integrated, both with upper levels and outdoor areas.

DAMP-PROOFING

One of the reasons why basement conversions remained unpopular for so long was that they were not always wholly successful in keeping out the damp. In the past, damp-proofing focused on keeping water out using water-resistant materials and waterproof coatings on the walls and floors. This process is often known as 'tanking'. Tanking can work moderately well in stable conditions, but if the level of the ground water rises, pressure can build up on the walls and floor of an underground area, creating movement and stress, particularly where planes meet. Under such pressure, cracks can appear, allowing water to penetrate.

New approaches to damp-proofing, developed in Europe, particularly in Germany, redirect and control ground water rather than attempting to exclude it. The walls and floor of the basement are lined with specially designed sheets of plastic that drain water down into channels, which then lead to a sump. From the sump the water is pumped into the main drains. Dry-lining panels are applied over the drainage membranes and final finishes go on top. The sump and pump are located in accessible positions to facilitate maintenance and inspection, which needs to be carried out annually. The efficiency of this new type of damp-proofing has made basement conversions much more achievable and the technology is used by many specialist basement conversion firms.

NATURAL LIGHT AND VENTILATION

Fresh air and daylight are not only essential for our well-being, they are legally required for all 'habitable' rooms. Only kitchens and bathrooms can be fully internal, although some form of mechanical extract will need to be fitted to ensure that there is adequate airflow. After damp-proofing, the greatest challenge presented by basement conversions is to provide good conditions of natural light and ventilation.

The standard means by which this is achieved is to sink lightwells into the ground. There are many different ways in which lightwells can be configured. Some operate essentially as skylights; others are shafts that are sunk right down to the basement floor level, with the basement wall infilled with glass. Where a basement has been excavated under a garden, lightwells can be installed directly overhead. In some cases, lightwells can be openable, which aids ventilation.

Solar tubes, which drawn natural light down through a reflective pipe, are another option (see page 117). Similar in principle are air pipes, which can be used as a source of fresh air.

Many basement conversions offer the opportunity to borrow light from upper levels. Open-tread staircases allow light to spill down from above. Cutting away part of a floor on the ground level and infilling with glazed panels is a dramatic way of toplighting.

Perhaps less desirable, from an eco point of view, is excavating an area to the rear of your house so that the end wall of the basement can be fully glazed. While this does offer the opportunity to make an easy connection with outdoor spaces, there will be a loss of ground area.

As with other naturally dark spaces, you can enhance the quality of light by using reflective surfaces and finishes and adopting a light decorative palette. Where areas need to be screened, glass or translucent panels or partitions are better than solid walls.

ACCESS

Providing access to a new or converted basement is generally more straightforward than providing access to a converted loft, simply because there is not the same pressure on space. Ideally, open-tread staircases, including spiral and cantilevered stairs, are best, as they allow light and air down from upper levels. However, depending on circumstances, fire regulations may stipulate a closed staircase or a fire door separating the basement from the ground-floor level.

If you are converting an existing basement or semi-basement, you may wish to make improvements to the present means of access. The stairs may be too narrow for regular use, or awkwardly sited.

Left: One way of providing natural light for a basement conversion is to excavate at the rear of the house, creating a large lightwell. This does entail the sacrifice of ground area.

Above: Sections of glass flooring installed on the level above lets light down to basement areas. Flooring glass is a special toughened variety and needs to be individually specified.

EXTENDING YOUR HOME

Right: Extending to the side of your house can make all the difference between a layout that is workable and one that is not. Here the main kitchen preparation area is located directly under the glazed roof. Plenty of natural light means good working conditions.

Home extensions occupy the middle ground between retro-fitting and new build. Most people extend their home for the same reasons that they make any other improvement – to give themselves more space and to improve the quality of the space they have. While most extensions entail the sacrifice of some garden area, the overall green benefits can be considerable. If you build an extension to high eco standards, especially in terms of insulation, the extra space you gain should not see an equivalent rise in energy bills.

Adapting or retro-fitting your home to make it more environmentally friendly means working within the existing framework to a large degree. Building an extension, on the other hand, allows you to branch out and adopt a more wholehearted eco approach, not merely in terms of servicing, surfaces and finishes, but also with respect to basic structure and fabric. In many parts of the world, all new extensions must meet fairly rigorous standards of energy efficiency, standards that are only likely to rise in the future. Advocates of green building go further and aim for zero carbon.

PLANNING AND ASSESSMENT

When you are converting a loft or a basement, you are essentially dealing with a potentially self-contained area, however closely it might be integrated with the rest of your home. Extensions, however, come in all shapes, sizes and configurations, from the extra few metres that absorbs a side return and enlarges an existing kitchen, to the two-storey rear addition that provides a significant increase in living area. When you take into account that building an extension almost always involves structural work and may well require planning permission, it is important to seek professional advice at the outset.

Ideally, an extension should not simply provide you with extra floor area wherever you are feeling the pinch, it should also improve what you've already got. At the very least, it shouldn't make matters worse. A poorly planned or sited extension can do just that, by taking light from internal areas, setting up awkward circulation routes or simply by being executed and finished in a substandard way. It is not uncommon for older properties to feature a ramshackle collection of lean-tos and additions, tacked on over the years in response to whichever need was most pressing at the time. A well-considered extension should look like it belongs, whether it is a sensitive match to existing architectural character or a bold and confident departure from it.

Professional advice can be invaluable in helping you turn your dreams into reality and ensuring that the money you spend on the extension will translate into real added value. Extensions that increase the size of the kitchen or that provide an extra bathroom or bedroom are generally most cost-efficient – studies show that such additions reliably increase sale value.

PERMISSIONS AND LEGALITIES

Building on to your home has an inevitable impact on the surrounding area. How much depends on the size of the extension and its location, as well as on the nature of your property. If your house sits in substantial grounds and is relatively isolated from neighbours, you may have more freedom when it comes to design and siting than would be the case if you were living in a terraced house in the middle of the city. Neighbours have the right to object if what you are proposing to do would reduce the amount of daylight in their home and this is one of the main grounds on which schemes are refused by the planning authorities. Inappropriate extensions to houses in conservation areas or those that are listed are also frowned upon. In this context, reasons for refusal can include insensitive use of materials and design that does not match up with existing architectural character.

Forewarned is forearmed. It is a good idea to consult your local planning department early on in the design process to find out whether what you are proposing is likely to win approval or not. The planning process is fairly lengthy – the last thing you want is to have to go through it twice simply because you were unaware of possibly contentious issues. Some extensions, generally those that are small scale and that do not increase the volume of your home by very much, are exempt from the process. Most extensions, however, do require approval. If you employ an architect – which is advisable, certainly for the design stage – he or she can have a preliminary discussion with the planners before the design is submitted to minimize the risk of refusal. The planner may advise, for example, that a

change of material would be a good idea, or that a different type of detailing would be more acceptable. Roof pitch can be a critical issue when it comes to whether or not natural light is blocked in adjoining properties.

Extensions that involve building onto a party wall require a party-wall award. As is the case with basement conversions that affect neighbouring foundations, you will have to pay for the services of a surveyor who will inspect the work at certain stages to confirm that there has been no adverse structural impact on your neighbour's property. As ever, it is always a good idea to let your neighbours know about your plans well ahead of making a planning application or seeking a party-wall award, both to forestall possible objections and also as a matter of courtesy. Extensive building works necessarily involve additional noise, disruption and mess, and you will need good will on your side for the duration.

All extensions are governed by local building codes, which are often the subject of revision and change. In many areas, new extensions need to meet very high standards of energy efficiency, whether or not your existing home does. This can mean, for example, that all artificial lighting must be low-energy and that the extension must have a high level of insulation. Other aspects of the build will also be subject to control and, in many cases, this may mean inspection at critical stages. Foundations are a key structural element and these will need to be approved before further work can be done. Changes to drainage and new structural frameworks will also be scrutinized.

While a design that incorporates many eco features may well impress the planners and help to win approval for your proposals, you may have more of a fight on your hands if you wish to use unconventional materials, particularly as structural elements. In such cases, it is worth contacting others who have successfully built in the same way to find out what documentation they needed to provide to back up their schemes, or what objections they had to overcome.

STRUCTURAL ISSUES

Building an extension is necessarily more involved than other types of conversion or home improvement – at their most ambitious, such projects present many of the same challenges as a new build. Planning authorities may insist that there is a certain amount of congruence between existing architectural character and the external appearance of a new extension, particularly if any part of it is visible from the street. Rear extensions, however, are likely to be given much more latitude. This opens the way for the use of green materials, such as timber cladding (or render, in an area where brick and stone predominate), and for an environmentally friendly design that departs from previous templates. If you do have to replicate existing character, think about using salvaged materials rather than new – old bricks, for example, or reclaimed stone.

Beneath the surface, there is also scope for the green designer when it comes to structural issues. Any extension that rests on the ground will need its own foundations, which in turn will need to be tied into the existing foundations. Architects or surveyors who have experience in green building may be able to come up with a way of specifying foundations to minimize disruption to the site and hence reduce the amount of concrete required – by using piled or pad foundations, for example. Structural frameworks can also be designed to make the most minimal use of material – for example, prefabricated timber systems manufactured off site, or lightweight steel frameworks (see page 146). There is no real reason why an extension could not be constructed out of an even more radical material, such as straw bale, although you may well encounter a greater degree of official resistance.

Aside from constructing foundations and structural frameworks, other types of work will be involved in building an extension. These include:

Changes to servicing. Electricity, heating and possibly drainage will need to be routed to the new extension. Depending on the location of the extension, existing drains may need to be rerouted.

Providing access. Connecting an extension to the existing building may involve enlarging an existing opening, such as a back door, or creating a new one. Both of these changes are structural and entail installing a beam or lintel over the new opening to take the weight of the walls above.

Adding insulation. A very well-insulated extension may need no supplementary heating at all.

Final finishes and fitting out. Installing fitted units, flooring and decorative finishes is the final stage.

Left: Extensions come in all shapes and sizes – and materials. This minimal glass box brings nature close to home.

SITING OPTIONS

Many different factors influence the siting of an extension – how much land you have at your disposal, ease of access and structural considerations may all have a bearing, as well as planning restrictions. In certain cases, there may only be one feasible option. Where you have a choice in the matter, however, it is important to keep green issues in mind.

Chief among these is to site an extension so that you lose as little of your garden as possible. Increasingly, living a low-carbon life means making the most productive use of outdoor areas – by growing food for the table, composting and collecting rainwater – and this means viewing gardens as our own mini green belts, protected from development.

A related issue is to design the extension so that the greatest possible spatial benefits are delivered from the smallest possible footprint. This may entail building a two-storey extension, so that you get twice as much room for the same loss of ground area. A terrace on the flat roof of an extension, where you can keep container plants, will offset the loss of garden. If there are issues to do with overlooking, an alternative would be to have a green roof instead.

Orientation is also an important consideration. The optimum orientation for an extension, from an energy-efficiency point of view, would be one where the new space benefits from passive solar strategies. In northern or temperate climates, a south-facing orientation would reduce the amount of supplementary heating required. In warm climates, siting the extension so that it faced away from the sun would help to keep the interior cool. But the best location for an extension may also be the best location for a vegetable plot. As ever, making the right decision is not always straightforward and a degree of compromise may be required.

Above: A quirky free-standing framework serves as a glazed garden room below and terrace above, shaded by trellising and a climber.

Right: Rear extensions are generally less contentious in planning terms than those that abut onto neighbours or that affect the appearance of the house from the street. Building up two stories gives you double the accommodation for the same loss of ground area.

Far right: An eco-friendly rear extension includes high-specification windows, skylight and sliding doors. Larch is used for the external cladding. The walls, ceiling and floor are highly insulated.

Side extensions

Extending your home to the side can be a good way of gaining extra space without sacrificing too much of your garden. Forget sprawling palatial wings built onto grand villas, many side extensions, particularly in urban areas, absorb the narrow passage or strip of land that runs between one property line and another. In terraced or semi-detached houses, these 'side returns' tend to be paved, used as access from the street to the rear of the house, and rarely provide hospitable conditions for planting. Although the amount of space is limited, such extensions can make a big difference to ground-floor areas, enlarging a kitchen, for example, so that it is big enough to include an eating area. If you glaze the roof of the side extension, natural light levels will be boosted dramatically.

Extensions at upper levels

If you already have a single- or double-storey extension at the side or rear of your house, you may be able to build on top of it. When you extend at an upper level, you lose no ground area at all. Rooftop extensions are another possibility – although these may be more contentious with the planners if all the houses in your area have the same number of storeys. Some loft and apartment dwellers have built an extra living area on their roof and transformed the rest of the space into a sustainable roof garden, introducing skylights and other types of toplighting to improve light conditions on the level below.

Rear extensions

The most common site for an extension is at the rear. Try to minimize loss of ground area as far as possible. One way of doing this is to demolish existing or redundant outbuildings, such as sheds and pantries, which may have accumulated over the years, and build over the top. Two-storey rear extensions provide double the space for the same footprint.

The challenge when it comes to designing a rear extension is to improve the connection with outdoor areas without detracting from spatial quality overall. Reorganizing the entire ground-floor layout may be necessary, otherwise existing rooms may lose their vitality and apparent purpose.

Garage conversions

One of the simplest and most straightforward types of extension is to convert an existing attached garage into habitable space. In many cases, you'll need planning permission to install the necessary window or windows because this type of alteration will affect the appearance of your home from the street. The building work, however, is not complicated – you can install windows in place of the garage doors without affecting the structure of your home. You'll also need to connect the garage with the rest of your house if there isn't already a door between the two. The rest of the work consists of insulating, extending services to the new space, and fitting it out with new surfaces and finishes.

Above: The all-inclusive kitchen is a perennial favourite and many people extend their homes to provide enough space for this type of open-plan arrangement.

Right: A glazed side extension serves as an eating area. Glazed porches or garden rooms can have a beneficial impact on a building's energy efficiency, serving as a buffer zone between indoors and out.

THE SUN SPACE: THE NEW CONSERVATORY

Conservatories or glazed garden rooms have long been popular types of home extension. In some areas they have almost become status symbols, a fact exploited by many companies offering off-the-shelf or prefabricated designs in the architectural equivalent of Victorian and Edwardian fancy dress. Rethought for the twenty-first century, however, the sun space can be an important element in passive solar strategies.

If you live in a cool or temperate climate and your home has a south- or southwest-facing aspect, building an enclosed glazed porch or sun room can make your home more energy efficient, provided that the sun room is not heated or cooled by any other auxiliary means. On sunny winter days it will pre-warm air and deliver the warmth to the walls of your home, also serving as a second skin for windows and other glazed openings. By night it helps to reduce heat loss by acting as a buffer zone.

Sun spaces or glazed porches make good intermediate areas for outdoor gear, bulky supplies and for firewood, which needs to be kept in a dry atmosphere. You can also dry clothes in a sun space, which helps to regulate moisture levels in the main house and prevents you from having to use a dryer when the weather is cold or rainy.

Overheating is a drawback of the sun space, especially in the summer. Shades and blinds are one way of minimizing heat gain. Windows that can be opened, especially at the top, to vent rising warm air, also keep temperatures within a reasonable range.

LARDERS AND COOL ZONES

Larders operate like sun spaces in reverse. In a temperate climate, building an enclosed area onto a north-facing facade provides natural refrigeration for a wide range of foodstuffs. In the days before fridges and freezers, the larder or pantry was where most households kept their food fresh. Stone floors and shelves and minimal or non-existent openings exploit thermal mass to maintain a cool ambient temperature.

After supermarkets arrived on the scene and shopping habits changed dramatically, people gradually lost confidence in their ability to manage their own store cupboards. 'Use-by' and 'sell-by' dates have encouraged vast amounts of food waste, with perfectly edible produce being consigned to the bin in many households on a weekly basis. In fact, many types of food, from vegetables to cheeses and cooked meats, keep well in larder conditions, if not better than in the fridge.

STAND-ALONE EXTENSIONS

If you have a big enough garden, one way of providing additional living space is to construct an outbuilding at some distance from the house. These stand-alone structures have become increasingly popular in recent years, thanks in part to the trend for working at home, and are often used as studios, consulting rooms or studies for home professionals. The size and siting of such buildings dictate whether or not they require planning permission.

Many of these up-market sheds come in prefabricated form, some with fixtures and fittings already pre-installed. Eco versions are also available. These are generally timber-framed, well-insulated, fitted with high-performance windows, and timber-clad.

NEW BUILDS

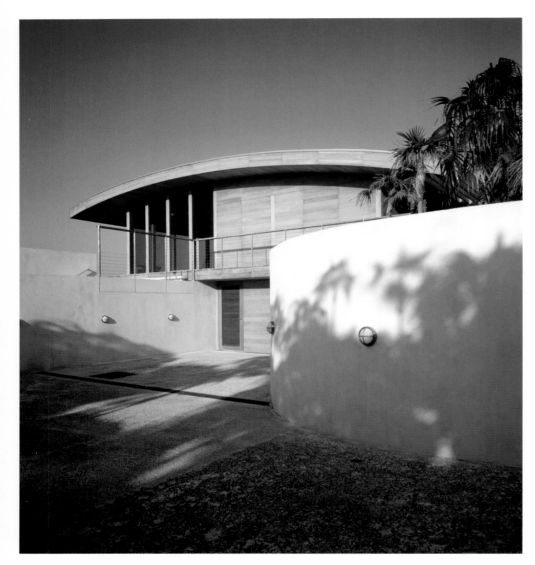

Left: A beach house in the West Indies, designed by Seth Stein, comprises a number of open unglazed pavilions linked by a timber walkway. The building plan was based on the module of the prefabricated 1.2 m (4 ft) timber panels used in its construction. Rainwater is collected on site.

Above: This contemporary three-storey house was constructed out of prefabricated timber panels and clad with board made of recycled glass. The corner floor-to-ceiling high-specification windows provide plenty of natural light and there is a large roof garden on the top level.

Right: An urban infill site in east London under construction. The completed house is an energy-efficient timber-framed structure, designed to adapt to changing family needs. A simple groundworks structure supports a prefabricated glulam larch post-and-beam kit that came as a flatpack for quick construction.

Many people who are committed to low-carbon living eventually begin to dream of building their own home – and some go on to achieve it. This is not surprising. Building from scratch provides the widest possible scope for greening the design process.

Eco homes have a longer history than one might think, but now it is increasingly hard to tell the difference between a house built to high eco standards and the type of sleek contemporary designs that fill the pages of glossy magazines. Some eco homes are proud to wear their green credentials on their sleeve; others are much less obvious about it.

A decade or two ago, you had to be a pioneer to build green. Many eco technologies were not far out of prototype

Below: In this vacation house in the Stockholm archipelago, a series of floor-to-ceiling glazed openings run along the two facades facing the water. Several of these are doors that allow access to the sun deck. From the inside of the house, the effect is that of a series of walls placed along an open facade.

Right: A new-build London mews house has large double-glazed windows infilled with argon. Special glazing reduces heat gain by 30 per cent. Slatted timber shutters also prevent the interior from overheating. The house is very well insulated. Three rooflights allow for natural ventilation and close automatically when rain begins to fall.

stage, sustainable materials were difficult to identify, let alone source, and local authorities were often intransigent in the face of proposed structures and building methods that departed from the norm. Today, things have changed dramatically. A far greater knowledge base is available for the green builder, much of it a mouse-click away online. Sourcing the right materials is also much easier; technologies have improved and in many cases become more affordable. And many of the battles to overturn local codes and regulations have been fought and won. If you meet with official opposition, chances are you will be able to find a built precedent for what you are proposing and use it in your defence.

While it isn't all plain sailing for eco builders, nowadays the major hurdles are not widely dissimilar to those faced by anyone who takes the self-build path. Finding a suitable site on which to build, especially in crowded urban areas, raising the finance and negotiating the complexities of the work as it progresses are pretty much the same whether you are aiming for zero carbon or not.

Building your own home, despite all the headaches, can be deeply rewarding, a way of ensuring that your surroundings fit you like a glove. For the green builder, there is the additional satisfaction of creating a home that harms the planet as little as possible and continues to pay eco dividends over the course of its lifetime.

SITE ISSUES

One of the first challenges faced by any self-builder is to find a site. In some parts of the world, plots of land are much harder to come by than others, due to population density and associated land value. For the same reason, urban locations, generally, are in much shorter supply than those in the countryside. In areas where property is at a premium, self-builders looking for an urban site often find themselves in competition with private developers with much deeper pockets. Online plot-finding agencies, local newspapers and self-build magazines can help you identify where to look and the sort of money you might be expected to pay. In the city, where sites are often snapped up the moment they are advertised, it pays to walk around and

investigate derelict patches of land tucked away off the beaten track. A title search can help you find a site's owner and discover whether or not it is for sale. Other options for finding a site include:

Land auctions. Sites are harder to value than houses, so many agents and vendors prefer to put land up for auction. Buying a site at auction means you must be sure that you can build on the land and that there are no nasty surprises waiting to derail your plans. It also means having financing in place.
In collaboration with others. Many self-builders realize their dreams after joining forces with like-minded people. Sites that are too big or too uneconomic for a single house can be developed into two or three units.
On your own property. If you have a large garden with the potential for street access you may be able to build a house on it. Similarly, one route often taken by self-builders is to buy a house that is dilapidated, tear it down and construct a new one. This is far from an eco option, however, if the existing house is in reasonable condition.

As is always the case with eco design, there are a number of competing factors to weigh in the balance when it come to choosing a site. Being sensitive about land use, a tenet of eco building, is generally interpreted to mean opting for brownfield over greenfield sites. However, city plots do not always offer optimum eco design conditions, particularly for passive solar strategies, due to the density of development. You may also find your options are limited when it comes to the way the new building will be orientated, which can affect how it responds to local climate conditions, such as prevailing winds. On the other hand, although building on virgin land leads to a direct loss of unspoilt countryside, there are ways of lessening the impact of a new build, by earth-sheltering, for example, installing a green roof, or minimising foundations so that the house sits lightly on the land. However, obtaining planning permission to build on a greenfield site can be very difficult. As building standards continue to improve it is unlikely that even a proposed scheme that incorporates many eco features will be approved if the site is outside the development boundary of a neighbouring town or village.

Above: Houses that are raised up on narrow supports or pilotis sit lightly on the land and minimize site disruption. This structure accommodates changes in ground level without the need for levelling.

Right: With no significant external elevations, this north London house makes use of retractable rooflights and passive energy systems to moderate the internal climate and flood the living space with light. The oval shape maximizes the volume of the house within the site constraints.

It is advisable to commission a thorough site survey before you go further with your plans. Relevant details include:

- **Soil conditions.** Is the land waterlogged or contaminated in any way? Ground conditions will dictate the type of foundations you will require and whether or not you can have a basement. Sites in areas that are prone to flooding or cliff erosion should be avoided.
- **Trees.** The position of mature trees will have an impact on design. An eco principle is to disrupt the site as little as possible, which means designing a building's footprint around existing trees. Tree roots may affect foundation design. In some areas, trees are protected by preservation orders.
- **Orientation.** Which part of the site gets the sun? Which part is shaded?
- **Exposure.** The direction of prevailing winds will also have an impact on design. In hot climates, orienting a house in line with prevailing winds can help to keep it cool. In cool climates, a sheltered location will reduce the wind-chill factor.
- **Slope.** A sloping site may offer the opportunity to build an earth-sheltered house.
- **Boundaries & exact dimensions.** Agents' and sellers' details can be imprecise.

PERMISSIONS

Not every plot of land that comes onto the market can be developed for residential use. Before you commit to a purchase, you must do your homework, otherwise you could find yourself owning a site that you can't build on.

Zoning ordinances in the United States specify which lots can be developed for residential purposes and which cannot. Other stipulations concerning building height and plot size will also be specified in local development plans. The situation is broadly similar in Britain. The safest bet is to buy a site that already has outline planning permission for residential development. Many site owners apply for such consent as a means of adding value to their property, not because they have any intention of developing the site themselves. If the site you are interested in does not have

outline permission, you can apply for it yourself before you buy it and make the sale contingent on gaining consent.

Outline permission is merely the first hurdle. The next step is to submit detailed plans for full planning permission. As ever, it is a good idea to involve your future neighbours in your scheme and explain what you propose to do. While this may not rule out every objection, it should at least prevent opposition that has no basis in fact.

Finally, whatever you build must conform to local codes and regulations. These vary widely from area to area and are constantly changing. Without final approval, which is granted after a number of inspections have been successfully passed, you might find it difficult to sell your home subsequently or to make an insurance claim.

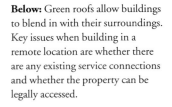

Below: Green roofs allow buildings to blend in with their surroundings. Key issues when building in a remote location are whether there are any existing service connections and whether the property can be legally accessed.

ACCESS AND SERVICE CONNECTIONS

Some sites that are offered for sale do not have a clear means of access from a public highway, which can effectively rule out development. Even if the site has a lane or road leading to it, you might not be legally entitled to use it. You may need the services of a legal professional to determine what the exact position is.

Another important consideration is to find out whether the site is connected to main services, such as drainage, water, electricity and gas. If there are no such connections, you will need to investigate whether it is both possible and cost-effective to create new lines of supply. Where there are existing services, their location may restrict options for design, or entail making costly diversions.

For green builders, especially those aiming for self-sufficiency, the issue of service connections may be less problematic. Tried and tested alternatives for mains sewerage do exist, such as the humble septic tank and its eco successors. A gas connection may not be essential, especially if you are considering some form of biomass heating. On the other hand, producing your own potable water on site is quite onerous, both logistically and in terms of regulations. A mains connection for electricity is also a useful backup for any off-grid renewable energy solution. In the case of photovoltaics and wind power, where it is necessary to even out the high and low output periods, the ability to sell surplus power back to the grid can determine whether a system is viable or not. While excess peak-output power can be stored in batteries, this is an expensive and technically challenging business.

Above left: Where access is limited, deliveries of materials may be more problematic. Installation of heavy elements, such as glazing, may need to be made by crane.

Left: Sites for development are harder to come by in urban areas, but many planners now look more favourably on designs that have eco features, such as solar panels.

STRUCTURAL SYSTEMS

The basic structure of a house can be constructed in many different ways and from a range of materials, most typically masonry, timber and steel. Less usual are various alternative materials sometimes adopted by green builders, such as adobe or rammed earth, straw bale and even recycled tyres.

For the eco designer, there is no one single answer and a number of factors will influence the final decision. One of the main considerations is the embodied energy of the material that forms the principal component of the structure. Timber structures, for example, consume 4 tonnes less CO_2 than masonry structures. In North American and Scandinavian countries, where timber is an abundant resource, most houses are timber-framed, even when they are faced with another material such as brick. Climate can also have a bearing. In hot semi-desert areas, vernacular houses have long featured thick earthen walls that keep interiors cool.

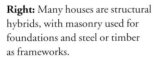

Right: Many houses are structural hybrids, with masonry used for foundations and steel or timber as frameworks.

FOUNDATIONS

The basis of a house's structure are the foundations. How they are designed and constructed will depend on two chief factors: the weight of the structure and the existing ground conditions. Where ground conditions are poor, there might not be much difference between those foundations required for masonry construction and those required for the lighter weight timber frame.

The standard type of foundation is the strip footing. Trenches are dug under the position of load-bearing walls. These trenches are then filled with a base layer of unreinforced concrete topped with masonry walling.

The most minimal foundations are pad foundations, which entail a minimum of site disruption and are preferred for that reason by many eco builders wherever conditions allow. Pad foundations are sufficient to support lightweight timber structures. Where there is a problem with tree roots or in heavily wooded areas, piled foundations may be necessary. However, these are expensive and require specialist construction.

Certain new technologies have been developed to minimize the amount of concrete used in foundations. One technique mixes soil that has been removed either from trenches (for strip foundations) or holes (for pad footings) with cement to reduce the amount of concrete required and the amount of soil that has to be dumped. This technique is suitable for only certain types of soil. Another method is to vibro-compact the soil in situ, removing the need for concrete completely.

TIMBER

Many eco homes are timber-framed; some are also timber-clad. For construction, green oak is a good choice. Glulam or paralam timbers, composed of laminated strips of softwood glued under pressure, are very strong and can span large distances. For external cladding, larch, western red cedar and Douglas fir are durable and relatively maintenance-free. The advantages of using timber include:

– Wood can be a renewable resource. Timber from FSC-certified plantations is guaranteed to be a sustainable material.
– Low embodied energy, especially if sourced locally.

– Timber structures are lightweight, which means foundations can be more minimal. Some timber structures rest on pad foundations, which entails less site disruption.

– Timber structures are easy to insulate to a high degree. For any given thickness, a timber-framed wall can be more heavily insulated than a masonry structure because it contains voids between its structural members that can be filled. In a masonry wall the thickness of the insulation is in addition to the structural depth, although there are inherent advantages of an inner masonry skin due to thermal mass.

– Relatively cheap, quick to construct and less labour-intensive than masonry construction.

– Timber has been rigorously tested for fire performance over the past few decades. Can be treated with borax, a natural salt, to promote fire-resistance and meet local building codes.

– Provided that timber structures are designed to promote water run-off and air circulation, there is little risk of insect attack. Features such as deep overhanging eaves will help to prevent water from collecting on the surface.

– Ideal for 'breathing wall' construction, where the cavity between outer and inner walls is insulated with recycled newspaper or other natural insulators to regulate moisture.

A disadvantage of timber buildings, particularly those that are also timber-clad, is that they have a relatively low thermal mass, heating up quickly and losing heat quickly. This can be addressed in hybrid types of construction, where a basic timber-framed structure clad in well-insulated timber panels has an inner masonry skin made of blocks or bricks.

Types of timber structure include:

–**Log cabin.** A traditional form of construction where solid logs are piled on top of each other to create the load-bearing walls that support the roof. Recent advances in technology mean that structures can be built from solid timbers without compromising insulation values or airtightness and they have become more popular as a result.

–**Stick-built on site.** A very common form of timber building in the United States, but much less common in Britain. The structural skeleton is initially braced by diagonal members. Subsequent sheathing stiffens the entire structure. This form of construction is usually bespoke, on site, with little standardization. 'Balloon frame' construction, which is the norm in the United States, has vertical framing members that span from the footings to the eaves. The first-floor joists hang off the inside of the external wall.

–**Open-panel systems.** The most common form of timber-frame in Britain is the open-panel system or 'platform-frame', where the vertical members are only a single storey high and the external first-floor walls sit on top of the ends of the first-floor joists. This has often meant that single-storey wall and floor panels, comprising wall studs or floor joists nailed to plywood sheets, can be manufactured in advance off site (although still in a more or less bespoke way) and delivered to the site for erection, often complete with glazed windows and doors. External wall finishes, insulation, internal wall linings and services are then added on site.

–**Closed-panel systems.** A variant of open-panel or platform-frame construction, in which insulation, internal wall linings and often first-fix services (pipework, electrical conduit and sometimes wiring) are installed in the factory. This form of construction has been developed to a high standard in Germany and the resulting buildings often have much better thermal performance and airtightness than examples of open-panel construction.

–**SIPs (structural insulated panels or 'stress skin' panels).** A form of platform-frame construction where the storey-height wall panels comprise sheets of 'Sterling-board' bonded to a core of polystyrene insulation. The board acts as a stressed skin for stability and provides impact resistance for the polystyrene core. Although polystyrene is a petrochemical product, the boards are made of waste wood. Panels are easier to transport because they are relatively light.

–**Post-and-beam.** Another traditional form of timber construction, dating back centuries, post-and-beam involves the erection of a timber frame composed of columns, floor beams, joists and roof rafters. Nowadays, stability is generally provided by sheathing and cross-bracing. Walls, either external or internal, do not play any supporting role. Post-and-beam offers the opportunity to create large interior spaces that are relatively uninterrupted. Suitable timbers include oak, Douglas fir and engineered timber such as glulam and paralam.

MASONRY

While there are a number of advantages to masonry construction from an environmental point of view, and eco houses may well contain masonry elements (floor slabs, for example), brick-and-block construction has a far higher embodied energy than timber, and many eco designers avoid it for that reason. The energy costs arise both during manufacture and transportation, although many of the raw ingredients are natural and plentiful. Locally sourced reclaimed bricks are perhaps the greenest choice for those building masonry structures.

In masonry construction the external walls support both the roof and the floors that span between them, with the combined load resting on the foundations. Some internal walls also play a load-bearing role. Floors on second levels can be solid, rather than timber as is the case with timber construction, which enhances insulating qualities.

In masonry construction, the external walls are doubled up, with the inner wall being the load-bearing element and the outer wall serving as a protection or skin for the building. In the gap or cavity between the two, which serves as a vapour barrier, goes insulating material. Masonry construction is much slower than building in timber and much more readily disrupted in periods of bad weather.

Eco advantages of masonry construction chiefly have to do with its high thermal mass. A brick or block house absorbs and releases heat slowly, which is an asset where the building has been designed in line with passive solar strategies. Masonry requires less maintenance than timber and is potentially longer lasting. It's also easier to make airtight.

STEEL

Structural steel frameworks result in light, airy buildings, where entire walls can be infilled with glazing. Because of steel's great strength, structures can be refined and elegant. The large spans that are also possible give rise to open internal layouts and free-flowing space. Frameworks are manufactured off site and can be assembled like a kit of parts very quickly.

Light-gauge steel framing is often used in 'volumetric' construction, where complete rooms or modules are delivered to the site and stacked one on top of the other.

Economies of scale and associated transport costs tend to rule out this method for small domestic projects. Another variant is where light pressed-steel members are used in lieu of structural timber members in either an open-panel or closed-panel system. Proponents of this method cite better fire- and rot-resistance.

For the eco designer, the use of steel and other metals is generally problematic because of the materials' high embodied energy. Steel, for example, has an embodied energy 300 times greater than timber. Extraction of ores can also scar the landscape and processing is a major polluter. A mitigating factor is that metals, including steel, are very easy to recycle, and because of their high value recycling is well-established in the industry.

Some eco designers argue that steel and other metals can play an important, if relatively minimal, part in the structures of environmentally friendly buildings, particularly where they promote a degree of durability and strength that would otherwise not be readily achievable. Steel connections and fasteners, for example, are largely seen as preferable to synthetic ones. The advice is to use recycled steel and other metals whenever possible, either metals that contain a high recycled content or those that have been directly reclaimed and salvaged from other buildings. To facilitate future salvage, steel or metal elements can be bolted in place rather than welded together.

A common feature of eco houses in Australia is the corrugated-metal sheet roof. The reflectivity of the material helps to keep the interior cool, while the corrugations promote rainwater collection.

ADOBE, RAMMED EARTH AND COB

Many eco builders are drawn to alterative methods of construction, even where this entails more protracted battles with local authorities to gain the necessary permissions. Nothing could be more direct than constructing a building from the earth itself.

Mud construction – using adobe, rammed earth or cob – is a vernacular tradition of building that has been employed since time immemorial. One third of the world's population still lives in earthen houses and there are examples that are hundreds of years old. This type of structure is best suited to moderate and warm regions; extra insulation may be required in cooler climates. Walls are thick and built up on concrete or stone walls so that they are not eroded by standing water. They may also be covered with stucco or rendering to make them more water-resistant.

Earthen houses have high thermal mass, absorbing heat slowly during the day and releasing it slowly at night. They are also good at regulating humidity. Because of the thickness of the walls, they are naturally sound-insulating.

– Adobe structures are made of adobe bricks – a mixture of earth, sand, straw and binders – which can be made on site or commercially produced. Structures can be curved and organic-looking.
– Rammed-earth structures are made out of dampened earth mixed with a small amount of cement or binder. The raw material is pressed into forms to dry, which generally results in a rectilinear structure.
– Cob is a blend of clay, sand, straw and water. The mixture is built up on top of low walls or applied over formwork.

STRAW BALE

Building a house out of straw may be a proverbial byword for fecklessness, but straw-bale structures combine high eco credentials with proven structural integrity. The method is gaining in popularity in various parts of the world, most notably in western areas of the United States.

Straw is a major agricultural waste product and in normal circumstances is generally burned. Using straw to make bales for construction, in earthen mixtures, or to create facing panels, cuts down on pollution and represents a direct form of recycling.

The basic building block is the straw bale, which is pre-compressed to prevent subsequent shrinkage and settlement. The bales can then be used either to make load-bearing walls, or as infill between other structural members. In either case, they must sit on raised concrete or stone walls that are as wide as the bales themselves in order to prevent moisture penetration.

In load-bearing construction, the bales are stacked flat in staggered rows and are secured in place by fine steel pins. Where they are used as infill, they may be placed edge-on, which gives thinner walls. After the walls have been built up, they are wrapped in wire mesh to create a ground for render. Both the external and internal finishes need to be of breathable materials, so that moisture does not build up inside the straw bales.

The density of straw bales makes them naturally fire-resistant and the risk of insect or vermin attack is prevented by adequate rendering. Like earthen houses, buildings made of straw bale are quiet and well-insulated.

Below left: Corrugated metal is a feature of vernacular Australian buildings. Although metal has high embodied energy, it is readily recyclable with no loss of quality.

Below: Earthen buildings have seen a comeback in recent years. They have high thermal mass and are good at regulating humidity.

OUTDOOR SPACES

Green space is precious. Contact with nature soothes the spirit and restores a connection with the living world. Many of us go on holiday precisely to reacquaint ourselves with the landscape, whether our destination is the seaside or the mountains. At home, there is a great deal you can do to make the most of whatever outdoor space you have, both as a place to relax and enjoy, and as a productive adjunct to a green lifestyle.

All too often in recent years, the garden as 'outdoor room' has been taken to its furthest and most unnatural extreme. I am all in favour of blurring the boundaries between indoors and out, and creating areas where people can sit, eat, drink and smoke cigars outdoors in fine weather. In some areas, however, this trend to annexe outdoor space as living space has resulted in gardens that are uniformly paved, warmed by unsustainable patio-heaters and where plants are treated as decorative accessories. If we need to green our homes, increasingly we also need to green our gardens.

Your home does not have to sit amid rolling acres for you to reap the benefits. Small gardens can be incredibly productive, supplying food for the table and providing a biodiverse habitat for local wildlife. Conservation begins at home.

Left: In hot dry climates, various strategies can be employed to reduce the need for supplementary watering. These include terracing to prevent water run-off and planting native and naturally drought-resistant species, such as agave, cactus, lavender and sedum.

EARTH-SHELTERING

Right: This earth-sheltered house in Spain has a green roof that incorporates a lattice or grille that provides ventilation and shading to the living spaces below.

Far right: These dome-shaped eco houses in Torup, Denmark, have turf roofs. The dome shape reduces materials and heat loss by 30 per cent. Renewable energy comes from solar panels and a wind turbine.

Earth-sheltering represents the ultimate integration of house and landscape. Like many green building strategies, it is far from new. Earth-sheltered houses have long been part of the vernacular tradition, particularly in Nordic or Alpine countries. Houses may be almost entirely buried in the ground or sheltered only on the roof and north-facing walls, leaving the southern aspect exposed to the sun for the purposes of solar gain.

The basic principle of earth-sheltering is to take advantage of the thermal mass of the earth. In the same way as massive materials such as stone and concrete absorb heat slowly during the day and release it slowly at night, the earth also modulates temperatures, but on a much longer time frame, measured in periods as long as several months. This is known as the 'thermal flywheel' effect.

Earth-sheltering in its traditional, vernacular form has essentially been practised as a form of energy conservation and insulation. But there are other benefits, too. An earth-sheltered house disrupts the landscape to a far lesser degree than a stand-alone structure – where a house is almost fully buried, its impact on the surrounding environment will be minimal. Many eco houses built in unspoilt natural landscapes are earth-sheltered for this reason. Roofs of earth-sheltered houses need to be far stronger than those of conventional structures in order to withstand the load, and be fully waterproofed.

GREEN ROOFS

At a time when London's mayor, Boris Johnson, has called for the greening of roofs across the city, the turf roof might be said to have come of age. Green, 'living' or turf roofs have long been a powerful symbol of the environmental movement; in the past, some critics have argued that they provided little more than that. However, with the right technical input, a green roof can deliver tangible and lasting benefits.

Like earth-sheltered houses, green roofs are part of a long vernacular tradition of building and are found all over the world, from Scandinavia to Africa. In cold climates, turf or sod roofs help to keep heat in; in hot climates, they keep buildings cool. The modern incarnation of the green roof dates from the late 1960s, when research was carried out in Germany and Switzerland into ways of updating the practice to make it more practical and cost-efficient for urban homes.

The principal advantages of a green roof is that it represents a direct replacement of the land lost to building, provides a habitat for local species of animals and plants, and absorbs pollution, carbon dioxide and other greenhouse gases from the atmosphere. In addition, a green roof will retain rainwater, easing pressure on sewers and storm drains, and, in the right circumstances, can help to insulate against both sound and excessive heat loss or gain. Studies have shown that a green roof costs about the same or less over its lifespan as standard types of roofing, taking into account the fact that green roofs are much longer lasting. The exception is greening an existing roof, where the roof structure needs to be substantially strengthened: such work can be very costly.

ELEMENTS OF A GREEN ROOF

A green roof consists of three key elements: a layer of waterproofing to protect the underlying roof structure, a drainage and aeration layer to regulate moisture, and a growing layer, which consists of the growing medium together with the vegetation.

The management of water is critical. The waterproofing or roof membrane is designed to prevent water from penetrating through to the roof structure and causing rot or damage. The edges of the roof and interruptions to the covering (by skylights and chimneys, for example) need particular protection. Because it is covered with plants, a waterproof membrane can last up to 50 years before it needs to be replaced.

In ordinary circumstances, a green roof will absorb and retain rainfall, but adequate drainage and aeration is also required to prevent the growing medium from becoming

Below: Green roofs don't come much greener than this Alpine pasture grazed by cows.

Below right: Providing a welcome oasis in the heart of the city, green roofs require specialist installation.

Far right: Planting depends on the type of green roof. Low-maintenance hardy species such as sedum are common choices for lightweight coverings.

Below right: A green or living roof can be installed on a sloping roof, but will require additional support and lateral strapping to prevent the covering from slipping.

Far right: Roof terraces are another type of green roof. You need to ensure that the roof structure can bear the weight of containerized plants, furniture and people.

Next page: Simple green roofs require little maintenance except for the occasional inspection. This garage in Seattle, Washington, built of wood salvaged from pre-existing deck, features a green roof that has proved to be very low-maintenance, aside from the watering required during the first summer to establish the plants. Planting is one-third 'eco turf' (a mix of yarrow, clover and fescues) and two-thirds drought-tolerant sedums, with the addition of some strawberries, nasturtiums and poppies.

waterlogged during prolonged periods of very wet weather and to hold moisture during dry periods. A root barrier prevents roots from growing down and piercing the waterproof membrane.

The depth of growing medium and height of planting can vary widely, from 50 mm (2 inches) for simple turfed or grassed roofs right up to 1,500 mm (5 ft) in the case of intensely cultivated roofs, where plants need deeper soil to become established. Where the soil or growing medium is relatively shallow, planting is generally a mixture of species that tolerate dry or Alpine conditions, such as mosses, grasses, sedum and wild flowers. Deeper soils can support a much broader range of planting, including shrubs and trees.

DESIGNING GREEN ROOFS

Most green roofs form part of a new structure or are installed when an existing roof needs an overhaul. Design and planting will be affected by a number of considerations. These include:

Function. Green roofs have a number of different uses and these will have an impact on design. Those whose chief function is aesthetic, for example, will require different planting to those whose purpose is to reduce water run-off.
Roof type and structure. Roofs have to be strong enough to bear the additional load. Simple self-sustaining coverings of moss, sedum, grass and herbs are the lightest forms of green roof. At the most elaborate and heaviest, a green roof can be a fully cultivated garden, with trees, shrubs and food crops. The slope of the roof will also have a bearing on the type of planting that is possible. Green roofs that are steeply sloped can slip, especially when they are wet, and additional support or lateral strapping may be necessary.
Microclimate. Exposure to wind, orientation, shade from surrounding buildings and other specific climatic factors will affect planting and design. Lack of shelter means that conditions on a roof can be much more extreme than at ground level. Hardy native species are relatively trouble-free.
Access. The simplest roof gardens require very little maintenance and no additional watering; after they are installed, access is limited to periodic inspection. More intensively cultivated green roofs and roof gardens will need to be accessed on a regular basis for on-going maintenance.

INSTALLING A GREEN ROOF

The design, specification and installation of a green roof is professional work – green-roof failures and leaks are generally the result of poor installation rather than adverse conditions. You will need the advice of consultants, such as a structural engineer to advise on roof loading, and a mechanical engineer to assess the impact on insulation and services. A number of companies specialize in green-roof manufacture and installation and are able to carry out the entire process from design to planting, and this is often the best route to take. Some provide warranties.

ROOF TERRACES

A more straightforward way of greening a roof is to set aside a portion of a flat roof as a roof terrace or garden. As with green roofs, loading is a critical issue – the roof structure must be strong enough to bear the additional weight of containerized plants, soil and water. A rooftop receptacle for collecting rainwater is an ideal way of meeting irrigation needs.

GARDENING AND LANDSCAPING

One of the basic principles of green building is to respect site conditions and design accordingly. The same is true of gardening and landscaping.

A garden may seem to be the epitome of nature in microcosm, but all too often it is a far from natural place. The use of chemicals, such as pesticides, fertilizers and weedkillers, often in higher concentrations than are commonly used on food crops, damage the environment and human health. Exotic plants and specimens imported from halfway around the world occupy valuable space in flowerbeds and greenhouses and require intensive nurturing. Power-hungry tools and appliances are employed for general maintenance and upkeep. And the predominance of the lawn turns what could be a rich and diverse habitat into a virtual monoculture.

Eco gardening means working with nature, rather than against it. It also means productive gardening – growing plants that support native wildlife and provide fresh food for the table.

Rather than impose an alien ideal on your garden, you should design and plant according to the specifics of the site: the type of soil, the amount of rainfall, the prevailing winds and the temperature range. Choosing native plants that are adapted to local conditions means less intervention will be required in the form of irrigation and pest and disease control.

Below: One way of greening your garden is to let your lawn go over into meadow. Lawns require energy-hungry mowing and watering, whereas meadows need only be cut once a year.

Right: Eco-friendly gardening means respecting the local conditions of the site and planting accordingly, rather than attempting to grow exotic or alien species in conditions that are not favourable to them.

LAWNS

Many gardens are defined by sweeping expanses of lawn. Even in crowded urban areas, where gardens can be the size of a pocket handkerchief, a lawn bordered by narrow flowerbeds is still a typical arrangement. But devoting most of your garden area to what is essentially one type of planting reduces biodiversity and entails unnecessarily high levels of upkeep in the form of watering and regular mowing. A lawnmower that runs on petrol generates the same amount of pollution in an hour as a car that is driven 558 km (347 miles).

In small gardens, there is a good argument for doing without lawns altogether and increasing the size of beds for growing shrubs, flowers, fruit and vegetables. If you have a larger garden and want to keep part of it grassed, consider using a push- or hand-mower instead of a petrol-driven or electric one. Choose grass varieties that are naturally hardy, root out weeds by hand rather than apply weedkiller and dress with natural fertilizers. Grass is one of the great survivors – if your turf dries out in hot weather and shows bare patches, don't rush to turn on the sprinkler. Instead, wait until rainier weather brings natural regrowth. Leave glass clippings on the lawn rather than rake them up – alternatively, add them to your compost (see page 166).

The most eco-friendly lawn is the meadow. Lawns that are allowed to go over into meadows only need to be cut once a year and will attract butterflies, bees and other pollinators. A meadow sown with a mixture of native wild-flower seeds is a glorious place.

XERISCAPING

Hot, dry climates pose particular gardening challenges. Xeriscaping is a relatively new term for an old practice of land management that involves conserving water and growing native drought-tolerant species rather than thirsty imports. This approach to eco gardening is growing in popularity in dry regions of the western and southern United States and is also well established in Australia.

Choice of species is a key consideration. Native plants that have evolved to cope with low rainfall require little additional irrigation. Other xeriscaping strategies include improving the soil with compost, mulch and organic matter

Below: Companion planting is a natural means of pest control. Marigold roots, for example, emit a substance that deters whitefly.

Opposite, top left: Don't neglect vertical surfaces. Green walls can encourage biodiversity in the garden.

Opposite, top right: Recycled planting containers, such as these enamelled teapots, have a great deal of charm.

Opposite, bottom left: The retaining walls of this raised flowerbed are made of wire cages filled with scrap masonry.

Opposite, bottom right: A sustainable garden at the Chelsea Flower Show features glazed pyramid sculptures incorporating solar panels. The fencing is made of recycled scaffolding boards. Planting includes foxgloves mixed with wild flowers, reed beds, vegetables and herbs.

to increase water retention, terracing the site so that water does not run off causing soil erosion, and grouping plants with similar needs.

Planting can help to regulate interior temperatures in hot climates. Screens of trees and shrubs provide shade, filter light and break the strength of the sun.

Some plants that thrive in dry locations need a free-draining soil so that they do not become waterlogged when it rains. Digging in organic matter and grit can help to promote drainage.

In temperate zones, as winters become milder and summers hotter and drier, it can be a good idea to increase the numbers of plants in your garden that are tolerant of dry conditions. Common examples include lavender, rosemary, sedum and cistus.

PEST CONTROL

Using chemicals to control pests upsets the natural balance by eradicating the food source of animal, bird and insect predators. Eco gardening means encouraging wildlife to control the pests for you – birds such as bluetits, which will feed on aphids; frogs and toads, which feed on slugs and snails; and predatory insects such as ladybirds, hoverflies and lacewings. One way of doing this is to plant species that attract them – for example, nectar-producing plants for butterflies and bees; fennel, calendula and dill for hoverflies. Another is to provide bird and bat boxes, ponds and other nesting sites. Hedgehogs, which prey on slugs and snails, will make their home at the bottom of a woodpile. Many green gardening specialists offer a number of feeders and houses for attracting both insects and birds.

When nature needs a helping hand, there are other options aside from chemical treatments. Barriers and traps can be used to prevent slugs and snails from nibbling on your plants. Nematodes, which are microscopic threadworms that attack slugs, can be bought from green garden suppliers. Alternatively, you can pick off larvae, slugs and snails by hand, and remove any leaves blotched with blackspot. A solution of soap and water sprayed onto roses will deter aphids.

Companion planting is a tried and tested method of natural pest control. Some plants naturally emit scents that deter pests; other combinations of plants provide nutrients

for each other. Beans, for example, fix nitrogen in the soil, so should be grown in rotation before nitrogen-hungry crops such as potatoes and carrots. Good pest-control companions include:

Alliums such as onions or garlic / carrots. The scent of the onions or garlic deters carrot fly.
Coriander, chives or chervil / roses. The scent of the herbs deters aphids, which prey on roses and other flowers.
French marigolds / tomatoes. The roots of marigolds exude a substance that deters whitefly. Marigolds are often planted in greenhouses as a natural all-round pest control.
Rosemary / cabbage, beans or carrots. The scent of rosemary repels cabbage fly.
Borage. An ideal companion plant for many crops, including cucumber, gourds, strawberries and tomatoes, borage deters many pests.
Dill / cabbages, lettuce, onions and cucumber. Dill repels aphids and spider mites.
Lovage. Another ideal companion plant, lovage improves the health of many different species.
Peppermint / brassicas such as cabbage, broccoli and kale. Peppermint repels cabbage flies.
Geraniums and petunias. There plants are 'trap crops', attracting pests away from roses and grapevines.

RECYCLING IN THE GARDEN

Composting waste is not the only form of garden recycling. Many types of salvaged materials, building elements and containers can be reused successfully. There's a certain charm in this make do and mend approach – I'm thinking of those allotment sheds cobbled together from old doors and windows, with a bit of corrugated tin roofing thrown in, or an array of plants grown in old olive-oil cans, a vibrant feature of many Mediterranean terraces and window sills.

Salvaged materials, such as railway sleepers and old bricks, have an obvious role in the creation of hard landscaping, terracing and pathways. While some reclaimed materials are more expensive than new, others can be picked up for a song, or even for free.

Containers are an essential part of gardening. Even if most of your plants are grown in beds, you will still need pots for nurslings and cuttings, and you will inevitably

Tips for green gardening

- Ditch the power tools – the lawnmower, strimmer, leafblower and so on. The physical exercise you get gardening manually will help keep you fit. Buy good-quality hand tools and look after them – they should last a lifetime.
- Buy wooden garden furniture and structures. Ensure that the wood is certified by the FSC as coming from a sustainable source.
- Treat wooden fences and furniture with non-toxic preservative.
- Reduce the amount of paving. Extensive paving prevents water from seeping into the water table and increases the risk of flooding.
- Plant seedlings in biodegradable pots made of paper, coir or plant fibre that can be put straight into the ground.
- Living or green boundaries extend the possibilities for creating diversity. Hedgerows, for example, support many different forms of wildlife, although they do take time to establish. Fencing made of woven willow or hazel looks more natural than ubiquitous timber panels. Dry-stone walling can provide a home for rock plants and insect life.
- Provide trellising and other supporting systems to make use of vertical surfaces – facades, walls and fences extend the garden into a new dimension.
- Avoid patio-heaters and electric lights in the garden. If you want to light your garden, choose lights that incorporate a solar panel. These are much easier to install than external wiring, too.
- Use citronella beeswax or vegetable-based candles to keep biting insects away.

acquire pots when you buy new plants. Unfortunately, the gardening industry – and it is big business – has a problem with packaging. Over 500 million plastic pots are used in Britain every year. A large proportion ends up in landfill. One answer to this burgeoning waste problem is to ensure that you buy plants from a supplier who uses pots that contain recycled plastic, or that are biodegradable, such as those made of coir or recycled woodchip. Another is to encourage nurseries to provide a recycling service so that old pots can be returned once you no longer need them.

Terracotta pots, which are a natural product, are more expensive but also more attractive than plastic pots. Once they have broken or cracked beyond repair, they can be broken up and the pieces used to promote drainage at the bottom of other containers.

A host of other receptacles can also be pressed into service as unusual and attractive containers for planting. Along with olive-oil cans, these can include metal buckets, watering cans and troughs, old basins and sinks, barrels and drums. A recycled container that may have started life serving a very different purpose brings charm and wit to your garden display.

PRODUCTIVE GARDENS

Recent reports suggest that the sale of vegetable seeds is booming. People are increasingly turning away from annuals and herbaceous perennials in favour of lettuces, carrots, cabbages and beans. Growing your own is back in fashion and allotments have never been more sought-after.

At my home in the country I have always grown a substantial proportion of the fruit, vegetables and herbs that we eat. I have to admit that the primary reason for this has more to do with flavour and freshness than eco-awareness. Home-grown food simply tastes better than supermarket produce that has been flown in from countries thousands of miles away and kept in cold storage. In some cases, there is simply no comparison. Asparagus, for example, whose flavour is fugitive, should be eaten as soon as possible after it is cut. A friend of mine, who became quite obsessed about this, used to take a primus stove into the garden so that he could drop the asparagus into hot water the instant it was cut.

For the green-minded, growing your own food has obvious advantages. You avoid reliance on supermarkets, with the waste and energy costs associated with packaging

Below: Recycling in the garden can take many forms. This path is made out of recycled tyres.

Below right: Empty cans make cheerful containers for growing seedlings and cuttings, and help to cut down on the enormous amount of wastage created by discarded plastic plant pots.

Opposite, left: The traditional Victorian terracotta cloche, used for blanching, makes a handsome addition to a vegetable garden.

Opposite, right: Urban allotments are incredibly popular. In many areas there are long waiting lists as a new generation discovers the pleasure of growing your own.

and air miles. As part of its 'One Planet Living' initiative, the World Wildlife Fund calculated that food production and its transport accounted for 23 per cent of the average British person's carbon footprint, more than home energy use. Where once we were exhorted to 'dig for victory', now we should seriously think about digging for sustainability.

At a time when food prices have seen significant increases, growing your own also saves you money. There is the added satisfaction of working with the seasons – having to wait until summer to taste the first strawberries or raspberries heightens the pleasure.

Many people who grow their own food go on to practise traditional methods of storing and preserving what they produce. Pickling, preserving and bottling are among many of the ways you can lay up a summer glut to see you through the winter months.

Interestingly, urban agriculture has recently received an added impetus by a number of community-based schemes that have transformed areas of public parks into vegetable beds. One such scheme in Grant Park, Chicago, was the inspiration behind a similar proposal to create an allotment garden in St James's Park, London.

WATER

and empty the bathtub or basin in a matter of minutes. Always use eco-friendly cleaning products, shower gel and soap if you are going to be recycling greywater. You can also recycle water from the kitchen sink if it is has been used to wash vegetables, for example, but not water that has been used to wash dishes – this will contain too much grease and organic matter.

Another method of collecting water is use a rainwater butt, which may be made out of either wood or plastic, with the more visually acceptable wooden varieties being the more expensive. Rainwater butts can be connected to gutters and downpipes to collect water that falls on the roof – but bear in mind that roof coverings are critical, since both lead and asphalt can taint the water and make it unusable. It is also essential not to leave the water standing for long periods, otherwise it can become septic. Rainwater butts that are fitted with pumps are easier to empty than those that simply rely on a tap.

Underground water tanks are much more expensive and disruptive to install but can hold upwards of 2,000 litres (528 gallons). These connect to hose pipes for garden irrigation, car washing and other non-potable uses.

NATURAL PONDS AND POOLS

A world away from the rather artificial 'water feature' beloved of so many garden makeover programmes is a natural pond or pool. Ponds attract wildlife – frogs, toads, insects that pollinate and insects that feed on garden pests – promoting biodiversity in your own back garden. An eco pond relies on aquatic plants such as reeds, lily pads and irises to filter waste and discourage algae bloom. Natural products, such as extracts of barley straw and lavender, can also be used as aids to filtration.

If you have a big enough garden, you might consider creating a natural swimming pool. These rely on purifying plants to keep the water clean without the use of harsh chemicals such as chlorine. Natural swimming pools are generally divided into two areas, a deep swimming area and a shallow zone where the water is filtered by aquatic plants. The shallow, warmer water of the planted area raises the temperature of the swimming area. Experts recommend planting mature specimens at the outset – waiting for smaller plants to mature can allow algae time to build up.

Above right: Rainwater butts connect directly to the downpipe. Those that are fitted with a pump are easier to empty.

Far right, above: Natural swimming pools rely on purifying plants to keep the water clean.

Far right, below: A natural swimming pool in Cottage Point near Sydney, Australia, provides somewhere to get away from it all.

Garden irrigation accounts for a large percentage of fresh-water consumption – all those sprinklers continually watering manicured lawns and hosepipes left running in flowerbeds. In dry or hot climates, the amount of water consumed in this way can reach staggering proportions. You shouldn't wait for a hosepipe ban to investigate the eco-friendly alternatives.

Part of the strategy for saving water in the garden is to enrich the soil with compost and add layers of mulch (see page 168) to help water retention. Another is to plant native or indigenous species (see page 158). In a hot country, this means opting for drought-resistant plants that are naturally adapted to surviving in dry conditions.

Collecting water to use on the garden can be done in a number of ways (see page 62). The simplest and cheapest is to recycle greywater directly from the bath, shower or handbasin. You can do this by hand – filling a bucket or washing bowl – or buy a water-moving device. There are a number of designs on the market. One type is a siphon pump – you put one end in the bath or basin and the other out of the window, and connect it to a garden hose. After you squeeze the pump a few times, gravity will take over

COMPOSTING

Making compost is one of those eco-friendly activities that provides multiple benefits. The organic matter you produce improves the fertility and productivity of your garden, while at the same time disposing of waste that would otherwise have to be recycled or put out with the rubbish. It is estimated that 40 per cent of the contents of the average dustbin can be composted.

Compost is an excellent way of improving the structure of your soil. It is also a rich source of humus, which provides nutrients essential for plant growth. Regular applications of compost to your vegetable beds means that you do not have to rely on chemical fertilizers, which can harm insects and animals as well as get into the food chain. You will also need to water less, since soil that is rich in nutrients does not dry out so readily.

COMPOST BINS

You can make compost simply by building a heap of organic matter and covering it with cardboard or polythene. Compost bins, however, are neater and can be easier to manage. Many local authorities now provide home composting bins at a low price. Alternatively, you can buy one from a garden centre or build your own from timber offcuts. Compost bins with turning handles save effort and help to speed up the process of decay. Bins come in various sizes; if you have enough room, consider having two or more, so that one can be rotting down while a second is being filled. Whatever container you choose for your compost, it must have a lid or cover.

SITING THE BIN

Some people view the compost heap or bin as an eyesore and keep it well out of view. However, having to make a long trek down to the bottom of the garden on a cold and rainy night to dispose of kitchen waste won't encourage you to compost, so make sure your bin is located where it is easily accessible. For best results, the bin should be placed directly on top of bare soil or turf and in a sunny or semi-shaded position, but not in deep shade. Keep it away from wet areas.

MAKING COMPOST

Compost isn't difficult to make provided that you use the right ingredients. You can simply add waste to the bin or heap as and when you want to. However, this rough and ready method will take time to yield usable compost – up to a year in some cases – and the end result may not be pleasant to handle. For high-quality compost and speedier results, you need to put more effort and thought into it. Ideally, compost should have a light, crumbly texture, be sweet-smelling and dark in colour.

It is important to ensure that you compost a balance of green and brown materials – the green materials rot quickly and exclude air, while the brown materials open up the mixture and create air spaces. You can either fill the bin with alternate layers of green and brown ingredients or add bulky brown materials to kitchen waste as you go. A filled bin will heat up in a matter of days; a bin that you add to gradually may never heat up.

Turning the compost on a regular basis will speed up the process of decay. Mix it well with a garden fork. If the mixture is soggy, add more brown materials to dry it out. If it is dry, add water. Manure and garden soil can also help to promote a more rapid breakdown.

Compost is ready when the contents of the bin or heap are dark brown, crumbly and earthy. This process may take anywhere between six weeks and a year to accomplish. When this stage is reached, leave the compost for a further month to mature before using it on the garden.

Safety. Making compost is generally a safe activity, provided that you follow basic rules of hygiene. Wear gloves, make sure that open wounds or cuts are bandaged and wash your hands after handling the compost.

Left: Successful compost requires a mixture of brown and green ingredients. Green ingredients, such as grass clippings, are fast to decompose. Brown ingredients give bulk to the mixture.

Right: Compost requires turning on a regular basis to speed up the process of decay. You can also add more green or brown ingredients to the mixture, depending on whether it is too dry or too soggy.

COMPOST INGREDIENTS

Any organic matter can be composted, with some important exceptions. Meat, dairy products and cooked food should not be added to the compost bin because these waste items will attract rats and other vermin. Similarly, don't compost cat litter, dog faeces or disposable nappies. You should also avoid composting diseased plants, particularly those suffering from soil-borne diseases, as well as really troublesome or invasive weeds such as bindweed and ground elder.

To make a good-quality compost, you need an equal amount (by volume) of 'green' and 'brown' material. 'Green' waste, such as grass clippings, are quick to compost and get the mixture going. On their own, however, they decay to a smelly sludge. 'Brown' waste, such as twigs and branches, are slower to decay and give bulk to the mixture. For best results, woody material should be shredded or chopped finely, otherwise the compost will take ages to break down.

Green ingredients include:
- Grass clippings.
- Raw vegetable peelings.
- Young weeds without seedheads; avoid invasive perennial weeds such as bindweed.
- Green prunings.
- Manure from cows, horses and chickens.

Brown ingredients include:
- Woody clippings and prunings, provided that they are shredded or chopped up small.
- Sawdust and wood shavings.
- Waste paper and cardboard.
- Straw and hay.
- Waste bedding from herbivores, such as rabbits and guinea pigs.
- Fallen leaves; alternatively use these to produce a mulch (see page 168).

Other ingredients include:
- Crushed eggshells.
- Natural fabric, such as all-wool or all-cotton material.

MULCHES

Mulching is another invaluable way of improving soil conditions. A layer of organic or inorganic material (no less than 5 cm/2 inches deep) helps to keep soil fertile and acts as an insulator, both in cold and hot weather. It also suppresses weeds and helps the soil retain its moisture.

In the past, the most popular types of organic mulch were peat-based. However, peat is a non-renewable resource and these days its use is strongly discouraged on environmental grounds.

A good organic mulch can be made using fallen leaves. Instead of adding raked-up leaves to the compost, bag them up separately or put them in a wire-mesh container. Allow about a year for the leaves to fully decompose into leaf mould. You can speed up the process considerably by shredding them first. Leaf mould can also be used as a basis for potting compost.

Another organic mulch is farmyard manure, left to rot for between three and twelve months. Don't mulch with fresh manure – it will burn plants. Manure mulches act as slow-release fertilizers.

Inorganic mulches include gravel and plastic sheeting.

WORMERIES

If you don't have a big enough garden for a compost heap or bin, try a wormery instead. These use worms to convert ordinary kitchen waste, including cooked food, into liquid feed and organic compost. If you are squeamish, you don't have to worry – the whole process takes place within a sealed, lockable container that is subdivided into separate chambers, with the worms feeding below the top layer where the food waste is added. Since the worms are sensitive to light, you are unlikely to see them. Compost collects beneath the worms and a drainage platform underneath the compost collects liquid feed in a reservoir that can be tapped off.

Although a wormery will begin to produce liquid feed after about eight weeks, it is usual to wait until the bin is full before emptying out the compost. You can add all kinds of kitchen waste to the wormery, including tea bags, eggshells and either cooked and uncooked food scraps, as well as paper products.

Right: Wormeries convert kitchen waste, including cooked food, into liquid feed and organic compost. They are ideal if you don't have much outdoor space for composting.

Far right: Because the process of composting takes a long time, it's a good idea to have more than one heap on the go – one can be rotting down while the other is being filled.

The compost produced by a wormery can be used directly on the garden. The liquid feed needs to be diluted with water first. It can be used as a feed for garden plants, house plants, vegetables and lawns.

Various sizes of wormery are available, including those that are small enough to place on a balcony. There are no restrictions about where you can locate a wormery, as the smell is negligible. The most common location is beside the back door or in a utility area, for easy access.

Bokashi food composters work in a similar way to wormeries, making use of digestive enzymes rather than worms to break down both cooked or uncooked food.

MAINTENANCE

The classic mantra of sustainability – Reduce, Reuse, Recycle – is what people of my generation knew as Make Do and Mend. As a child growing up during the war, I could not help but be aware of the shortages that were such a feature of everyday life. No petrol, precious little butter, nasty powdered egg. Yet it was not simply wartime privation or rationing that made people thrifty. Wasting as little as possible by repairing, mending and reusing was simply good housekeeping. In the majority of families, socks were darned, shoes were resoled, children's clothes were handed down and many a Monday supper was made from Sunday's leftovers. In recent years that way of life has seemed almost quaint. Yet now that the past few decades of consumerism have come down with the bump of a credit crunch, newspapers and magazines are full of advice on how to rediscover the skills that every family knew and practised back in the days when I was growing up – such as knitting, mending, preserving food and growing your own vegetables. A thrifty lifestyle is naturally green. So, too, is using traditional recipes for cleaning that rely on harmless ingredients such as lemon juice, vinegar and baking soda, rather than the chemical concoctions that line the shelves of supermarkets.

Left: Certain materials and finishes are naturally low in maintenance, which reduces the need to apply protective surface treatments such as paints or seals.

REDUCING WASTE

Ever since planned obsolescence was introduced by manufacturers in the postwar period as a way of ensuring steady sales, we have increasingly been living in a throwaway society. The lifespans of many consumer goods are incredibly short, and as the pace of technological change accelerates, they are getting even shorter. It is not unusual for a laptop to break down after three or four years, or for new software to be introduced that is not compatible with existing hardware. Even when products continue to work, new models with additional functions appear on a regular basis, encouraging people to upgrade before they really need to. Once the idea of calling someone on a mobile phone was revolutionary in itself. Now we expect our mobiles to take pictures and connect to the Internet. Rapidly succeeding generations of mobiles and computers have contributed to an explosion of electronic scrap. It is estimated that 4 million PCs are discarded in China every year. In the UK, 2 million working Pentium PCs end up in landfill during the same period.

Reducing waste is a three-pronged attack. The first strategy is to buy better quality and use less, which represents a direct reduction in consumption. The second is to reuse products – repairing and mending is a way of reusing – and the third is to recycle so that the minimum ends up being disposed to landfill or incinerated.

CONSUME LESS

- Buy only what you need or really want. Some brave souls have taken up the challenge of buying nothing superfluous to basic requirements for a period of months and discovered that many of their previous purchases had been made unthinkingly. Impulse buys rarely satisfy true needs and are often the items that are most likely to be discarded at a later date or hang around indefinitely occupying valuable space.
- Buy better things. When you buy less, you will be able to afford products of higher quality, which will last longer and perform better.
- Avoid buying products made of plastic or other materials that cannot easily be recycled or that are not biodegradable. Choose glass bottles over plastic containers, for example.
- Packaging is a huge source of waste. Buy loose fruit and vegetables from a local market or grocer; buy staple items in bulk; use reusable shopping bags and baskets.
- Avoid disposable products such as plastic razors, paper napkins and tissues, paper plates, cups and plastic cutlery.
- Join a library to borrow books or read periodicals. Read newspapers online. Rent DVDs or videos from a store.
- Join a toy library to rotate your children's toys, rather than buying new every time.
- Hire tools rather than buying them, or borrow from your neighbours. Many DIY jobs are tackled rarely and there is no need to keep a vast array of power tools on hand for the odd occasion when you feel moved to put up a shelf.
- Stop junk mail at source by removing your name from direct mailing lists or joining a mail preference service.
- Don't buy bottled water unless absolutely necessary. Reuse old plastic bottles or use a water flask if you need to take water out with you. Ask for tap water in restaurants.
- Send e-cards instead of paper ones.
- Don't print your emails unless absolutely necessary. Try to print on both sides of the paper if possible. Special software is available that reduces toner and paper consumption.
- Don't buy single-use cameras.
- Make a packed lunch to take to work and save money as well as packaging.
- Give an 'experience' as a present. Unwanted gifts account for a significant degree of waste (and wasted money). Instead, buy gift vouchers, cinema, theatre or concert tickets, spa treatments or other experiences.
- Learn the art of cooking leftovers to reduce food waste. Soups, stews and casseroles are good ways of making use of spare ingredients.

Right: Individual bins concealed within a fitted kitchen unit make recycling simpler.

Far right: In many areas, recycling happens on the doorstep. In the most effective schemes, waste is collected once it has been separated into type: paper, glass (clear, green and brown), metal and organic food waste.

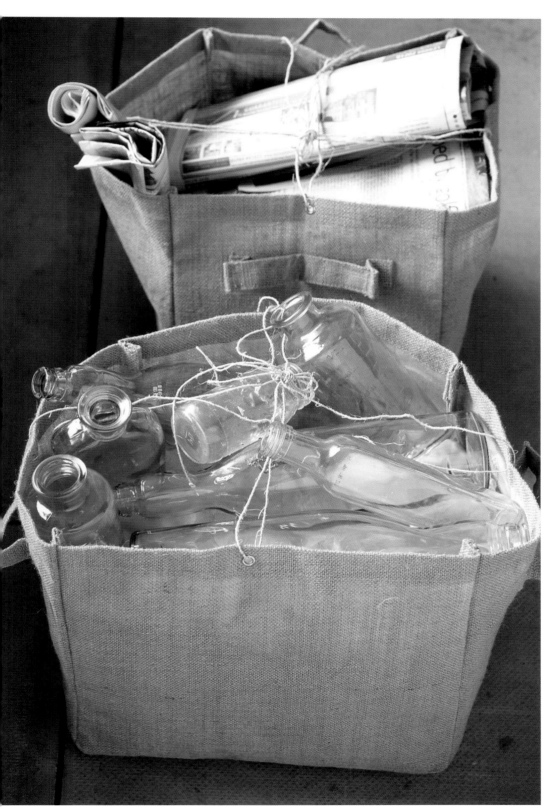

REUSE AND REPAIR

One pernicious side-effect of our throwaway society is that we are all too ready to discard things that could easily be repaired. Basic mending skills are not difficult to acquire. If you are all fingers and thumbs, it only takes a little effort to find a repair service. Many dry-cleaners, for example, will do simple alterations to clothing.

However, repair is sometimes not an option. Manufacturers often collude in this by building in obsolescence or discontinuing parts that might keep an appliance functioning for longer if they were available. Products made of synthetic materials, including plastics, are also more difficult to repair. If your wooden floor looks battered, you can always resand and reseal it. A worn vinyl floor, on the other hand, is heading for landfill sooner rather than later. Buy goods that are made of natural materials as far as possible and you stand a better chance of prolonging their life with proper maintenance.

- Don't buy disposable batteries. Use rechargeable ones that contain no mercury or cadmium. Use a solar-powered recharger.
- Reuse old containers for home storage needs. Jam jars, yoghurt pots with lids and ice-cream cartons can be used to organize your home workshop or food cupboards. Use resealable and reusable containers to store leftovers rather than cover them with foil or plastic wrap.
- Reuse envelopes and padded bags.
- Repair and mend furniture and furnishings. Have chairs and sofas reupholstered rather than buying replacements. Refinish scratched or stained wooden furniture.
- Buy reconditioned electrical appliances from approved outlets.
- Visit charity shops – you can find some amazing bargains.
- Buy vintage. Scour flea markets, secondhand shops, car boot sales and other outlets for 'pre-loved' goods. Skips, auction houses and salvage yards are good sources for secondhand building materials, such as bricks, paving stones and timber, as well as building elements, such as fireplaces, windows, doors, and fittings and fixtures.
- Old knitted garments can be unravelled for a source of yarn you can reuse.
- Practise good housekeeping on your computer. Upgrade to new software when it becomes available and install extra memory rather than buy a new model.
- Downcycle old sheets and towels as cleaning rags rather than buy disposable cloths or paper towel.
- Many local areas provide scrap materials for children's art projects.

RECYCLE

In many parts of the West, local recycling schemes are well-established. If you don't have one in your area, campaign to have one introduced. Doorstep collections are more successful than centralized banks located in supermarket car parks and so on, because they remove at least some of the effort from recycling and provide households with greater incentives to reduce their waste. Schemes, however, do vary. In some areas different bins are provided for separating and collecting different types of waste; in others all recyclable materials are collected in one go, which is less satisfactory.

Facilitate home recycling by investing in separate recycling containers. Closed bins are best – labeled or colour coded for ease of sorting. Ideally, glass should be sorted into clear, green and brown, with corks and metal caps removed. Separate steel from aluminium cans with the use of a magnet – steel will stick to a magnet, but aluminium will not. Some areas also have facilities for recycling plastic or certain types of plastic.

The most preferable form of recycling is when waste materials are recycled into material of the same quality – what is generally known as 'closed-loop' recycling. For example, glass and metals can be recycled with no loss of quality. Making recycled aluminium uses 95 per cent less energy than making aluminium from scratch.

Lending or leasing products for the duration of their lifespan – such as carpeting and washing machines – and then recycling them afterwards is another form of recycling that some manufacturers have put in place. The consumer pays a fee for the period of use.

There are many online resources that give information about waste management and recycling, a number of which are listed at the back of this book. You can consult these to find out how to recycle specific items in your area, or how to acquire products and goods that have a recycled content. Many charities, such as Oxfam, will recycle problematic items, such as mobile phones, computers and ink cartridges.

Right: Good housekeeping means getting the recyling habit. Separate bins for different types of waste encourage everyone to do their bit.

- Before you make a purchase, think about how that item or material will be recycled at the end of its life. Try to avoid buying things that are not readily recyclable. Patronize those retailers that will collect and recycle the items or products you are replacing.
- Divert your food waste from landfill where it generates methane. Instead, compost raw vegetable matter such as peelings (see page 166). All kinds of food waste, cooked and uncooked, can go in a wormery or a bokashi food-composter (see page 168). Some areas will collect food waste in separate bins. Biodegradable bin liners are available to keep recycling bins clean. Don't use a waste-disposal unit – these add a slurry of pulverized waste to the water supply.
- Recycle old clothes and shoes by donating them to a local charity shop. Children often grow out of their clothing before it is worn out – pass items on to younger siblings, friends or family

members, or take them to a charity shop. Some charities run schemes where very worn clothing can be recycled by shredding the fibres and reweaving them.
- Instead of donating clothing and other unwanted items to charity, you can freecycle them on a freecycling website, where items are swapped, or put them up for auction on eBay and earn a bit of extra money.
- Plunder skips for cast-off elements that you can assemble into desirable furniture using a little inventive DIY. It doesn't have to be as basic as scaffolding boards on bricks – the shelving solution of countless bedsits – with more craft and ingenuity you can knock up a storage unit from discarded drawers, or a table from a door or sheet of glass supported by a pair of sawhorses.
- Old reading glasses can be donated to charity. Some high-street opticians will recycle glasses to those in need in different parts of the world.

- Buy recycled paper products, such as toilet paper and stationery. Avoid pure white paper products; these have been bleached and bleach contains harmful dioxins.
- Many companies that sell print cartridges operate recycling schemes, whereby you send back the spent cartridge in pre-paid packaging.
- Discarded or hoarded mobile phones are fast becoming a waste nightmare, particularly as their batteries contain harmful heavy metals. Cadmium, found in mobile phone batteries, is one of the most dangerous substances on earth – the cadmium from a single mobile phone battery can pollute 600,000 litres (158,550 gallons) of water. Never dispose of mobiles to landfill. Instead investigate charities or other organizations that guarantee to recycle them safely.
- Computers also require careful disposal. If your old computer still works, you can donate it to one of a number of different charities, educational institutions or similar

bodies. Broken or defunct computers can be scrapped for their parts, with harmful heavy metals safely removed. Again, there are specialist organizations that will do this, sometimes for a fee.
- Old fridges and freezers often contain CFCs and HCFCs, which are harmful to the environment. Some retailers will collect your old fridge or freezer when you buy a new 'green' model and either send it to be reconditioned for future sale or to have CFCs removed.
- Donate working appliances and bulky furniture to schemes that specialize in recycling and reconditioning goods to sell to low-income families.
- Hazardous or non-recyclable waste needs careful disposal. Car batteries, motor oil, low-energy fluorescent tubes, synthetic paints, solvents and garden chemicals all fall within this category. Never dispose of such materials with the household rubbish. Contact your local authority for details of hazardous waste collection centres.

RECYCLE

CLEANING

In recent years many people have become concerned about additives and preservatives in processed food and switched to a healthier diet. It's a natural progression to apply the same attitude to household cleaning products, many of which contain an arsenal of chemicals that are potentially harmful to both human health and the environment. What is worse, common household products are often not fully labelled, which means you don't know exactly what chemicals you are exposing yourself to and in what concentrations. Instead, what you will find on the label are cautions not to swallow, to keep out of reach of children and to avoid contact with the skin – which tells you all you need to know about the risks you are running.

Back in the days of gaslighting and coal fires, cleaning was arduous. Today, our electrically powered and centrally heated homes simply don't get anywhere near as dirty. Yet many people have become almost hysterical about hygiene, falling on each labour-saving appliance and new 'miracle' cleaning products as if they were the answer to all their anxieties about germs. I'm not advocating squalor, but

NATURAL CLEANING PRODUCTS

Many common ingredients that you can find in your store cupboard or can buy easily and inexpensively from a supermarket, health store or chemist can be used as highly effective cleaners, detergents, stain removers, polishes and deodorizers.

Chief among these are lemon juice, baking soda and vinegar, all of which have a multitude of uses. Traditional recipes for natural cleaners can be found in old household manuals or on various Internet sites.

Lemon

Lemon juice is a natural sanitizer and deodorizer and leaves behind a pleasant citrus scent.

Uses include:

− Dissolving soap scum, grease and hard-water deposits.
− Cut a lemon in half and dip the cut end into baking soda or salt and use to scour and deodorize chopping boards, to scrub dishes and wooden surfaces, and to remove stains.
− Cleaning and polishing brass and copper.
− Mixed with vinegar or baking soda, lemon juice makes a good all-purpose cleaning paste.
− Removing perspiration and other stains from clothing.

exposure to some common bacteria has been shown to boost immune systems – you simply don't need the same standard of cleanliness at home as you would be entitled to expect if you were undergoing a medical procedure.

Many of the cleaning products on the market today are products of the petrochemical industry, which developed rapidly in the second half of the twentieth century. Before these cleansers, detergents, deodorants, air fresheners and polishes came on the market, and were heavily advertised to persuade us to buy them, people relied on traditional remedies using common ingredients from the store cupboard. In many cases these work just as well, especially if you are prepared to use a little elbow grease. They are also often multipurpose in their applications, so you don't, for example, need a separate cleanser for the bath and for the kitchen sink. Other alternatives include products specifically marketed as eco-friendly.

Get into the habit of cleaning little and often. Wipe down surfaces, hobs and ovens after use; don't allow grime to build up so you need to rely on a powerful caustic product to shift it. Similarly, sweep floors regularly rather than get the vacuum cleaner out. Dry clothes on a line or an air dryer rather than use a power-hungry tumble dryer.
– Choose eco cleaners for washing dishes and doing the laundry. Unlike chemical-based cleaners, eco products are generally fully labelled so you know what the ingredients are. Most laundry detergents contain phosphates, which is a major pollutant. Common ingredients of eco cleaners are citrus oils to provide scent, chamomile to act as a softener, and coconut or palm oil as cleaning agents.
– Cloths with dust- and dirt-trapping weaves – generally marketed as 'eco cloths' – reduce the need for polishes. These can be washed and reused over and over again.
– Use beeswax, tung oil or linseed oil to polish and seal wooden surfaces and furniture.
– Be aware of 'greenwashing' when selecting products for cleaning and personal grooming. 'Natural' is a vague term and may not mean that the product is environmentally friendly. Organic plant extracts are common ingredients of eco cleaners.

Previous page: Dry wet laundry on a clothesline rather than use an energy-hungry tumble dryer.

Left: Label your recycling bins so you can see at a glance what needs to go where.

Next page: Timber cladding, which requires no subsequent sealing or finishing, makes a low maintenance exterior finish.

Vinegar

Like lemon juice, vinegar is also a natural sanitizer and deodorizer. Don't worry about making your home smell like an old fish-and-chips wrapper – the vinegar smell disappears almost immediately.

Uses include:
– Cleaning glass and windows. Mix vinegar half and half with water and put into a spray bottle. Spray onto windows or glass surfaces and wipe clean. Wiping with a crumpled newspaper won't leave any streaks.
– Clearing sluggish drains. Put two tablespoons of baking soda down the drain and add some vinegar. The fizzing reaction between the two will clear the blockage. Afterwards, flush through with boiling water. The same procedure can be used for deodorizing drains.
– As an astringent. Vinegar mixed half and half with water clears the skin of soap residue.

– As a toilet cleaner. Pour neat vinegar into the toilet and around the rim, leave overnight and scrub well in the morning.
– As an all-purpose cleaner. A solution of vinegar and water can be used as an all-purpose cleaner for kitchen and bathroom surfaces. You can add a little salt to make a more abrasive cleaner.
– As a descaler. To remove hard lime deposits, soak paper towels in vinegar and place them around the taps. Leave for an hour, then clean.
– As a fabric/water softener. Half a cup of undiluted vinegar can be added to the rinse cycle instead of fabric conditioner.
– As a hair rinse. A rinse of neat vinegar helps to remove shampoo residue and prevent dandruff.
– As a stain remover. To remove water stains from leather shoes, rub with a cloth dipped in a solution of vinegar and water.

Baking soda

A mild abrasive, baking soda (sodium bicarbonate) has so many uses it's worth buying in bulk. It's highly effective at removing odours and makes a good all-purpose cleaner.

Uses include:
– Put an open container of baking soda in the refrigerator to absorb odours.
– All-purpose cleaner. Sprinkle baking soda on kitchen and bathroom surfaces to clean and deodorize them. A scouring paste can be made of baking soda mixed with a little water.
– As an oven cleaner. A paste of baking soda and water will remove baked-on grime.
– As a rug and carpet deodorizer. Sprinkle baking soda onto the carpet, leave for fifteen minutes, then vacuum.

Borax

A mineral that is naturally antifungal and antibacterial, borax (sodium borate) can be used as an alternative to bleach. However, unlike lemon juice, baking soda and vinegar, borax is toxic and should be kept well out of the reach of children and pets.

Uses include:
– To pre-soak soiled clothing. Mix up a solution of borax and water (1 tablespoon per 4½ litres/ 1 gallon) and soak clothing before washing.
– As a disinfectant. Mix a solution of borax and water (half a cup to 4½ litres/1 gallon) to use as a cleaner.
– Borax sprinkled onto a damp cloth can be used to scour surfaces in the bathroom.

Insect repellents

Proprietary brands of insecticide contain harmful chemicals and are highly toxic. Many herbs and essential oils, however, can be used as natural pest repellents.
– *Moths.* What attracts moth larvae, which do the damage, are proteins in natural fibres, as well as food residues on your clothing. Launder or dry-clean all garments before you put them away. Don't overfill drawers or cram hanging rails or closets to bursting. Natural moth repellents include: lavender oil, cedar shavings, nutmeg, cloves, cinnamon, thyme and rosemary.
– *Flies.* Strong smells repel flies. Natural fly repellents include: cloves, rosemary, thyme, lavender, rue and basil.
– *Fleas.* Pet fleas, which flourish in our warm homes, are generally treated with chemicals. For a natural alternative, try bathing pets in tea-tree oil shampoo.

CASE STUDIES

Left: Detail of Sunken House (see page 196–7) showing the dark stained timber cladding. The structure is made of prefabricated timber panels.

Many advocates of green living jump at the opportunity to build their own homes – or to give their existing houses a radical overhaul. As the following examples show, eco building does not mean adopting a one-size-fits-all approach. Designs can be inspired by traditional vernacular forms, such as barns or farmhouses, or display a cutting-edge modernist sensibility. Materials may range from the humble and low-tech to the latest high-specification products. What all have in common, however, is the desire to create homes that harm the planet as little as possible.

NATURAL RESPONSE

WALSH HOUSE | KANGAROO VALLEY | AUSTRALIA | ARCHITECTS: GLENN MURCUTT

Award-winning architect Glenn Murcutt designs houses that are uniquely responsive to their local surroundings, seasonal conditions and natural elements. Environmental issues, in their broadest sense, have been a feature of his work long before they were taken up by the design community at large.

The Walsh House in Kangaroo Valley shares certain similarities with other Murcutt designs, combining an Australian rural vernacular with an elegant and restrained modernism. Like all of Murcutt's work, the house sits lightly on the land and is constructed of materials that have both consumed as little energy as possible during their manufacture and will consume as little as possible over the lifetime of the house.

The house is situated in open grassland. Its long axis runs east to west, capitalizing on the movements of the sun, which, in the southern hemisphere, travels through the northern sky. Along the main north facade, which overlooks a wooded ridge, the overhanging roof protects windows from direct summer sun. External Venetian blinds provide further solar control. The southern and western sides of the house, which are more rustic in appearance, have smaller, fewer windows to shelter the house from the cold winter winds that blow from that direction.

The construction of the building is what is known as a 'reverse brick veneer'. The basic structure is brickwork. The internal surface was rendered with a light coat of cement and painted. Stud timber framing was applied to the outside, highly insulated and then clad in timber boarding stained ebony. The inner brickwork acts as thermal mass. The foundations of the house comprise a concrete raft slab. Flooring is grey stone tile. The roof is highly insulated. Made of galvanized-iron sheeting, it serves to collect rainwater.

During winter the warmth of the sun penetrates deep into the house, gradually warming up the floor and walls. At night the house is closed up and the warmth gathered during the day radiates within the spaces. The reverse applies in the summer.

Above: The north side of the house, seen from the west. Three projected bays fitted with louvres clearly announce different rooms.

Right: One of the bays is fitted as a writing desk to form a study area. The louvres allow fine adjustment of levels of daylighting and help to keep the interior cool in summer.

Far right: Rainwater is collected from the roof and stored in large corrugated cisterns, an essential conservation strategy in an area prone to drought.

Opposite: The main sitting area is separated from the kitchen/dining area by a large wood-burning stove that provides supplementary heat in the winter.

Murcutt is known for his open-plan layouts and free flow of space. In the case of the Walsh House, however, space has been arranged as a series of individual rooms, each with its own glazed bay projecting from the facade. The bays are fitted with movable louvres, so that the daylighting of each room can be adjusted to suit the needs of the occupant. The bays themselves fulfil different functions, serving respectively as a writing desk, daybed and small greenhouse.

Controlling daylight is an important means of ensuring comfortable living conditions. So, too, is manipulating through-breezes. In the Walsh House, the two end windows on the north facade can be slid back, as can the glazed east wall, uniting the sitting room with the veranda. Air playing over a shallow pool helps to temper the heat of the summer.

The only area in the house that has both a northerly and southerly aspect is the kitchen/dining area. Separating the kitchen/dining area from the sitting room is a large heat-exchange wood-burning stove. Like most of Murcutt's designs, this house has been so sensitively attuned to light and air that it requires no further heating or cooling.

A particular feature of the south side of the house are the large corrugated cisterns that collect rainwater from the roof. This is used for everything from drinking to cooking to flushing toilets. One cistern is dedicated to fire-fighting use, as the area is subject to wild fires during the summer.

Below: A large south-facing window in the kitchen frames a view of an ancient tree on a neighbouring hill. The kitchen is fully fitted in an L-shaped layout.

Below right: Another glazed bay window in a bedroom serves as a daybed. The ribbon of high transom windows provides good conditions of natural light and is shaded from direct sun by the overhanging roof.

Left: A number of bathrooms are slotted in between the bedrooms. The elegance of the fittings is characteristic of Murcutt's attention to detail. Rooms connect with one another or can be alternately accessed from an external walkway sheltered by the roof.

Right: Adjustable vents allow the occupants to control natural ventilation and promote cooling through-breezes.

ECO FACTS:

- Use of humble materials that consume as little energy as possible to produce
- Exceptional site sensitivity.
- Adjustable louvres, blinds, vents and sliding windows to control daylighting and ventilation and prevent the need for artificial cooling.
- Sloping overhanging roof to shade windows from direct summer sun.
- Water conservation in large cisterns.
- Efficient use of space, incorporating many fitted elements.

PLAN KEY:

1 - Utility
2 - Garage
3 - Bedroom
4 - Bathroom
5 - Entrance/foyer
6 - Kitchen/Dining room

7 - Writing desk
8 - Living area
9 - Pond
10 - Veranda
11 - Barbecue

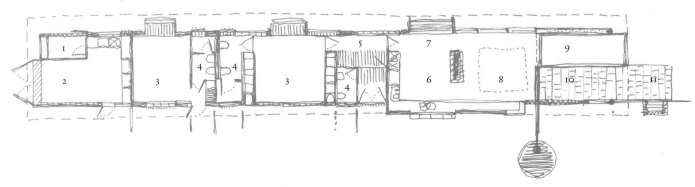

NORWEGIAN WOOD

FINRUD CABIN | HEMSEDAL | NORWAY | ARCHITECTS: HENRIK E NIELSEN

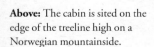

Above: The cabin is sited on the edge of the treeline high on a Norwegian mountainside.

Above right: Extensive glazing on the south-facing elevation allows the building to benefit from passive solar gain. The north-facing facade is much more sheltered.

Right: Concrete walls are left exposed inside. The concrete floor slab incorporates underfloor heating and is tiled in slate.

Far right: The entire cabin is highly insulated and clad in timber panels. None of the timber has been treated. With time, it will weather to a soft grey.

The product of a highly successful collaboration between client and architect, this timber cabin sits high on a mountainside in the Hemsedal Valley in central Norway. The owners wanted to be close to nature; during the winter the cabin is accessible only on skis.

Great care was taken to integrate the house with its spectacular setting. From the other side of the valley, it appears almost transparent, due to the huge glass windows that face south. In this particular area, the treeline is further up the slopes than anywhere else in the vicinity, an indication that temperatures are higher. The house is sited at the edge of the treeline and oriented to make the most of passive solar gain.

Houses in such remote locations are often far from mains servicing. In this case, fresh water comes from a well situated under the cabin.

Glazed curtain walls on the south, east and west facades allow light and heat to penetrate into the interior. Openings are minimal on the northern side of the cabin to provide shelter from cold northern winds.

Right: The main living areas of the cabin are arranged in an open-plan layout along the south-facing facade. Inside the roof is clad in birch panels, left untreated. Furnishings are simple and rugged in keeping with the setting.

Far right, above: An additional sleeping area is provided by a mezzanine level tucked under the slope of the room. Other bedrooms are on the ground floor.

Far right, below: Supplementary heating is provided by a wood burner. Fresh water comes from a well underneath the house.

The floor slab and the spine walls are made of concrete, which has high thermal mass, absorbing heat slowly during the day and releasing it slowly overnight. In the interior, the concrete walls have been left exposed; externally, they have been highly insulated and clad in larch panels. The concrete floor incorporates underfloor heating and is covered in slate. There is also a wood burner to provide supplementary heating and create a warm focal point in the living area.

The sloping roof is clad with cedar panels on the outside and birch panels on the inside. None of the timber used in the house, either internally or externally, has been treated with oil, paint or any other finish. Instead, it has been left to weather naturally.

The layout of the cabin is essentially open plan, with the main living areas – kitchen, sitting area and dining area – ranged along the south-facing facade, benefiting from natural light and the views across the valley. In the warmer months this free-flowing space opens out onto terraces to the east and west, both of which are sheltered by the overhanging roof. Bedrooms are located on the sheltered north side of the cabin, with additional sleeping space on the mezzanine level. Below, on the basement level, are the bathrooms.

Raised on pillars, the cabin sits lightly on the land. Refined detailing, the use of extensive glazing and natural timber cladding allow it to blend almost imperceptibly with its location.

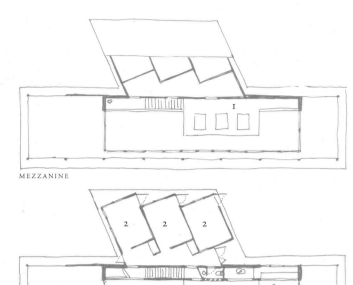

MEZZANINE

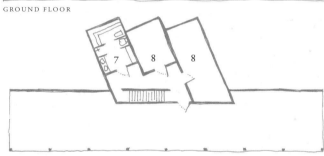

GROUND FLOOR

LOWER GROUND FLOOR

ECO FACTS:

- Siting and orientation to make the most of passive solar gain.
- High degree of insulation.
- Use of concrete for its high thermal mass.
- Untreated timber cladding internally and externally.
- Water supplied by a well on site.
- Extensive glazing bathes the interior in natural light.

PLAN KEY:

1 - Mezzanine
2 - Bedroom
3 - West terrace
4 - Living area
5 - Dining area
6 - Kitchen
7 - Bathroom
8 - Garage

OPEN HOUSE

PFANNER HOUSE | CHICAGO, ILLINOIS | USA | ARCHITECTS: ZOKA ZOLA

Designed by an architect for herself and her family, the house was conceived as an exploration of openness, both in terms of the way the interior spaces are planned and in the house's relationship with passersby. Part of a phased development that will eventually include the installation of geothermal heating and cooling, along with photovoltaic and solar thermal panels on the roof of an extension, the existing building incorporates many environmentally friendly features, reflecting the family's energy- and health-conscious lifestyle.

The positioning of the house on its corner lot both articulates the spaces that surround it and maximizes natural light. On the south side, there is a 2.4 m (8 ft) yard separating the house from its immediate neighbour. Wider than required by law, it allows low winter sun to penetrate deep into the interior. Four cottonwood trees provide shade during the summer.

The building's section was influenced by the building code, which stipulates that two-storey single-family homes can only have one staircase. Since the whole area of garage, studio and studio mezzanine, along with its staircase, counts as a basement level, this allows the house to conform to the code while achieving an optimum density.

Right: The house occupies a corner lot in Chicago. On the west side is a garage and above it a large open terrace. The orange brick is the same colour as other houses in the area.

Below left: Narrower from north to south than east to west, the building is flooded with natural light.

Below right: The south-facing side yard has been planted with deciduous cottonwood trees, which provide shade in the summer months. During the winter natural light penetrates to the living areas.

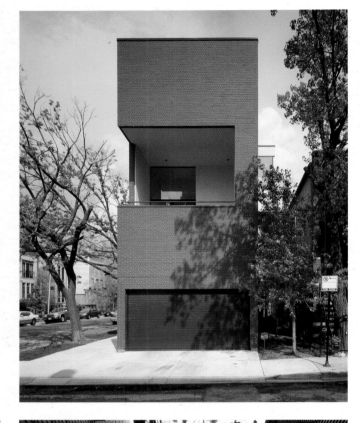

This page: The basement studio and its mezzanine, with the main entrance to the house on the right. Large windows dissolve the boundaries between public and private space and provide good lighting conditions.

Right: The north side of the house at night, showing the rear balcony and the large window that lights the studio space. There is no fencing around the plot.

Below: The kitchen is clad entirely in wood. A penetrating or hardening oil has been used to treat the wood and make it water-resistant, rather than a plastics-based sealant.

Because the house is shallower from north to south, all of the rooms have plenty of natural light. The architect has noticed that people who live in houses that are naturally bright during the day tend not to turn on all the lights at night, because they actually enjoy the darkness, and it has proved to be the case here. Artificial lighting is provided almost completely by low-energy compact fluorescent bulbs, except for a handful of downlighters fitted with dimmable low-voltage bulbs.

The entire building is highly insulated, in keeping with Chicago's cold winters and hot summers. Wall insulation is 10–25 cm (4–10 inches) thick and the roof is insulated to a depth of 30 cm (12 inches). The basement slab, which is below the frostline, is insulated with rigid panels to a depth of 13 cm (5 inches).

Windows, too, are of a high specification – argon-filled, low-E insulated units framed in aluminium encased in wood. To reduce the build-up of heat in the interior and to prevent a heat island effect, the roof is painted with a bright white commercial roof paint. The cladding of orange bricks serves as a raincoat, with a 1 cm (2 inch) air gap behind the cladding to drain rainwater.

Throughout the house, heating is provided by radiant or underfloor heating, which uses 5 per cent less energy than the forced-air systems that are the norm in the United States. Radiant heating is also quieter and more comfortable, as it does not result in air movement.

A ventilating heat-exchange system in the studio provides tempered fresh air to the whole house. Cross-ventilation ensures cooling through-breezes and the provision of ample outside living spaces on the front terrace and back balcony also reduces the need for cooling.

Materials and finishes have been chosen for their environmental friendliness. Wooden surfaces have been treated by a hardening oil that penetrates the wood and acts as a seal. All paints, including the studio floor paint, are non-VOC. The studio tables are made out of straw board.

The planting on the site is equally sensitive. In the side yard, in addition to the four cottonwood trees, four smaller trees have been planted as a understorey, with winter creepers and ivy as ground cover. On the north-facing 'parkway' side of the house, the city was persuaded to plant three maples. Rather than grass, which requires constant watering, the ground cover here is clover.

Left: The house enjoys an enviable quality of natural light. The large windows are highly insulated and argon-filled.

Below left: Bedrooms are on the second floor. All the paints and finishes used throughout the house are non-VOC.

SECTION KEY:

1 - Storage
2 - Bedroom
3 - Terrace
4 - Living room
5 - Living room
6 - Balcony
7 - Library
8 - Bathroom
9 - Garage
10 - Entrance
11 - Boiler
12 - Studio

ECO FACTS:

- High degree of insulation in walls, ground slab and roof.
- High-specification argon-filled insulated window units.
- White reflective paint on the roof to prevent heat build-up.
- Underfloor heating.
- Orientation to promote natural light and cross-ventilation.
- Non-VOC finishes and paints.
- Water-saving fixtures.
- Sensitive planting and compost maker on site.

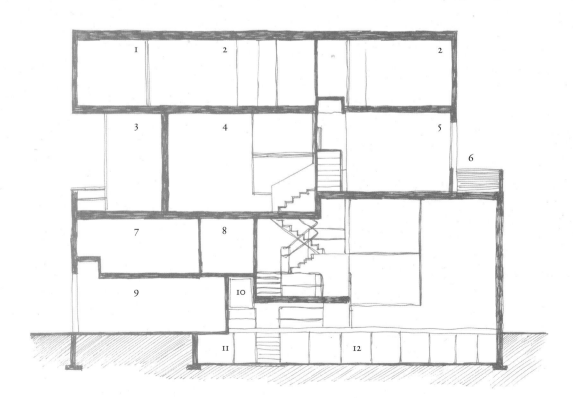

BOX CLEVER

Above: A view of the dining area on the lower ground floor looking in from the sunken patio. The prefabricated timber frame, with its consistent thickness, allowed for precise placement of openings.

Above right: The front elevation of the house faces east. The form of the building is deceptively simple.

Far right: All the facades of the house are clad in timber rainscreen, providing a continuous surface.

A surprising addition to a north London neighbourhood, where most of the houses are brick-built Victorian terraces, this sleek timber building was designed for a photographer who specializes in the fields of interiors and design. To achieve the accommodation that was required, the entire site was excavated to basement level, creating a sunken patio on which the house was built. The foundations are a concrete slab, which was necessary because subsidence is common in the area.

The defining element of the design is the bold use of timber. The simple form of the building could have been achieved in a number of different ways – reinforced concrete, for example, or brick or breezeblock. Instead, the structure is made of solid engineered timber panels, prefabricated off site. Using large prefabricated elements is much cheaper and quicker than standard construction. It is also more environmentally friendly. Each cubic metre (35 cubic feet) of timber saves almost 1 tonne of carbon emissions compared to masonry construction. There are also energy savings in the production process and a much

lower degree of material wastage. Large panels mean fewer joints and consequently a higher degree of airtightness, enhancing thermal and acoustic performance.

In this instance, the use of solid timber panels also helped to address a number of technical challenges, posed by the arrangement of the openings and the positioning of the staircase immediately behind the front elevation. The panels have a consistent thickness, which delivers the necessary structural performance, gives thermal stability to interior spaces and provides an element of durability (both physical and psychological) that can be missing from high-tech structures. Unlike timber-frame, a solid timber-shell building performs very well when it comes to regulating temperature and humidity levels, ironing out variations and creating a comfortable interior climate.

The large wall, roof and floor panels – up to 3 tonnes in weight – are made of spruce, the roof panels pre-insulated with natural hemp. These were delivered to the site and simply placed on top of each other, an installation process that took a total of five days, including delivery time.

Above: The main living area is at the top of the house and is lit by a long horizontal window along the west wall.

Left: Detail of a bathroom. White fittings contrasting with dark wood panelled walls.

Below: The dining area on the lower ground floor overlooks the sunken patio.

Left: Sleek fitted storage in the study houses books, files and CDs.

Below: The kitchen is laid out in an L-shape and forms part of an open-plan area that includes space for dining.

The entrance to the house is at street level, across part of the lower ground floor roof, which also serves as off-street car parking. The lower ground floor or basement level is where the kitchen and dining area are located, as well as a study and bathroom, with the sunken terrace wrapping around three sides of the building. The bedrooms, bathroom and utility are on the ground floor, with the entire first floor given over to a living area.

All the facades of the house, as well as the horizontal and vertical surfaces of the patio, are clad in timber rainscreen, to create the impression of a continuous skin. The cladding is 'thermowood', heat-rectified spruce dried to a point where the timber cannot reabsorb moisture, with the result that it is also very durable. The grooved boards have been given a dark translucent coating. The timber structure itself is hidden, although the underside of the pre-insulated roof panels remains exposed.

ECO FACTS:

- Use of timber for main structure, which has a low carbon footprint.
- Large prefabricated panels reduce energy and wastage.
- High degree of thermal performance.
- Insulation with natural hemp.

PLAN KEY:

1 - Living room
2 - Nursery
3 - Utility
4 - Bedroom
5 - Bathroom
6 - Deck terrace
7 - Kitchen
8 - Dining room
9 - Bathroom
10 - Study

FIRST FLOOR

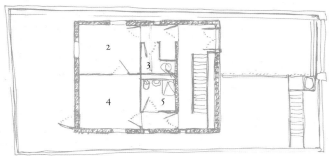

GROUND FLOOR

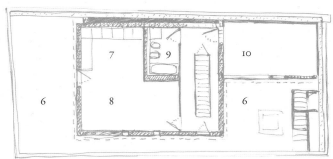

LOWER GROUND FLOOR

ECO BARN

Above: The gable end of the house faces south to take advantage of passive solar heating in the winter months. The simple form of the building has been inspired by traditional agricultural buildings.

Right: The weekend retreat is not connected to mains electricity. After dark, the house is lit with storm lanterns and candles.

Below right: The exterior of the house is clad in red cedar shingles, which were imported from Canada. The cedar naturally weathers over time to a silvery grey.

Far right: The main living area is a soaring space that rises up to the pitched roof. Supplementary heating is provided by a wood-burning stove made of brick.

A modern version of a traditional agricultural building, this weekend retreat is sited in the middle of a field in Normandy. The tall, pointed structure is built entirely out of wood, except for the minimal concrete piles that anchor it to the ground. The building, which is not connected to the electrical grid, has many eco features.

Chief among these is its orientation. The glazed gable end of the house faces south. During the winter, low sunlight penetrates into the interior and warms it, while in the summer, the sun is too high to cause overheating. Natural stack ventilation is promoted by six trapdoors under the house and openings high up.

Supplementary heating is provided by a wood-burning stove clad in masonry, similar to the traditional 'kachelofen', which is common in northern Europe and in parts of France, such as Alsace. Using the same principle of the brick in the storage heater, these masonry stoves warm up slowly and release heat gradually. To operate most efficiently, it is necessary to place the stove centrally and leave the doors open so that heat can circulate – not a problem here, where there are minimal partitions.

The structure of the house is made of timber. Exterior cladding consists of red cedar shingles imported from Canada. These naturally weather over time to an attractive silvery colour. No applied finishes or treatments were used on the external joinery, which is made of recycled local timber. Instead, the wood was lightly charred to protect it from ultraviolet light and to increase its water-resistance – a time-honoured method of timber protection that was much used in vernacular construction.

Left: A long horizontal box, reached by a short flight of stairs, provides an enclosed private space for sleeping and bathing.

Below: A mezzanine level above the floating corridor provides room for another sleeping area. It is accessed by a ladder.

ECO FACTS:

- Siting to take advantage of passive solar strategies.
- Minimal foundations.
- Timber structure, recycled timber joinery, cedar cladding.
- No timber treatment.
- Wood-burning masonry stove.
- No connection to electrical grid.
- Lighting provided by candles and storm lanterns.
- Natural ventilation provided by vents and high-level windows.

SECTION KEY:

1 - Bedroom pods
2 - Floating corridor
3 - Bathroom
4 - Living room
5 - Ladder

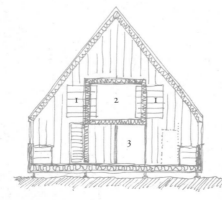

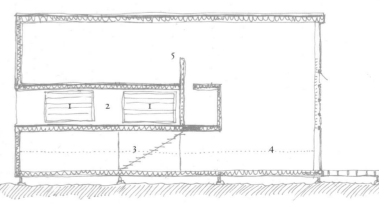

The building rests lightly on the land. Instead of a concrete slab foundation, which would disrupt the site, foundations are provided by 20 mini concrete piles.

Apart from the basic structure, which was erected by a team of carpenters, the architect/owner built this house entirely by himself, a process that took eighteen months. The result offers the opportunity to experience the simple life, attuned to natural rhythms. After dark, candlelight and storm lanterns provide the only illumination.

The internal layout of the house is very simple, with the entire ground floor devoted to living, eating and cooking areas. The insertion of a long horizontal box creates a private area for sleeping and bathing, with two bedroom pods, reached by a flight of stairs, and a bathroom. Above, on a mezzanine level under the eaves, is another sleeping space, which is accessed by a ladder.

In keeping with the back-to-nature approach, the interior finishes are simple and rustic. The walls are clad in unfinished timber panels, which provide physical and psychological warmth.

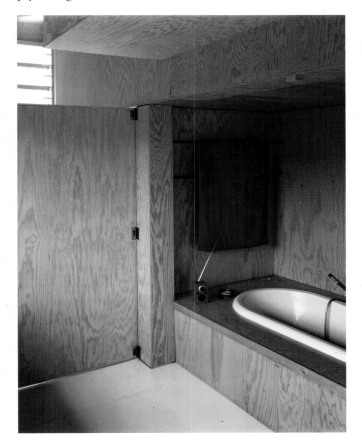

Above: Unfinished timber cladding is used on the walls. Furnishings echo the back-to-basics approach.

Far left: The bathroom is on the middle level.

Left: A pair of sleeping alcoves or pods are minimally screened with curtains.

GOLD STAR

SMOG VEIL RECORDS BUILDING | CHICAGO, ILLINOIS | USA | ARCHITECTS: WILKINSON BLENDER ARCHITECTURE

Above: The open-plan living area/kitchen on the second floor leads to a bedroom beyond. A clerestory window brings light down from above. Kitchen cabinets contain no formaldehyde and are recyclable.

Above right: The new house is a reworking of an existing building that occupied the plot. Over 80 per cent of the demolition materials and construction waste were recycled.

Far right: Two wind turbines are installed on the top of the roofline. Zoning ordinances had to be changed to allow the wind turbines to be installed. The planes of the roof help to define interior and exterior spaces as well as introduce natural lighting to areas below.

The fundamental concept behind the design of this award-winning live/work family home in Chicago is sustainability. When the clients, husband and wife record producers, acquired the site it was entirely occupied by an existing tavern, which they intended to demolish and rebuild. The brief they gave to their architects included few specific requirements, except that the new house should have a green roof to make up for the lack of outdoor space. Otherwise, what they wanted were comfortable surroundings that suited their tastes and routine, and which would serve as a built expression of their newly adopted commitment to sustainable living and working.

As a starting point, the green roof had a significant influence on the development of the design. The way the roof plane steps up and down allows light to be admitted to the spaces below, provides views over the Chicago skyline and helps to define indoor and outdoor areas. It also serves as a platform for sustainable technology used to generate energy for the home.

The completed house addresses the issue of sustainability in three major ways. Firstly, various forms of alternative technology have been installed to generate energy. Secondly, significant energy savings have also been achieved through insulation and other means. And thirdly, every effort was made during construction and fitting out to save material and reduce waste. The success of the strategy can be gauged by the fact that the building received a Gold LEED (Leadership in Energy and Environmental Design) for Homes rating, the first given to a domestic residence in Illinois and only the eighth given so far in the United States.

The house represents a major reworking of an existing building. While the building itself was saved through reuse, its masonry structure was also reconfigured using bricks salvaged from its demolition. The original wooden roof structure was reclaimed and used for butcher-block stair landings and treads. Of the original gutted material, both demolition materials and construction waste, 80 per cent was recycled. Interior finishes include 99 per cent recycled gypsum board and flooring composed of 100 per cent recycled glass terrazzo incorporating recycled vinyl records.

Energy generation is provided by wind turbines and photovoltaic panels located on the roof. In order to install energy-generating wind turbines in a residential area, the project team first had to work with the city to amend the zoning ordinance that prohibited it. The two vertical axis turbines stand 3 m (10 ft) above the top of the roofline

Above: Many of the materials used in the house are recycled. The flooring is recycled glass terrazzo, which incorporates recycled vinyl records.

Right: The roof garden provides green space and a natural environment that attracts bees and butterflies. A trellis of PV panels creates shading for the outdoor terrace.

Far right: Timber reclaimed from the original roof structure has been reused to create butcher-block stair landings and treads. Masonry walls on the first floor are left exposed.

and are projected to provide 20 per cent of the energy required to run the house. Enclosed in bright orange steel frames, they look like pieces of kinetic sculpture and are designed to be visible to (and avoidable by) birds. An array of 30 170-watt PV panels generates another 30 per cent of the household's energy requirements, while also providing rooftop shade for outdoor areas.

One of the principal ways in which the house saves energy is through the use of geothermal heating and cooling. A loop of 16 wells carefully located within the existing building shell provides a heat sink/source that is anticipated to save 30–60 per cent of the energy required for heating and cooling. The building was insulated using soya-based spray foam, chosen not only for its natural components, but also because it has a superior seal and reduces infiltration. Windows are high-specification. Their careful positioning, particularly with respect to skylights and clerestory windows, reduces the amount of energy needed for artificial lighting. All appliances were selected for their low energy usage and surpass the standards set by the Energy Star programme.

The green roof plays its own conservation role. The plant cover adds an insulating layer, reduces rainwater run-off to Chicago's overburdened sewer system and cools the local area. The roof garden also attracts bees and butterflies and provides a pleasant environment for relaxing and entertaining.

ECO FACTS:

- Energy generation using PV panels and wind turbines.
- Geothermal heating and cooling.
- Soya-based insulation.
- High-efficiency windows.
- Energy-efficient appliances.
- Green roof to reduce water run-off and provide a natural habitat.
- Reclaimed materials used in construction and fitting out.
- Recycling of demolition materials and construction waste.

SECTION KEY:

1 - Wind turbines
2 - Solar panel trellis
3 - Roof terrace
4 - Living area
5 - Kitchen/dining area
6 - Bedroom
7 - Office
8 - Studio
9 - Garage
10 - Storage

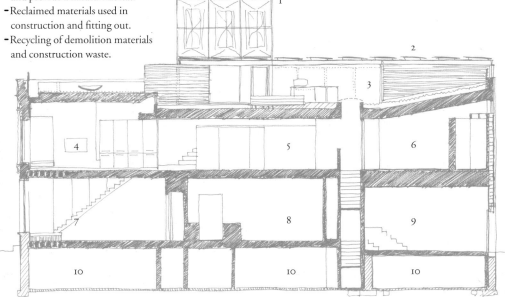

GREEN MAKEOVER

TERRACED HOUSE | SYDNEY | AUSTRALIA | ARCHITECT: ROTH ARCHITECTS PTY LTD

Right: The rear elevation of the house, showing the glazed doors on the ground floor and the balcony above. The house was extended to the full width of the plot at the rear.

Far right: A mezzanine level in the master bedroom provides a private place for a study in the roof cavity, without blocking light and air. Storage is built in below.

Opposite: The central staircase serves as a lightwell, drawing daylight down into the middle of the house. It is minimally screened with glass balustrading.

In many ways, terraced houses can be viewed as potentially more environmentally friendly than free-standing houses. Shared walls reduce the amount of materials used in construction, provide thermal mass, and reduce heat gain and loss because the external surface area of the building is smaller. However, natural daylighting and ventilation can be a problem, especially if orientation is less than ideal, which can mean that terraced houses are dark and stuffy, and either too cold or too hot.

This renovation and extension of a house in Sydney's eastern suburbs addresses many of the problems associated with older terraced properties. Originally the house, which is just 4 m (13 ft) wide, was subdivided into a number of small, poorly lit and ventilated rooms. A key aim was to maximize natural light and cross-ventilation, and to employ various passive strategies to cut down on the need for supplementary heating in winter and cooling in summer.

A related aim was to open up the interior as far as possible and achieve more usable and flexible space with a minimum of materials. The house was extended at the rear to the full width of the plot to make the most of available space.

Sunlight was introduced deep into the house through a combination of skylights, large windows and glazed roofs, making artificial lighting completely unnecessary during daylight hours. A glazed roof above the kitchen floods the rear living area with light, while the large double skylight above the central staircase turns it into a lightwell that brings daylight down into the middle of the house. Bathrooms and utility areas are lit by borrowed light from internal opaque windows in the staircase, which maintain privacy and acoustic separation.

The conversion opened up the entire ground floor of the house, creating two large spaces partially divided by the stairs and the laundry. This allows cooling through-breezes

Right: The kitchen/eating area at the rear of the house has a glazed roof fitted with energy-efficient low-E glazing.

Below: The all-white colour scheme used throughout the house makes the most of natural light and helps to reduce the heat load on the building. Internal opaque windows in the staircase provide borrowed light for the bathrooms.

Below right: The central staircase.

Left: A child's bedroom at the rear of the house has door that open onto the balcony. The balcony overhangs the large glazed kitchen doors below, shading them from the summer sun.

to circulate the interior. The white decoration both enhances the sense of space and light, and reduces the heat load on the building. A mezzanine level above the master bedroom creates space for a private study.

The new tiled concrete slab to the rear half of the ground floor, along with a stone bench, provides passive heating in winter. Sunlight streaming in through the new large glazed rear doors and kitchen skylight warms the slab, which releases the heat slowly. The balcony that overhangs the doors prevents unwanted heat gain during the summer. Low-E glass was used in the glazed roof. Other materials were chosen for their insulation properties, including a type of lightweight masonry panel that has good acoustic as well as thermal qualities.

New landscaping has been designed to minimize water consumption, while providing an outdoor entertaining area directly accessible from the kitchen and family room. At the rear of the site, the roof of a lowered car port serves as an additional play area or place for outdoor eating.

FIRST FLOOR

GROUND FLOOR

PLAN KEY:

1 - Bedroom
2 - Bathroom
3 - Bedroom/office
4 - Balcony
5 - Skylight
6 - Sitting/dining room
7 - Laundry
8 - Kitchen/family room
9 - Car port

ECO FACTS:

- New top-level openings, glazed roof and internal windows reduce the need for artificial light.
- Low-E glass.
- Thermal mass of concrete slab provides passive heating in winter.
- High degree of insulation.
- Cross-ventilation reduces the need for air conditioning.
- Flexible planning maximizes space and uses fewer materials.
- Landscaping cuts down on water consumption.

HOME COMFORT

PASSIVE HOUSE | MUTTELSEE | GERMANY | ARCHITECTS: SELF-BUILT BY OWNER

'Passive houses' are designed and constructed in such a way that they require very little supplementary energy to maintain comfortable living conditions. The 'Passivhaus' concept was pioneered in Germany and recent technological developments have seen thousands of these houses built, chiefly in central Europe.

A passive house is designed to lose as little heat as possible, which means a high degree of insulation and airtightness. Stagnant air and the growth of mould used to be a problem with buildings that were hermetically sealed; nowadays this problem is avoided by the use of heat-exchange units that recover heat from exhaust air and transfer it to fresh air coming in. On very cold days, integral heat pumps warm the air up further. On hot days, the reverse happens and air is pre-cooled.

This clean-lined timber structure was built on the site of an existing house in a village in southern Germany. It's a pleasant rural location near Lake Constanz, just 15 minutes from the Swiss border. The owner, an engineer who knows a fair amount about architecture, taught himself the necessary skills to design the house himself. Technical support was provided by the Fraunhofer Institute of Freiburg, which has developed integrated heat pump systems for this type of high-performance house. The house actually cost less to build than a conventional house of the same size, partly because of government subsidy that favours green building and partly because, apart from mains water, costly servicing connections did not need to be made.

As might be expected, the levels of insulation are incredibly high. The prefabricated timber walls are 55 cm (21½ inches) thick, with panels enclosing a gap 50 cm (19¾ inches) deep infilled with cellulose insulation. The heavily insulated roof is 48 cm (18 inches) thick. All the windows are high-specification, triple-glazed with argon infill. All pipes, wires and cables exit the house through the floor and run about 1–2 m (3–6½ ft) underground so as not to compromise the insulation. Similarly, the windows are inset into the walls so that only a tiny proportion of the frames are exposed – the frames being where cold bridges are more likely to occur.

Passive houses have to meet high standards of airtightness, measured by a blow test to demonstrate that minimal air is lost under pressure. That means barely any

Below: The Passive House is a timber structure, highly insulated and virtually airtight. Sliding panels shade the windows and keep the house cool in the summer.

Below right: The house is compactly laid out, which is more energy efficient. Large south-facing openings allow the house to benefit from passive solar gain.

Far right: The house is located in the countryside of southern Germany. Passive house design and construction is increasingly popular in central Europe.

Right: The flooring throughout the house is local limestone tiles, which adds to the thermal mass of the building. The walls are made of gypsum plasterboard.

Below: A mezzanine level provides another bedroom as well as an additional seating area above the main living spaces.

Below right: The dining room is located just off the main living area. The ventilation system ensures that there is a constant supply of fresh air, even when windows are shut.

- Timber structure. Thick walls and roof heavily insulated with cellulose insulation.
- High-specification windows, triple-glazed and argon-filled.
- High degree of airtightness; detailing to prevent cold bridges.
- Heat-exchange unit to recover heat from exhaust air.
- Heat pump system to warm or cool air as required.
- Solar thermal panels for hot water heating.
- PV panels for generating electricity.
- Rainwater collection to flush toilets and run washing machine.

heat escapes and barely any cold seeps in. Heat recovered from exhaust air and transferred to fresh air keeps the indoor temperature at a steady 20–21ºC (68–70ºF).

Most of the time, the house is warmed solely by the body heat of those living there and the heat given off by the washing machine, computers, lighting, cooker and so on. On very cold days, extra heat is provided by a heat pump. This system consists of pipework about 50 m (164 ft) long and buried underground at a depth of 3 m (10 ft), where the ground temperature all year round is about 13ºC (55ºF). Fresh air is warmed as it is pumped through the pipework before it passes the heat exchanger. In summer, on hot days, the reverse happens.

Hot water is provided by solar thermal panels, which produce about 80 per cent of annual requirements. Photovoltaic panels produce about a third more energy every year than the house actually requires to run.

Rainwater is collected from the roof and used to flush toilets and to run the washing machine. Drinking water comes from a mains connection.

Proponents of this type of construction maintain that living in a passive house is very comfortable. The ventilation system means that there is always fresh air, even on the coldest days when the windows are shut. Walls and floors are evenly warm (or cool), the same temperature as the air.

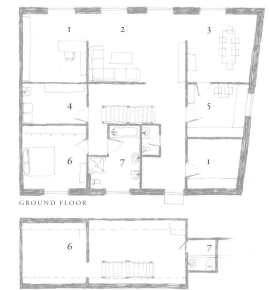

GROUND FLOOR

MEZZANINE

PLAN KEY:

1 - Office
2 - Living room
3 - Dining room
4 - Laundry
5 - Kitchen
6 - Bedroom
7 - Bathroom

Right: Toilets are water-saving fixtures. Rainwater is collected from the roof and used to flush toilets. The walls are clad with the same limestone tiles used on the floor.

Far right: The staircase up to the mezzanine level is made of brushed stainless steel, which needs no maintenance and will never corrode.

GARDEN LOFT

BROADWAY PENTHOUSE | NEW YORK | USA | ARCHITECTS: JOEL SANDERS ARCHITECT AND ANDARCHITECTS

Above: The loft was opened up internally to create a series of free-flowing spaces. The master bedroom is not screened at all. At the heart of the loft, an open staircase rises to the rooftop bulkhead.

Right: Planting surrounding the base of the staircase serves as an indoor garden, introducing nature to the interior.

Far right: The glazed bulkhead opens out to a decked area and a roof garden. Urban features such as water towers are treated as part of the 'natural' landscape.

The guiding idea behind this project, a renovation of a Broadway loft in downtown Manhattan, was to blur the distinction between the inside and outside in such a way as to convey an experience of nature in the heart of the city. The penthouse, the home of a developer who also collaborated in the design process, includes two bedrooms, two and a half bathrooms, living and dining rooms, kitchen and outdoor entertaining space. The redesign incorporated many environmentally friendly materials, fixtures and fittings, from FSC-certified decking to 100 per cent recycled cotton insulation.

During the design process, the architects explored what it means to be 'natural' in an urban setting. A critical element of this creative investigation was deciding how

Right: Light spilling down from above creates a dynamic quality. The walnut used for flooring and cladding came from sustainably managed sources.

Below: The view across the indoor garden to the green wall of the master bathroom. Switchable glazing means that the bathroom can be obscured for privacy.

to deal with the infrastructure of the existing building. 'Found' urban objects, such as water towers, piping, valves, vents and railings, which are 'natural' to the city, were not suppressed or concealed but treated as evocative contrasts to the planting indoors and out.

The principal strategy was to weave the natural world into the interior by setting up a series of progressions. An indoor garden at the base of the staircase that leads to the roof serves as a hint of what is to come. From this green carpet, open timber treads rise to the new outdoor space and roof garden surrounding the bulkhead. In keeping with this sense of connection, the interior of the loft was also opened up to create a free flow of space that is minimally portioned. Formerly the loft had felt cramped, having been subdivided into poky spaces. Now the wooden walls and ceilings guide the eye from area to area and serve as a backdrop for the ever-changing quality of natural light, reaching a culmination on the outdoor deck with its view of the surrounding city.

The roofscape incorporates different levels and supports a range of activities, including an outdoor shower, outdoor kitchen, spa and lounging area. A large cistern collects

Right: The guest bathroom. A palette of natural materials, used throughout the loft, echoes the indoor/outdoor aesthetic.

Below right: The master bathroom features a green wall that links visually to the roof garden above.

rainwater, which supplies all the garden irrigation. One portion of the roof is planted with sedum, which is commonly used in green roofs and hardy enough to be walked on. The decking is FSC-certified ipe, a water-resistant hardwood than needs no further treatment.

The glazed bulkhead spills light down into the centre of the interior, creating a dynamic, uplifting quality. The open treads of the walnut staircase similarly allow light to spill through. The main bedroom is located on one side of the loft and is not screened at all. Switchable glazing allows the bathroom to be obscured for privacy. One wall of the main bathroom features greenery that appears to tumble down from the rooftop planting above.

As well as these more poetic 'green' elements, the loft incorporates many environmentally friendly features. Greywater is processed for reuse and kitchen waste is composted. Toilets are water-saving dual-flush fixtures. Paints and wood glue are low-VOC and appliances are Energy Star rated. The walnut flooring and cladding comes from sustainably managed sources and the plasterboard (sheetrock) is made of recycled gypsum. Furniture is locally made, either of recycled or sustainable materials.

ECO FACTS:

- Planting enhances the experience of nature in an urban setting, creating a green oasis in the city.
- Rainwater collection, greywater recycling, kitchen composting.
- Low-VOC paints and glue.
- Use of sustainable, salvaged, recycled materials.
- Energy-efficient appliances and dual-flush toilets.

PLAN KEY:

1 - Rain catchment/cistern
2 - Spa/lounge area
3 - Outdoor kitchen
4 - Seating area
5 - Roof planting
6 - Outdoor shower
7 - Bedroom
8 - Lounge
9 - Bathroom
10 - Interior garden
11 - Living room
12 - Kitchen/dining room

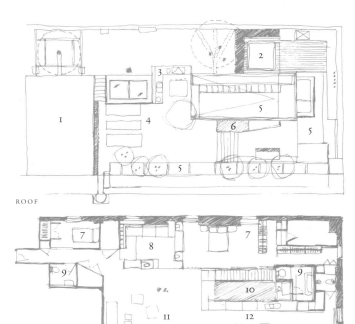

ROOF

PENTHOUSE

NORTHERN LIGHT

PLUS HOUSE | STOCKHOLM | SWEDEN | ARCHITECTS: CLAESSON KOIVISTO RUNE

Above: On the ground floor, the long walls are fully glazed, bathing the interior in natural light. The windows are triple glazed.

Above right: The perpendicular glazing on the long ground-floor walls and gable ends look like a plus sign in plan, hence the name. The spruce panels were prefabricated and assembled on site in just 20 days.

Far right: The central staircase has open treads to preserve the sight lines across the house.

Prefab houses comprise over 70 per cent of the single-family housing market in Sweden, an astonishingly high percentage compared to other countries. In other parts of the world prefab has been slow to shake off its trailer-park image, but here it is simply a way of building that has developed in the postwar years as a way of rationalizing resources and time. Known as 'kit' or 'catalogue' houses, most of the designs offered by manufacturers are traditional in feel, with small windows, pitched roofs and painted clapboard cladding.

Arkitekthus, a Swedish development company dedicated to improving the architectural quality of prefab housing, recently approached a number of Swedish architects to submit designs. 'Plus House' (AH#001) is the work of Claesson Koivisto Rune, an up-and-coming design and architecture practice based in Stockholm.

What might be said to distinguish prefab design from 'pure' architecture is that prefab by its nature can never be site-specific. However, what the architects have achieved with this design manages to distil a generic Swedish building type – the traditional barn house – into a clean, contemporary form that can adapt to any setting.

Plus House gets its name from the long glazed walls and gable ends that are such a striking feature of the design. Seen in plan, the two lines of vision are perpendicular to each other like a plus sign. The orientation of the house is symmetrical and no single wall is intended for sun or shade. Instead, all the windows are recessed from the facade so that however the house is situated, a 90cm (3 ft) overhang shades the windows from summer sun.

The pitched roof and proportions of the two-storey house meet local planning requirements and conform to market tastes. But the house, with its clean lines and abundance of natural light, remains distinctly modern, not backward-looking.

Left: The view from the dining/kitchen area through to the living area. Although the layout is essentially open plan, an element of enclosure and partitioning maintains a sense of privacy.

Above right: The master bathroom is the only room in the house that is fully internal. It opens off the light-filled master bedroom.

Above far right: The house features plenty of concealed storage to keep everyday clutter at bay.

Altogether the house took 40 days to construct: 20 in the factory and another 20 on site. The prefabricated timber panels, comprising beams, walls and roof trusses, were assembled in the factory. The spruce exterior cladding will gradually weather to a grey colour, as will the zinc-coated steel window frames. The panels are highly insulated and the windows are triple glazed.

The internal layout is simple and uncluttered, in order to preserve the long sight lines that contribute so much to the sense of space. The central staircase has open treads that allow light to spill through. (This is an optional extra – the basic house model has a closed staircase incorporating storage underneath.) Unglazed walls have been fitted with seamless cupboards to keep clutter under control. Upstairs, doors slide rather than swing open, which takes up less space and is visually neater.

Although the layout of the house feels open and airy, the architects have been careful to balance openness with enclosure, recognizing that fully open-plan layouts can leave people desperate for some private space. However, any hint of compartmentalization is banished by the large expanses of glazing. The only fully internal room in the house is the master bathroom.

ECO FACTS:

- Prefabricated timber structure.
- High degree of insulation.
- Triple glazing.
- Recessed windows prevent summer sun from overheating the interior.
- Abundant natural light.

PLAN KEY:

1 - Bedroom
2 - Bathroom
3 - Lounge
4 - Sitting room
5 - Kitchen
6 - Utility
7 - Dining area

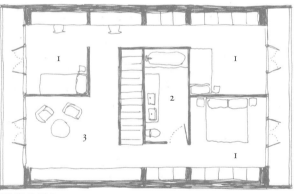

FIRST FLOOR

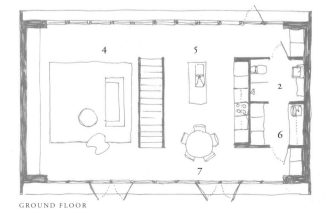

GROUND FLOOR

LAKESIDE PAVILIONS

WEEKEND HOUSE | SMITHS LAKE, NEW SOUTH WALES | AUSTRALIA | ARCHITECTS: SANDBERG SCHOFFEL ARCHITECTS

Right: The pavilions that make up the Weekend House are set on a sloping site, connected by a covered staircase. Only one tree needed to be felled during construction.

Below: The main living pavilion extends out to a deck overlooking the lake. Cross-ventilation and overhanging eaves help to keep the interior cool.

Far right: The corrugated roofs of the pavilions and walkway collect rainwater that is stored in large tanks under the living pavilion. The collected rainwater is used for garden irrigation and to supply a bushfire sprinkler system.

Minimizing site disruption is a central aim of all new eco building, but never more crucially than in an unspoiled area of natural beauty. Smiths Lake in New South Wales is a popular vacation spot for weekending Australians. Surrounding bushland supports a wide range of native species. Situated on a north-facing slope that falls down from the road to the lakeside, this weekend retreat comprises separate pavilions for living and sleeping connected by a staircase covered by a butterfly roof.

The house was designed with many eco strategies in mind: minimizing energy use, rainwater collection, passive heating and cooling, but most particularly, site sensitivity. Screw piles used as footings for the buildings meant that there was no disruptive site excavation or damage to tree roots. The pavilions were so carefully sited that only one tree on the heavily wooded plot needed to be removed for their construction. The retention of the existing tree canopy both preserves the appearance of the local environment and maintains a habitat for native animals. The fact that the house is not enclosed by a fence or retaining walls also means less disturbance and minimizes the use of materials.

Arranging the accommodation in two distinct pavilions – one for living, eating and cooking, and one for bedrooms and bathrooms – resulted in an efficient use of space and savings in overall servicing. The main structure consists of lightweight prefabricated steel framing, representing a minimal use of material. Pavilion platforms were used as working areas during construction so that disruption to the site under the tree canopy could be kept to a minimum. The exposed galvanized steel reflects the colour of the surrounding trees, as does the form of the roof structure over the staircase that connects the two pavilions. Colours for the exterior were specifically chosen to make the house appear to recede in its setting, allowing the trees to dominate. The use of corrugated iron, combined with flat-sheet cladding, also creates a natural pattern of light and shade. The use of galvanized steel and pre-finished cladding meant that very little painting needed to be done on site. Because the basic structure is made of steel, which is naturally insect-resistant, no chemicals were required to provide protection against termites.

The pavilions are oriented to the north, so that all rooms have a good quality of natural light, as well as views of the lake. Sloping eaves and shade from the tree canopy help to

screen the house from summer sun, while the positioning of the house on the slope, with the land rising to the south, protects it from the cold winter winds that come from that direction. Storage walls to the south and east – towards the street and neighbouring house, respectively – provide insulation and privacy.

All walls, roofs and floors are thermally insulated and all rooms have cross-ventilation, which means that no air conditioning or supplementary heating is required. Hot water is provided on demand by a gas-fired unit.

Drought and attendant bushfires are an ever-present risk. Rainwater is collected from the sloping corrugated roofs and stored in tanks under the living pavilion. This collected water is used for garden irrigation and for the bushfire sprinkler system, which can be remotely operated by phone. Sprinklers can also be activated to cool the house down during heatwaves.

Respect for a site also means avoiding the introduction of plant species that are not local to the area. New planting, designed to provide a screen to future neighbouring houses, comprises native drought-tolerant species that require little additional irrigation.

Below: The lower pavilion houses the living, eating and cooking areas. Louvred windows foster natural ventilation. All the rooms have views of the lake.

Right: The kitchen is built into one side of the lower pavilion.

Opposite, left and right: The upper pavilion houses the bedrooms and bathrooms. External cladding helps the buildings to blend in with the natural setting.

ECO FACTS:

- Minimal site disruption due to careful positioning, lightweight steel framework and the use of screw piles for foundations.
- Cross-ventilation avoids the need for air conditioning.
- Thermal insulation and a sheltered position keeps the pavilions warm during winter.

- No supplementary heating or cooling, except for hot water.
- Rainwater collection for garden irrigation and a sprinkler system.
- Pre-finished cladding avoids the need for paint finishes.

SECTION KEY:

1 - Decked living and kitchen area
2 - Walkway under rain collector
3 - Bedrooms and bathrooms
4 - Parking

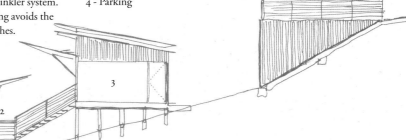

CUSTOM PREFAB

RESIDENCE FOR A SCULPTOR 3 | SANTA ROSA, CALIFORNIA | USA | ARCHITECTS: SANDER ARCHITECTS

Right: The house, sited on a hillside, is clad in metal panels that are normally used for roofing. These require no subsequent maintenance.

Below: The 'great room' on the first floor is an open-plan space used for living, dining and cooking. The lightweight steel frame allows for large high-ceilinged rooms.

Far right: The tall, vertical entrance on the ground floor echoes the form of the sculptor's pots, which are prominently displayed. A curved staircase leads up to the first floor.

In design and construction, the term prefabrication covers a wealth of different approaches. The common denominator is that elements of a building, which may or may not include its structure, are manufactured in a factory, transported to the site and slotted into place. At the most extreme, these elements may take the form of whole modules or rooms, which can be configured in a number of ways according to how much accommodation is required. Prefab is generally considered to be eco-friendly because manufacturing off site reduces the amount of materials that are wasted and also the amount of energy consumed in production. It's also speedy. Once the foundations have been laid and the prefab elements have been delivered, construction can take a matter of days, rather than months, which represents an efficient use of site labour.

The architects of this hillside house in California specialize in a form of 'hybrid' construction that allows the ultimate freedom of design. Unlike most forms of prefab, which have limited scope for customization, the lightweight recycled steel structural system that they employ enables them to create individual houses that meet their clients' particular requirements. With no restrictions on scale or proportion, great spans and soaring spaces can be achieved. The prefab structure has the further advantage of being extremely economical, with costs estimated to be a third less per square foot than an equivalent one-off custom design.

The house, designed for a sculptor, projects from a hillside with views over the evocatively named 'Valley of the Moon'. Careful siting maximizes passive heating and cooling. The arrangement of the windows has also been designed to accomplish the same goal, as well as to promote cross-ventilation and make the most of natural light. The result is that no artificial lighting is required during daylight hours and no air conditioning is needed.

The lightweight recycled engineered steel frame represents a minimal use of materials. At the end of the lifetime of the house, the frames can be easily unbolted and disassembled to be recycled or reused. The owners stipulated that they wanted a house with no external upkeep, and the exterior is clad in pre-finished metal panels that are normally used as roofing and require no further maintenance or repainting. A similar economy of materials has been achieved by using the ground floor construction slab as the final floor on this level.

Below: The steel framework is expressed throughout the house. In the future, it could be disassembled and reused or recycled. The kitchen counter is made of low-ash concrete and the flooring is bamboo.

Right: A 6.7 m (22 ft) curving torqued steel wall runs from the ground floor to the first floor, making sculptural reference to the glazed clay vessels.

Far right: Careful placement of windows ensures maximum natural light and through-ventilation.

The rest of the materials and fittings used in the house have been chosen for their eco credentials. On the upper level, flooring is environmentally friendly bamboo. Heating is by underfloor radiant heating. In the kitchen, eco-friendly cabinetry is combined with counters made of low-ash concrete. The studio and all the bathrooms are lit by low-energy light bulbs; other light fittings are designed to take compact fluorescent bulbs. Appliances are Energy Star rated, toilets are low-flush and the paint used throughout the interior is low-VOC. Outside, landscaping has been kept to a minimum. Native drought-resistant plants reduce the need for garden irrigation.

The internal spaces have been carefully choreographed to provide richness of experience. The entrance is to the rear of the property and uphill. Immediately inside is a tall vertical space, reminiscent of the form of the sculptor's pots, which were a significant influence on the design. This entrance leads, via stairs and across a bridge, to a large open living/dining/cooking area with views across the valley. The ground floor, where the studio, kiln room and office are located, is more inward-looking and enclosed.

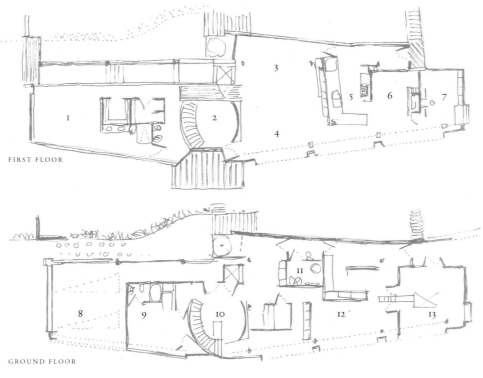

FIRST FLOOR

GROUND FLOOR

ECO FACTS:

- Siting and window placement to maximize passive heating and cooling; no supplementary air conditioning required.
- Prefab structure of lightweight recycled engineered steel, capable of being recycled and reused at the end of the house's life.
- Ground-floor slab used as final floor; bamboo flooring upstairs.
- Underfloor radiant heating.
- Exterior cladding requires no maintenance.
- Low-energy lighting, low-flush toilets, Energy Star rated appliances, low-VOC paint.
- Low-ash concrete used for kitchen counters.
- Minimal landscaping with native drought-resistant plants.

PLAN KEY:

1 - Master bedroom/bathroom
2 - Entrance
3 - Dining area
4 - Living area
5 - Kitchen
6 - Family room
7 - Den
8 - Car port
9 - Bedroom
10 - Entrance
11 - Office
12 - Studio
13 - Kiln room

RAISING THE ROOF

MAISON A AND STUDIO B | PARIS | FRANCE | ARCHITECTS: JACQUES MOUSSAFIR, ISABELLE DENOYEL AND ERIC WUILMOT

Below: High-performance glazing, minimally interrupted by framing, brings light and a soaring sense of volume into the existing house. The roof was raised away from the street elevation to provide more space.

Below right: The large windows in the living room are screened along the alleyway with a wooden trellis up which climbers are trained.

Far right: The conversion of the existing building and the extension blend seamlessly together. The redesign means that the house is now flooded with light and highly energy efficient.

Tucked away in a picturesque alley in the heart of Paris's 14th arrondissement, and dating from the end of the nineteenth century, this house and studio have been transformed into airy spaces in tune with modern living. The result marries contemporary design and environmentally friendly technologies and materials. Its energy performance is 40 per cent better than comparable new builds.

The clients' brief to the architects was to increase the amount of space and make the existing space more liveable, and to open the house to the garden and increase the amount of natural light, while minimizing carbon emissions through the use of alternative technologies and sustainable materials. The basic design concept was to raise the roof, increasing the volume dramatically, and to reconstruct and extend the house along the alleyway to provide the extra accommodation required. Avoiding the joint pitfalls of pastiche and stark, glaring contrast, old and new have been conceived as a harmonious whole.

The new raised roof is covered in zinc, with standing seams giving a crisp appearance. Zinc, which is 100 per cent recyclable, is a material commonly used as a roof covering in the immediate vicinity. Velux windows in the roof encourage natural ventilation, while 6 sq m (19½ sq ft) of solar panels provide almost half the energy required to heat the hot water. These have been so inconspicuously installed that they could almost be mistaken for windows set into the plane of the roof.

High-specification double glazing was chosen for the new windows. The particular glass specified is a type that can be angled around corners without the interruption of joinery. With its thermal- and acoustic-insulating properties, the glass helps to make the interior more comfortable and energy efficient. The walls, roof and floors of the house are also highly insulated.

On the side of the living area facing the lane, the large picture windows are covered in trellising as a support for

Right: The redesign of the existing house entailed moving the position of the staircase to provide a better allocation of space.

Far right: The kitchen now occupies a central position in the heart of the home. The dining area has views over the garden.

Below: The living area is raised up three steps from the kitchen/dining area. The wood-burning stove, which provides supplementary heating, is highly efficient.

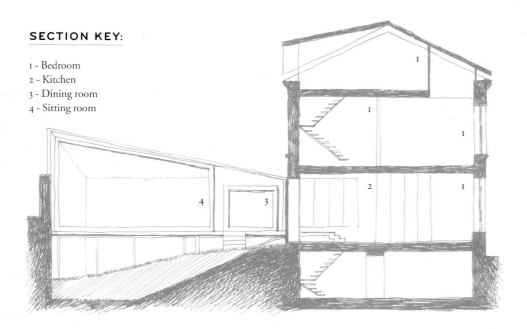

Above right: All the doors in the house are full-height, a tried and tested strategy for enhancing the sense of space.

Right: Corian, a composite material that includes recycled and recyclable ingredients, has been used as a finish in the bathrooms.

climbing plants. This solution provides privacy for the house, while satisfying concerns of the neighbours.

A geothermal system and heat-recovery ventilation unit further reduce the need for supplementary heating or cooling. In winter, the heat-recovery unit captures 85 per cent of the heat of extracted air, transferring it to fresh air coming in. In the summer, air is forced underground and pre-cooled before it enters the house, avoiding the need for air conditioning; in the winter, when the temperature underground is higher than air temperature, the fresh air is pre-warmed before entering the house.

Supplementary heating is provided by a highly efficient gas condensing boiler and a wood-burning stove. The stove, which has an energy efficiency in excess of 80 per cent, is cylindrical. As well as being an attractive feature in its own right, it can be used in three different ways according to whether or not the hearth is exposed – it can be covered either by using a glazed door to provide a view of the fire, or with a solid metal door so that fuel can be burned overnight. Alternatively, it can be left fully open for a fireside ambience, which is less fuel efficient.

Two large cisterns in the garden collect rainwater for garden irrigation. Toilets are also water-conserving and highly efficient, with powerful jets using only 4 litres (7 pints) per flush. The garden, a rarity in Paris, has been transformed into an intimate productive area, planted with a vegetable plot, aromatic plants and a fruit tree.

THIN END OF THE WEDGE

FOCUS HOUSE | LONDON | UK | ARCHITECTS: JUSTIN BERE, BERE:ARCHITECTS

Right: The new zinc-clad eco house occupies a wedge-shaped plot at the end of a terrace of Victorian houses. The house widens towards the rear.

Far right: The stairs leading up to the second floor are decorated in a neutral palette that is naturally space-enhancing.

Below: The ground floor is an open-plan living, dining and cooking area. The floor is oak and the fitted units are clad in rosewood. Large Scandinavian high-performance windows flood the interior with light.

Opposite: The view from the dining area to the front of the house reveals the way the plot tapers. Every opportunity was taken to build in storage space.

Finding a site to build a new house can be difficult, particularly in dense urban areas. When the owners of this striking zinc-clad building wanted to build a new eco-friendly home for their family, the solution came in the form of a wedge-shaped parcel of land attached to a four-bedroom Victorian house in north London, which at the time was being used for car parking. The clients bought the Victorian house and sold it on minus the 'bit on the side' to finance the new project.

The awkward shape of the plot dictated the form of the new house. It's tall and wedge-shaped, stepping back from a width of 2.8 m (9 ft) at the front to 7 m (23 ft) at the rear. The entire ground floor is designated as a general living space and dining area. Large Scandinavian sliding windows open out onto the back garden and allow light to flood in.

Upstairs on the first floor is a study jutting out over the front entrance, and two bedrooms and a bathroom arranged in a linear fashion and connected by a corridor. A second flight of stairs leads up to a second bathroom and master bedroom that overlooks the neighbourhood at the rear.

ECO FACTS:

- Timber structure with low embodied energy, derived from sustainable sources.
- High degree of insulation using 'Foamglas'.
- High-specification Scandinavian windows.
- Heat-recovery ventilation.
- Solar thermal installation to provide hot water heating.
- Low-maintenance and durable exterior.
- Efficient use of space.

SECTION KEY:

1 - Existing house
2 - Bedroom
3 - Study
4 - Bathroom
5 - Living room
6 - Kitchen

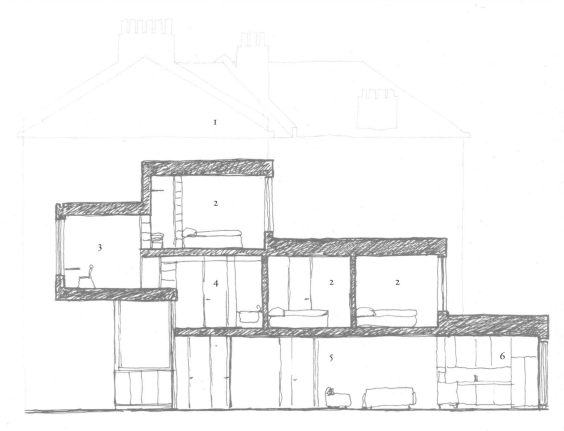

Far left, above: Coming from a larger house, the family had to learn to live with fewer possessions. The kitchen occupies the rear of the main living space.

Far left, below: The garden is simple and low in maintenance. Surfaces include paving, pebbles and wooden decking. In addition to a kumquat tree in the centre, there are also olive trees grown in containers.

Left: The master bedroom is up a short flight of stairs from the study.

Central to the brief was to create a low-cost, low-energy and low-maintenance family home that offered more flexible living space than the Victorian property the family had previously occupied. The walls, floors and roof panels consist of cross-laminated timber slabs, 200 mm (7¾ inches) thick, made from sustainable sources and imported from Austria. Compared to conventional concrete and steel structural systems, the timber structure has low embodied energy. What embodied energy does exist is offset by the carbon dioxide locked within the timber over the course of its lifetime. Used in kit form, the timber slabs can span large distances and be erected very quickly – the entire building, including all final finishes and fittings, was completed in only six months.

A high degree of insulation was provided by wrapping the exterior in a 200-mm (7³/4-inches) thick layer of 'Foamglas', a black insulating material that serves as an impermeable vapour barrier. This was covered with a zinc skin, which further insulates the structure and serves as a durable low-maintenance cladding. High-specification Scandinavian windows add to the energy efficiency.

Following the same general guidelines as those used in the German 'Passivhaus' system, the house is sufficiently airtight and well-insulated to require only minimal supplementary heating. The Foamglas insulation also helps to keep the house cool in summer. Heat-recovery ventilation is used throughout the house and half the household's annual hot water requirements are supplied by a solar thermal installation. Electricity bills are very low.

A number of strategies were adopted to enhance the sense of space. Every opportunity was taken to build in storage and rooms are subdivided by partitions, rather than floor-to-ceiling walls. A neutral colour palette of grey and white makes the most of the natural light that spills through the generous windows. For the clients and their family, coming from a larger house meant a considerable degree of downsizing. Possessions were shed, a process that they found ultimately liberating, a 'less is more' approach well in keeping with an eco-friendly lifestyle.

Building a home from scratch can present daunting financial and organizational challenges, particularly when you factor ecological issues into the equation. Recognition of the success of Focus House came when it won three prestigious awards: RIBA London Awards Winner, Grand Designs Awards Best Eco Home and British Homes Awards Small House of the Year.

REVIVAL

PRIVATE HOUSE | LE VAR | FRANCE | ARCHITECT: BERTRAND BONNIER

After a long search for a rural property that would offer the opportunity to explore both environmental and traditional agricultural practices, the owner stumbled across this ancient smallholding in the Var, a region in the south of France. Although terraces for cultivation were clearly visible in old photographs, they were so overgrown they were barely discernible on the ground. The property included a modest, semi-derelict dry-stone house. Fortunately, it also came with a building permit.

The restoration and extension of the house were an integral part of the regeneration of the surrounding land. Formerly the land had been planted with wheat, vines and olive trees, but the terraces had been neglected for 70 years. The ground was cleared, and the terraces and stone walls were restored. A grove of 600 olive trees were planted, the four varieties of olive chosen to suit the soil, the orientation, the strong winds and climatic conditions.

The old house was restored and a new extension, forming a long narrow bar, was built immediately behind it in line with the terraces, partly earth-sheltered in the slope facing the hills behind. A vaulted terrace, open from midday to sunset and shaded by split-cane matting in the summer, completes the basic layout.

Timber was used for the main structure of the new extension and for the cladding on the sides and north-facing facade. At the rear, rock and earth excavated from the site were built up to form a bank, contributing thermal mass to the building and helping to keep it cool during the summer and warm during the winter. The main living spaces are partitioned by concrete walls to add to the thermal-mass effect. The entire new building is covered with a terrace planted with hardy shrubs.

Above right: The original house is a dry-stone construction. The new extension runs behind it. Solar panels on the terraces provide energy for the house.

Right: The old house and new extension blend together seamlessly.

Far right: An outdoor terrace is shaded by split-cane matting to keep off the heat of the summer sun.

Far left: Stone walling, with its high thermal mass, helps to keep heat in during the winter and keep interiors cool in summer.

Left: Supplementary heating is provided by a wood-burning stove.

The new building has large windows facing south to capture the warmth of the sun, with sliding shutters to act as screens. On the north-facing side of the extension, a series of fanlights high up encourage natural cross-ventilation. The building is highly insulated. The aluminium-framed windows are semi-inset.

Miles from the nearest village and too remote for electrical or water connections, there was no alternative but for the property to be as self-sufficient as possible. A borehole was dug to serve as a source of water. This is augmented by rainwater from the roofs and the terraces, which is collected in a new pool (225 cubic metres/378 cubic feet in capacity). The collected rainwater provides irrigation for the olive grove and for fire-fighting – the area is prone to forest fires.

Most of the energy required for the house comes from the sun. Beside the pool, solar panels, angled at 60 degrees,

capture direct sunlight in the winter months, when the sun is at a lower angle in the sky, as well as indirect reflections of sunlight falling on the water in the basin. This provides energy for the underfloor heating and hot water. Further away, on the terraces, photovoltaic panels produce the electricity needed for the house. This is supplemented by energy from a generator in bad weather.

The original dry-stone building is one of those vernacular structures that seem to grow naturally out of their surroundings in an almost organic fashion. The new extension blends with the existing house perfectly and is just as at home in the pastoral landscape. With modern technology harnessing the sun's power to provide the required energy, and the olive grove now producing olive oil of an exceptional quality, a piece of rural history has been restored to productive life.

ECO FACTS:

- Restoration of existing building and regeneration of landscape.
- Solar panels providing hot water and electricity.
- Borehole and rainwater collection to provide water.

- Extensive use of materials with high thermal mass.
- Timber structure and cladding.
- High degree of insulation.
- Natural cross-ventilation.

PLAN KEY:

1 - Bedroom
2 - Bathroom
3 - Living/dining room
4 - Utility
5 - Boiler room
6 - Garage
7 - Kitchen/living room

Above: Rainwater is collected in a new pool with a capacity of 225 cubic metres (738 cubic feet). Solar panels angled at 60 degrees capture winter sunlight and light reflected from the water.

Left: The living area in the new extension is lit by large south-facing windows. Fanlights high up on the north-facing side promote natural cross-ventilation.

INSIDE OUT

1532 HOUSE | SAN FRANCISCO, CALIFORNIA | USA | ARCHITECTS: FOURGERON ARCHITECTURE

Above: The main street frontage of the house is louvred to provide privacy. On the street level is the garage; above is an artist's studio.

Above right: The house consists of two distinct volumes arranged around a central courtyard. There are many different outdoor spaces, including a deck on the roof of the studio.

Right: A central two-storey staircase connects the bedrooms on the lower level with the main living space and the master bedroom above.

Far right: The view of the rear section of the house from the inner courtyard. Glass and wood walkways connect indoors and out. Generous floor-to-ceiling windows are openable for natural ventilation.

Occupying a narrow 7.6-m (25-foot) wide plot in San Francisco, this modern infill consists of two distinct volumes separated by an inner courtyard. Altogether, there are seven different outdoor spaces, from the front deck through to the backyard, all surrounding the main living areas and bringing a sense of openness to the design. Floor-to-ceiling windows, glass floors and skylights allow natural light to penetrate deep into all the rooms. From the street, you can see right through the house to the rear of the plot.

The front section of the house incorporates a garage at street level with a painting studio above for the artist/owner. Across the inner courtyard, the rear section of the house is where the main living space is located. An open-plan kitchen, dining and living area is on the same level as the rear garden. The master bedroom is on the floor above, which is stepped back to provide spectacular views of the bay and the Golden Gate Bridge. Below the living area, on the same level as the garage, are additional bedrooms.

The sense of clarity that arises from the expanses of glazing and courtyard spaces has not been achieved at the expense of energy efficiency. Urban infills can be dark and inward-looking. Here generous openings mean the interior is bathed in natural light, which reduces the need for artificial lighting and generates a feel-good factor. All

Above: The open-plan living area has sliding doors that provide access to the garden at the rear.

Right: Generous overhangs shield the glazing from the hot summer sun, while allowing low winter to penetrate into the interior.

glazing is insulated to protect against heat loss and has a low-E coating that reduces solar gain. The street frontage is louvred for privacy.

The largest openings are on the north and south facades to take advantage of thermal mass. Windows on the west and east are smaller. Overhangs on the south elevation block summer sun, while allowing low winter light to enter and warm the space.

All the windows in the living spaces can be opened. Large sliding glass doors provide access to the courtyard on all levels. Together with an open stairwell, this promotes natural stack ventilation and allows the building to expel excess heat without mechanical extract.

The house is powered by photovoltaic panels installed on the roof, which provide more electricity than is required for daily life. Solar thermal panels pre-heat the water used in the underfloor heating system. The radiant concrete floors eliminate the need for ductwork. Energy use is significantly lower and more efficient than that required by a forced-air system.

All the paint used in the house is low-VOC and finishes have been chosen for their sustainability. Wall insulation is formaldehyde-free. Artificial lighting is by highly efficient dimmable fluorescent tubes.

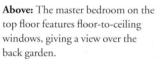

Above: The master bedroom on the top floor features floor-to-ceiling windows, giving a view over the back garden.

Above right: The open toplit staircase encourages natural stack ventilation to help cool the interior.

ECO FACTS:

- Photovoltaic panels provide more electricity than required.
- Solar thermal panels pre-heat hot water for the underfloor heating.
- Radiant underfloor heating.
- Concrete provides thermal mass.
- Highly insulated low-E glazing to prevent heat loss/gain.
- Operable windows encourage natural ventilation.
- Generous openings bathe the interior in natural light.
- Low-VOC and sustainable finishes.

SECTION KEY:

1 - Bedroom
2 - Deck
3 - Living area
4 - Studio
5 - Garage

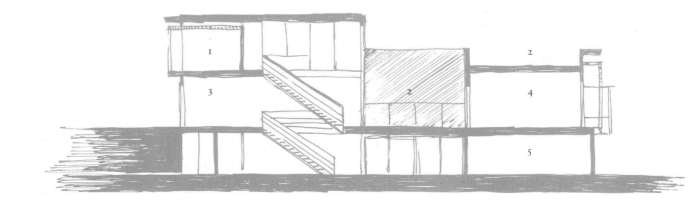

POWER STATION

LACEMAKERS HOUSE | NOTTINGHAM | UK | ARCHITECTS: MARSH: GROCHOWSKI ARCHITECTS

Right: A former factory, the eco house now features solar panels on the roof. The building has been insulated to a high degree.

Below: One wall of the living area is clad in old cardboard tubes, a cheap and highly effective solution.

Below right: Rock wool insulation applied to the exterior has been covered with render.

Far right: A steel girder provides a reminder of the building's industrial past. The flooring in the living area is composite boarding. The kitchen floor is linoleum.

Alan Simpson, Labour MP for Nottingham South since 1992, traces his mission to promote sustainable housing back to the days when he was campaigning against fuel poverty and raising awareness of the plight of pensioners who were dying of hyperthermia because they couldn't afford to heat their homes in winter. Unlike other politicians whose lifestyles are often somewhat at variance to their declared principles, Simpson has put his into practice with the renovation of a former derelict brick mill into an eco home.

The former mill is located on the fringes of a car park in central Nottingham in an area that is known as Lace Market, in reference to the textile industry that once made its home there. The building was in a terrible state when Simpson bought it, but rather than build on a greenfield site, he was determined to show that it was possible to convert and renovate an existing building into one with a much smaller carbon footprint. Given that well over 80 per cent of people in Britain live in existing housing stock, if carbon emissions are to be cut to any significant degree, it is these homes that must be adapted.

A substantial part of the money invested in the conversion of the mill was spent on insulation. Victorian masonry structures are notoriously bad at keeping in heat. The solution here was to wrap the exterior of the building in rock wool insulation and then apply rendering on top. Insulation was also applied internally in the roof space and to the inner wall surfaces.

Another significant investment was the photovoltaic solar panels that cover the south-facing part of the roof. These will save up to eight tonnes of carbon dioxide emissions over their lifetime and represent a direct saving of 15 per cent on energy bills. Other alternative technologies used in the house include a gas-fired CHP (combined heat and power) boiler that provides hot water and heating and generates some of the electricity the family uses. Because of

Right: A skylight draws natural light down into the centre of the house. Some of the brick walls have been left exposed.

Far right: View looking down into the main double-height living area. The house generates all its own electricity and exports 50% back to the National Grid.

these technologies, and the fact that the house is so highly insulated, the family is able to export 50 per cent of their electricity back to the National Grid.

Water conservation is also addressed. A greywater recycling system collects water from baths, showers and basins and uses it to flush toilets. Flushing toilets accounts for a high proportion of domestic water use; this system saves 40 per cent of an average household's consumption.

The four-storey house is simply laid out. The ground floor is a double-height open-plan space. Exposed steel girders reveal the building's past. On the first floor is the main bedroom and bathroom, with two additional bedrooms on the level above.

Site boundary conditions meant that it was impossible to create new openings in the exterior walls of the living area. To improve natural daylighting, shafts were built into the roof terrace above. These are topped with glass and lined in mirrored Perspex. Similarly, a triple insulated

polycarbonate rooflight was inserted over the new stairwell. Below this, a sandblasted-glass floor allows light to fall down through three stories.

Many of the materials and finishes used in the house have been chosen for their environmental friendliness – and cheapness. Sterling board, a wood composite from managed Scottish forests, is used as flooring in the living area. Marmoleum, a type of linoleum, is used as kitchen flooring. Linoleum is a natural product made of renewable ingredients. The roof terrace is tiled in 'Glasscrete', made from 80 per cent recycled glass. The roof itself was recovered with reclaimed slate.

Other eco features are more eye-catching. One wall of the living room is clad in old cardboard rolls, which bring visual warmth and tactility to the former industrial space. A window in the staircase tints and filters the light flooding through the coloured bottles stuck end-on to the double-glazed unit, creating interesting patterns.

Far left: A window on the staircase filters light through coloured bottles, stuck end-on to the glass.

Left: The conversion of a derelict factory into a sustainable home reveals the potential for adapting existing buildings.

Below left: A gas-fired CHP boiler supplies hot water and heating, and also generates some of the electricity used in the house.

SECTION KEY:

1 - Solar panel
2 - Rooflight
3 - Loft
4 - Bedroom
5 - Terrace
6 - Master bedroom
7 - Dressing room
8 - Dining room
9 - Snug

ECO FACTS:

- Renovation of existing building on a brownfield site.
- High degree of insulation.
- PV panels for electricity generation.
- Gas-fired CHP boiler for hot water, heating and some electricity.
- Greywater recycling system to flush toilets.
- Sustainable, recyclable and recycled materials.
- Energy efficient (A-rated) appliances and low-energy light bulbs.

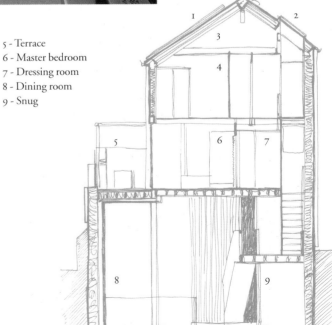

USEFUL ADDRESSES

USEFUL ADDRESSES

ARCHITECTS

Adjaye & Associates
23–28 Penn Street
London N1 5DL
Tel. +44 (0)20 7739 4969
www.adjaye.com

Alex Fergusson Architects
3 Elfin Grove, Teddington
Middlesex TW11 8RD
Tel. +44 (0)20 8977 7323

Andrea Steele
ANDArchitects
198 Betsy Brown Road
Rye Brook, New York NY 10573
Tel. +1 914 939 1951
www.ANDarchitects.com

Backen Gillam Architects
1028 Main Street
St. Helena, CA 94574
Tel. +1 707 967 1920

Bark Design Architects
PO Box 1355
Noosa Heads Queensland 4567
Australia
Tel. +617 54710340
www.barkdesign.com.au

Baufritz (UK) Ltd
T: +44 (0)1223 235 632
www.baufritz.co.uk
www.baufritz.de
UK and Germany

Belsize Architects
48 Parkhill Road
London NW3 2YP
Tel. +44 (0)20 7482 4420
www.belsizearchitects.com

Bertrand Bonnier
Les Adrechs
83570 Cotignac
France
Tel. +33 4 94 77 70 04

Bill Dunster
The Zed Factory
21 Sand Martin Way
Bedzed, Wallington
Surrey SM6 7DF
Tel. +44 (020) 8404 1380

Bischof Partner Architektur
Bahnhofstraße 40
8590 Romanshorn
Switzerland
Tel. +41 (0)71 466 76 76
www.bischof-partner.ch

Bryan Roe
The Green Shop
Cheltenham Road, Bisley
Gloucestershire GL6 7BX
Tel. +44 (0)1452 770629
www.greenshop.co.uk

Claesson Koivisto Rune
Östgötagatan 50
116 64 Stockholm
Sweden
Tel. +46 8 644 58 63
www.claessonkoivistorune.se

Ecoscene
Empire Farm
Throop Road
Templecombe
Somerset BA8 0HR
Tel. +44 (0)1963 371700
www.ecoscene.com

Eric Gizard & Associés
14 rue Crespin du Gast
75011 Paris
France
Tel. +33 (0)1 55 28 38 58
www.gizardassocies.com

Eurban (Constructors)
5 Bickels Yard
151–153 Bermondsey Street
London SE1 3HA
Tel. +44 (0)20 7749 3929

Fougeron Architecture
431 Tehama Street, Suite 1
San Francisco
CA 94103
Tel. +1 415 641 5744
www.fougeron.com

Frieder Gros
Friedrichstraße 71
D-88045 Friedrichshafen and
Muttelsee 8/1, D-88069 Tettnang
Germany
Tel. +49 (0)171 2712285

Harrison Architects
1932 First Avenue, Suite 200
Seattle
WA 98101
Tel. +1 206 956 0883
www.harrisonarchitects.com

**Henrik E Nielsen Arkitektkontor
AS**
Bispegata 12
PO BOX 9208 Greenland
NO-0134 Oslo
Norway
Tel. +47 2300 2140
www.hen-arkitektur.no

Interieurs
151 Franklin Street
New York, NY 10013
Tel. +1 212 343 0800
www.interieurs.com

Jean-Baptiste Barache
32 rue Sainte-Marthe
75010 Paris
France
Tel. +33 (0)1 42 01 33 87

Joel Sanders Architect
106 East 19th Street
New York, NY 10003
Tel. +1 212 431 8751
www.joelsandersarchitect.com

Kevin Fellingham Architecture
Wharf Studios
Baldwin Terrace
London N1 7RU
Tel. +44 (0)20 7354 0677
www.kfellingham.com

Marcus Lee
FLACQ
4 John Prince's Street
London W1G 0JL
Tel.+44 (0)20 7495 5755
www.flacq.com

Marsh:Grochowski Architects
16 Commerce Square
The Lace Market
Nottingham NG1 1HS
Tel. +44 (0)115 9411761
www.marsh-grochowski.com

Michael Wilkinson
Wilkinson Blender Architecture
1714 n. damen 3m
Chicago, IL 60647
Tel. +1 773.772.7787
www.wbarch.com

Michael Winter Architect
The Boundary House,
Upper Cumberland Walk,
Tunbridge Wells, Kent TN2 5EH
Tel. +44 1892 539709
www.michaelwinterarchitect.com

bie G. Bowman Architect
P.O. Box 1114
Healdsburg, CA 95448
Tel. +1 707-433-7833
www.obiebowman.com

Pulltab Design
10 East 23rd Street, No 710
New York
NY 10010
Tel. +1 212 727 9448
www.pulltabdesign.com

Robert Dye Associates
Unit A2, Linton House
39–51 Highgate Road
London NW5 1RS
Tel. +44 (0)20 7267 9388
www.robertdye.com

Roth Architects Pty Ltd
Level 1 / 202 Oxford Street
Paddington
Po Box 3176 Bellevue Hill
NSW Australia 2023
Tel. +61 (2) 9361 6364
www.rotharchitecture.com.au

Sandberg Schoffel Architects
Unit 2A, 3 The Postern
Castlecrag, NSW 2068
Australia
Tel. +61 2 9958 5088
www.sandbergschoffel.com.au

Seth Stein Architects Ltd
15 Grand Union Centre
West Row
London W10 5AS
Tel. +44 (0)20 8968 8581
www.sethstein.com

Sheppard Robson
77 Parkway
Camden Town
London NW1 7PU
Tel. +44 (0)20 7504 1700
www.sheppardrobson.com

Steven Holl
450 West 31st Street
New York
NY 10001
Tel. +1 212 629 7262
www.stevenholl.com

Stutchbury and Pape
5/364 Barrenjoey Road
NSW 2106
Australia
Tel. +61 2 9979 5030
www.stutchburyandpape.com.au

Tim Pyne
m-house, 10 Charlotte Road
London EC2A 3PB
Tel. +44 (0)7855 493932
www.m-house.org
www.timpyne.com

Whitney Sander
Catherine Holliss
Sander Architects
2434 Lincoln Blvd.
Venice, CA 90291
Tel. +1 310.822.0300
www.sander-architects.com

Zoka Zola
1737 West Ohio Street
Chicago IL 60622
Tel. +1 312 491 9431
www.zokazola.com

ECO AUDIT

www.carbonfootprint.com
Calculate your carbon footprint

www.clevel.co.uk
Calculate your carbon level

www.stylewillsaveus.com
An independent digital magazine with a focus on ethical, fairtrade, eco-friendly, vintage, recycled and sustainable issues

www.waterfootprint.org
Calculate your water footprint

www.whatsmineisyours.com
Swap clothes at this fashion swap website

www.freecycle.org
An email list where people give away things that they no longer need for free

www.eBay.com
The World's Online Marketplace where millions of items are traded each day

RuralZED
www.ruralzed.com
Information on zero-carbon home design.

ADVICE

The Building Centre
Store Street
London
WC1E 7BT
Tel. +44 (0) 207 692 4000
www.buildingcentre.co.uk
Information on everything to do with building and building materials; advice service

Federation of Master Builders (FMB)
Gordon Fisher House
14-15 Great James Street
London WC1N 3DP
Tel. +44 (0)20 7242 7583
www.fmb.org.uk
Publishes and index of members

National House Building Council
NHBC House
Davy Avenue
Knowlhill
Milton Keynes
MK5 8FP
Tel. +44 (0)844 633 1000
www.nhbc.co.uk
Publishes a list of members and registers newly-built houses

Royal Institute of British Architects
66 Portland Place
London W1B 1AD
Tel. +44 (0)20 7580 5533
www.architecture.com
Publishes a list of members

Royal Institute of Chartered Surveyors
RICS Contact Centre
Surveyor Court
Westwood Way
Coventry CV4 8JE
Tel. +44 (0)870 333 1600
www.rics.org
Publishes a list of members

ECOLOGICAL ORGANISATIONS

Association for Environment-Conscious Buildings (AECB)
PO Box 32
Llandysul SA44 5ZA
Tel. +44 (0)845 456 9773
www.aecb.net
Publishes magazine

Better Planet
www.betterplanet.co.uk
Information on green technologies

Building Research Establishment (BRE)
Bucknalls Lane
Watford WD25 9XX
Tel. +44 (0)1923 664000
www.bre.co.uk
Information on reducing the environmental impact of construction projects; includes information on eco-homes and a materials exchange for second-hand and unused building materials

Centre for Alternative Technology
Machynlleth
Powys SY20 9AZ
Tel. +44 (0)1654 705 950
www.cat.org.uk
Publications and demonstration centre

Construction Resources
111 Rotherhithe Street
London SE16 4NF
Tel. +44 (0)20 7232 1181
www.constructionresources.com
Ecological builders' merchant for sustainable building materials and systems; detailed technical information available

Environmental Building News
122 Burge Street, Suite 30
Brattleboro VT 05301
Tel. +1 802 257 7300
www.BuildingGreen.com
US newsletter

The Findhorn Foundation
Communications
The Park, Findhorn, Forres
Morayshire IV36 3TZ
Tel. +44 (0)1309 690311
www.findhorn.org

Friends of the Earth
26–28 Underwood Street
London N1 7UQ
Tel. +44 (0)20 7490 1555
www.foe.co.uk

Greenpeace
www.greenpeace.org
Information on pollution, solar energy, pvc and other environmental campaigns

Scottish Ecological Design Association
28 Albert Street
Edinburgh EH7 1LG
www.seda2.org
Promotes the design of materials, products and systems that are benign to the environment

The Soil Association
South Plaza
Marlborough Street
Bristol BS1 3NX
Tel. +44 (0)117 314 5000
www.soilassociation.org

Wrap
www.wrap.org.uk/construction
Advice on waste minimisation and management

ENERGY

Allbrite Group
Tel. +44 (0)800 781 3908
www.allbriteuk.co.uk
Underfloor heating & flooring

American Aldes Ventilation Corp
4521 19th Street Court East,
Suite 104
Bradenton FL 34203
Tel. +1 941 351 3441
Freephone 800 255 7749
www.americanaldes.com
Manufacturers of heat-recovery ventilators

American Solar Energy Society
2400 Central Avenue, Suite A
Boulder, Colorado
CO 80301
Tel. +1 303 443 3130
www.ases.org

Atlantis Energy Systems
9275 Beatty Drive, Suite B
California
CA 95826
Tel. +1 916 438 2930
www.atlantisenergy.com
Manufacturere of solar slates

BioHeat USA
4 Britton Lane
PO Box 285
Lyme
NH 03768
Freephone 800 782 9927
www.woodboilers.com
Manufacturer of multi-fuel boilers and domestic hot-water heaters

Bergey Windpower Co. Inc
2200 Industrial Blvd
Norman
Oklahoma
OK73069
Tel. +1 405 364 4212
www.bergey.com
Manufacturere of small-scale wind turbines

BP Sola
www.bpsolar.com
Largest manufacturer of photovoltaic modules on the world

British Eco.com
268 Bath Road
Slough SL1 4DX
Tel. +44 (0)845 257 0041
www.britisheco.com
Solar thermal water heating

British Wind Energy Association
Renewable Energy House
1 Aztec Row, Berners Road
London, N1 0PW
Tel. +44 (0)20 7689 1960
www.bwea.com

Carbon Energy Solutions
Unit 6, Twisleton Court, Priory Hill
Dartford DA1 2EN
Tel. +44 (0)1322 271932
www.carbonenergysolutions.com
Photovoltaic panels

Consolar
Holbrook Garage
Cheltenham Road
Bisley GL6 7BX
Tel. +44 (0)1452 77 20 30
www.consolar.co.uk

Danfoss Heat Pumps UK
Unit 3 Parkwood Business Park
Parkwood
Sheffield S3 8AL
Tel. +44 (0)114 270 3900
www.ecoheatpumps.co.uk
Specialists in new builds, complete renovations, barn conversions and commercial developments

Ecohometec UK Ltd
Unit 11e Carcraft Enterprise Park
Carcraft
Doncaster DN6 8DD
Tel. +44 (0)1302 722266
www.eco-hometec.co.uk
Energy-efficient condensing boilers

Energy Saving Trust
21 Dartmouth Street
London SW1H 9BP
Tel. +44 (0)20 7222 0101
www.energysavingtrust.org.uk

EVALON Solar
www.alwitra.de
The power-generating roofing membrane

first.utility
www.first-utility.com
Electricity, gas and telecoms – environmental solutions to technology

Jaga
www.theradiatorfactory.com and
www.jagaexperiencelab.com
Energy savers – radiators and other heating systems

Kingspan
7 Balloo Crescent
Balloo Industrial Estate
Bangor
Co. Down BT19 7UP
Northern Ireland
Tel. +44 (0)28 91270411
www.kingspansolar.co.uk
Solar energy systems custom made to suit individual needs

NEF Renewables
The National Energy Foundation
Davy Avenue
Knowhill
Milton Keynes MK5 8NG
Tel. +44 (0)1908 665555
www.nef.org.uk
Advice and contact details for suppliers and installers of renewable energy

Redring
Applied Energy Products Ltd
Morley Way
Peterborough PE2 9JJ
Tel. +44 (0)1733 456789
www.redring.co.uk
Heating and hot water solutions

Solar Century
91–94 Lower Marsh
London SE1 7AB
Tel. +44 (0)20 7803 0100
www.solarcentury.com
Suppliers of solar technology, including photovoltaic panels and solar slates

Solar Energy Industries Association
805 15th Street NW
Suite 501
Washington DC 20005
Tel. +1 202 682 0556
www.seia.org
National trade association of companies providing solar products

Solar Sense
Long Ashton Business Park
Yanley Lane
Long Ashton
Bristol BS47 9LW
Tel. +44 (0)1275 394139
Suppliers of solar products, photovoltaics, solar heating systems

Solar Twin
2nd Floor, 50 Watergate Street
Chester CH1 2LA
Tel. +44 (0)1244 404 410
www.solartwin.com
Solar hot water energy systems

SunEarth Inc
8425 Almeria Avenue
Fontana
CA 92335
www.sunearthinc.com
Solar water-heating equipment

Sustainable Buildings Industry Council
1112 16th Street NW
Suite 240
Washington DC 20036
Tel. +1 202 628 7400

Syntonic Solar
63–65 Penge Road
London SE25 4EJ
Tel. +44 (0)20 8778 7838
www.solarheating.uk.net/
Design and specification of high technology green energy solutions

Thermo-Floor
Unit 1, Babsham Farm
Chichester Road
Bognor Regis PO21 5EL
Tel. +44 (0)1243 822058
www.thermo-floor.co.uk
Underfloor heating and cooling

The Unico System
Tel.+44 (0)1443 843261
www.unicosystem.co.uk
*Heating and air conditioning
solutions to save energy and costs*

Wind & Sun Ltd
Humber Marsh
Leominster
Herefordshire HR6 0NR
Tel. +44 (0)1586 760671
www.windandsun.co.uk

WATER & WASTE

American Standard
1 Centennial Plaza
Piscataway
NJ 08855
Tel. +1 800 442 1902
www.american-standard-us.com
Manufacturers of gravity-flush toilets

Cistermiser Ltd
Unit 1 Woodley Park Estate
59–69 Reading Road
Woodley
Reading RG5 3AN
Tel. +44 (0)118 969 1611
www.cistermiser.co.uk
*Manufacturers of water-conserving
devises for cisterns*

Clivus Multrum Ltd
15 Union Street
Lawrence
Maine 08140
Tel. +1 978 725 5591
Freephone 800 425 4887
www.clivusmultrum.com
Manufacturer of composting toilets

Envirosink
PO Box 98231-2564
Blaine
Washington
Tel. +1 888 663 4950
www.envirosink.com
*Suppliers of kitchen sinks that
drain to grey water system*

Kingsley Plastics Ltd
Western Barn Industrial Park
Heatherleigh Road
Winkleigh
Devon EX19 8AP
Tel. +44 (0)1837 83154
www.kingsleyplastics.co.uk
*Manufacturers of low-flush and
composting toilets*

Marley
Tel. +44 (0)1622 852585
www.marleyplumbinganddrainage.com
Recycling the rain that falls on your roof

Niagara Conservation Corp
45 Horsehill Road
Hanover Technical Center
Suite 106
Ceder Knolls
New Jersey 07927
Tel. +1 973 829 0800
Freephone 800 831 8383
www.niagaraconservation.com
*Suppliers of wide range of water-
conserving showerheads, toilets
and taps*

Rainharvester Limited
268 Bath Road
Slough
SL1 4DX
Tel. +44 (0)845 466 4797
www.rainharvester.co.uk
*Rainwater harvesting solutions
(pumps, filters etc.)*

Rainharvesting Systems
The Greenshop
Cheltenham Road
Bisley, Stroud
Gloucestershire GL6 7BX
Tel. +44 (0)845 223 5430
www.rainharvesting.co.uk
Water conservation for domestic use

INSULATING MATERIALS

**Cellulose Insulation
Manufacturers Association**
136 S. Keowe Street
Dayton OH 45402
Tel. +1 888 8812462
www.cellulose.org
*Association of American cellulose
insulation producers*

Eco Merchant
Head Hill Road
Goodnestone
Faversham
Kent ME13 9BU
Tel. +44 (0)1795 530130
www.ecomerchant.co.uk
*Isonat hemp and recycled cotton
based insulation*

Excel Industries Ltd
Maerdy Industrial Estate
Rhymney
Gwent NP22 5PY
Tel. +44 (0)1685 845200
www.excelfibre.com
*Information about 'breathing wall'
construction; cellulose insulation*

Klober Ltd
Ingleberry Road
Shepshed
Loughborough LE12 9DE
Tel. +44 (0)1509 500660
www.klober.co.uk
Wool insulation

Natural Insulation
Plant Fibre Technology Ltd
The BioComposites Centre
Deiniol Road
Bangor
Gwynedd LL57 2UW
Tel. +44 (0)1248 388486
www.naturalinsulation.co.uk
Natural fibre insulation

Second Nature UK Ltd
Soulands Gate
Dacre, Penrith
Cumbria CA11 0JF
Tel. +44 (0)17684 86285
www.secondnatureuk.com
Home insulation

MATERIALS – GENERAL

Barausse
Via Parmesana, 31
36010 Monticello Conte Otto
Vicenza
Italy
Tel. +39 0444 900 000
www.barausse.com
*High quality designer interior
doors using innovative composite to
replace wood*

Butcher Living
29 The Woolhouse
74 Back Church Lane
London E1 1LX
Tel. +44 (0)20 7481 2705
www.butcherliving.com
*Innovative interior design using
sustainable and eco-friendly materials*

Calch Ty-Mawr Lime
Tel. +44 (0)1874 658249
www.lime.org.uk
*Manufacturers & suppliers of
traditional & ecological building
materials*

The Conran Shop
Michelin House, 81 Fulham Road
London SW3 6RD
Tel. +44 (0)20 7589 7401
www.conran.com

Construction Resources
111 Rotherhithe Street
London SE16 4NF
Tel. +44 (0)20 7232 1181
www.constructionresources.com
Building materials and products

Ecohaus
4121 1st Avenue South
Seattle WA 98134
Freephone 800 281 9785
www.ecohaus.com
*Flooring, FSC-certified wood, tiles,
furniture, finishes*

Glatthaar
www.glatthaar.co.uk
*Makers of the ThermoSafe
Basement – state of the art lower
ground floor living*

Green Building Store
Heath House Mill
Heath House Lane
Bolster Moor
West Yorkshire HD7 4JW
Tel. +44 (0)1484 401705
www.ecoproducts.co.uk

Green Depot
222 Bowery
New York
NY 10012
Tel. +1 212 226 0444
Freephone 800 238 5008
www.greendepot.com

The Green Shop
Cheltenham Road
Bisley
Stroud GL6 7BX
Tel. +44 (0)1452 770629
www.greenshop.co.uk
Finishes, solar- and wind-powered equipment

Lime Green
Coates Kilns
Stretton Road
Much Wenlock
Shropshire TF13 6DG
Tel. +44 (0)1952 728 611
www.lime-green.co.uk
Renders for buildings that conserve rather than use energy

Natural Building Technology
The Hangar
Worminghall Road
Oakley HP18 9UL
Tel. +44 (0)1844 338338
www.natural-building.co.uk

Planetary Solutions
2030 17th Street
Boulder
CO 80302
Tel. +1 303 442 6228
Freephone 800 488 2089
www.planetearth.com
Cork, linoleum, wool, recycled plastic carpet, reclaimed and certified wood, bamboo, recycled glass tiles, natural finishes

Plant Fibre Technology Ltd
The BioComposites Centre
Deiniol Road
Bangor
Gwynedd LL57 2UW, UK
Tel. +44 (0)1248 388486
www.plantfibretechnology.com
Ultra-light, sustainable furniture panels

Springvale
Dinting Vale Business Park
Glossop
Derbyshire SK13 6LG
Tel. +44 (0)1457 863 211
www.springvale.com
Manufacturers of expanded polystyrene and structural insulated roofing panel systems

BAMBOO

Bamboo Hardwoods Inc
4100 4th Avenue South
Seattle
WA 98134
Tel. +1 206 264 2414
www.bamboohardwoods.com

Plyboo Smith & Fong
475 6th Street
San Fancisco
CA 94103
Tel. +1 415 896 0583
www.plyboo.com

Teragren
12715 Miller Road NE
Suite 301
Bainbridge Island
WA 98110
Tel. +1 206 842 9477
Freephone 800 929 6333
www.teragren.com

TongLing Flooring (UK) Ltd
6 Camellia Drive
Priorslee, Telford,
Shropshire TF2 9UA
Tel. +44 (0)1952-200032
www.tlflooring.co.uk

BRICK AND TILE

Bulmer Brick and Tile
The Brickfields
Bulmer, Sudbury
Suffolk CO10 7EF
Tel. +44 (0)1787 269232

Decorum
31 Wornal Park,
Menmarsh Road, Worminghall
Buckinghamshire HP18 9JX
Tel. +44 (0)1844 338749

21–22 Oldfields Business Park,
Galvaston Grove
Fenton, Stoke-on-Trent
Staffordshire ST4 3PE
Tel. +44 (0)1782 325500
www.decorumtilestudio.co.uk
ceramic floor and wall tiles

Fired Earth
Twyford Mill
Oxford Road
Adderbury, Banbury
Oxford OX17 3SX
Tel. +44 (0)1295 812088
www.firedearth.com

Ibstock Building Products Ltd
Leicester Road
Ibstock LE67 6HS
Tel. +44 (0) 1530 261999
www.ibstock.com

Natural Tile
150 Church Road
Redfield
Bristol BS5 9HN
Tel. +44 (0)117 941 3707

Terra Green Ceramics
1650 Progress Drive
Richmond
IN 47374
Tel. +1 765 935 4760
www.terragreenceramics.com
Tiles made from recycled aviation glass

CONCRETE & PLASTER

British Gypsum Ltd
East Leake
Loughborough
Leicester LE12 6HX
Freephone 08705 456 123
www.british-gypsum.com

The Concrete Centre
Tel. +44 (0)1276 606 800
www.concretecentre.com
Concrete solutions for the changing climate

Davis Colors
3700 East Olympic Blvd
Los Angeles
CA 90023
Tel. +1 323 269 7311
Freephone 800 356 4848
www.daviscolors.com
Mineral pigments for self-colouring concrete flooring slabs

ECO-Block LLC
11220 Grader Street
Suite 700
Dallas
TX 75238
Tel. +1 214 503 1644
www.eco-block.com
Insulating concrete forms

Greenblock Worldwide
759 S. Federal Hwy
Suite 213
Stuart
FL 34994
Freephone 800 216 1820
www.greenblock.com
Insulating concrete forms

Quad-Lock Building Systems Ltd.
7398 - 132nd Street
Surrey, BC V3W 4M7
Canada
Tel. +1 604 590 3111
Freephone 888 711-5625
www.quadlock.co.uk
A key to sustainability in construction using insulating concrete formwork

CORK

Natural Cork Inc
Freephone +1 800 404 2675
www.naturalcork.com

Siesta Cork Tile Co
Unit 21, Tait Road
Gloucester Road
Croyden CR0 2DP
Tel. +44 (0)20 8683 4055
www.siestacorktiles.co.uk

Amorim Flooring (Wicanders)
7513 Connelly Drive
Suite M
21076 Hanover
Maryland
Tel. +1 410 553 6062
www.wicanders.com

GLASS & WINDOWS

The Efficient Windows
Collaborative
1850 M Street NW
Suite 600
Washington DC 20036
Tel. +1 202 530 2254
www.efficientwindows.org

Paramount Windows Inc
105 Panet Road
Winnipeg
Manitoba R2J 0S1
Canada
Tel. +1 204 233 4966
www.paramountwindows.com
*Long-established producer of
energy-efficient windows*

Paxton Restoration
Tel. +44 (0)8700 27 84 24
www.paxtonrestoration.co.uk
Double glazing for sash windows

Pilkington Group Ltd
Alexandra Business Park
Prescot Road
St Helens
Merseyside WA10 3TT
Tel. +44 (0)1744 629000
www.pikington.com
Manufacturer of low-E glass

Preedy Glass
Lamb Works
North Road, Islington,
London N7 9DP
Tel. +44 (0)20 7700 0377
www.preedyglass.com
*design and installation of glass
flooring*

Swedish Window Co Ltd
Earls Colne Business Park
Colchester
Essex CO6 2NS
Tel. +44 (0)1787 223931

Velfac
The Old Livery
Hildersham
Cambridge CB21 6DR
Tel. +44 (0)1223 897100
www.velfac.co.uk
*High specification aluminium and
wood framed windows*

Velux
Tel. +44 (0)870 240 0617
www.velux.co.uk
Roof windows and skylights

LIGHTING

Glidevale
2 Brooklands Road
Sale
Cheshire M33 3SS
Tel. +44 (0)161 905 5700
www.glidevale.com
*Sun scoops and solar tubes for natural
daylighting*

Crescent
Tel. +44 (0)1635 87888
www.crescent.co.uk
Low-energy downlights

Solatube
SolaConcepts
Sola House, 17 High Street,
Olney MK46 4EB
Tel. +44 (0)1234 241466
www.solaconcepts.co.uk

LINOLEUM

Armstrong Flooring
Armstrong World Industries Ltd
Fleck Way
Teeside Industrial Estate
Thornaby on Tees
Cleveland TS17 9JJ
Tel. +44 (0)1642 768660
www.armstrong-flooring.co.uk

PO Box 3001
Lancaster
PA 17604
Tel. +1 800 233 3823
www.armstrong.com

Forbo Flooring North America
8 Maplewood Drive
PO Box 667
Humboldt Industrial Park
Hazleton
PA 18202
Tel. +1 866-MARMOLEUM
www.forbolinoleuma.com

Forbo Nairn Ltd
PO Box 1
Kirkaldy
Fife KY1 2SB
Tel. +44 (0)1592 643777
www.forbo-flooring.co.uk

Sinclair Till Flooring Company
791–793 Wandsworth Road
London SW8 3JQ
Tel. +44 (0)20 7720 0031
www.sinclairtill.co.uk

METAL

Steel Recycling Institute
680 Andersen Drive
Pittsburgh
PA 15220
Tel. +1 800 876 7274
www.recycle-steel.org
*Association promoting recycling of steel
products*

Corus
www.corusgroup.com/en/
Sustainable steel construction

NATURAL FABRICS & FLOOR COVERINGS

**The Alternative Flooring
Company**
3b Stephenson Close
East Portway, Andover,
HampshireSP10 3RU
Tel. +44 (0)1264 335111
www.alternativeflooring.com
100% natural wool carpets

Blenheim Carpets
41 Pimlico Road
London SW1W 8NE
Tel. +44 (0)20 7823 6333
www.blenheim-carpets.co.uk
*Design and fitting of body and
border carpets*

Christopher Farr Contemporary
Rugs & Carpets
6 Burnsall Street
London SW3 3ST
Tel. +44 (0)20 7349 0888

748 N. La Cienega Boulevard
Los Angeles CA 90069
Tel. +1 310 967 0064
www.christopherfarr.com
*Specifiers and design commissioners
of contemporary handmade rugs
and carpets*

Christy Carpets
4 Danbury Court
Linford Wood
Milton Keynes MK14 6PL
Tel. +44 (0)1908 308777
www.christycarpets.com
*Durable carpets for reducing
environmental impact*

Contemporary Life & Textiles Ltd
PO Box 428
Blackburn BB2 2WQ
Tel. +44 (0)1254 296829
www.contemporarylife.co.uk
Carpet made from natural materials

Crucial Trading
79 Westbourne Park Road
London W2 5QH
Tel. +44 (0)20 7221 9000
www.crucial-trading.com
Natural fibre floor coverings, from coir and sisal to jute

Greenfibres
99 High Street
Totnes
Devon TQ9 5PF
Tel. +44 (0)845 3303440
www.greenfibres.com

The Healthy House
The Old Co-op
Lower Street
Ruscombe
Stroud
Gloucestershire GL6 6BU
Tel. +44 (0)1453 752216
www.healthy-house.co.uk
Pure untreated cotton bedding and other products

Ian Mankin
109 Regent's Park Road
London NW1 8UR
Tel. +44 (0)20 7722 0997
www.ianmankin.co.uk
Natural fabrics

Roger Oates Floors and Fabrics
1 Munro Terrace (off Riley Street)
London SW10 0DL
Tel. +44 0845 612 0072

The Long Barn, Eastnor
Herefordshire HR8 1EL
Tel. +44 (0)1531 632718
www.rogeroates.com
hand-woven rugs, carpets and stair runners

PAINTS, VARNISHES & SEALS

Auro Paints UK
Cheltenham Road
Bisley
Stroud
Gloucestershire GL6 7BX
Tel. +44 (0)1452 772020
www.auro.co.uk

Biofa
45 Gloucester Street
Brighton BN1 4EW
Tel. +44 (0)1273 808370
www.biofa.co.uk
Natural paints

Nutshell Natural Paints Ltd
Unit 3, Leigham Units
Silverton Road
Matford Park
Exeter EX2 8HY
Tel. +44 (0)1392 823760
www.nutshellpaints.com

Old Fashioned Milk Paint Co
436 Main Street
Groton,
MA 01450
Tel. +1 978 448-6336
Freephone 866 350 6455
www.milkpaint.com

PAPER AND STRAW

Amazonails
Hope Mill
Crescent Street
Todmorden OL14 5HA
Tel. +44 (0)1706 814696
www.strawbalefutures.org.uk
Straw bales

Duro Sweden AB
Durovägen 15
Box 907
801 32 Gävle
Sweden
Tel. +46 26 65 65 00
www.durosweden.se
Environmentally friendly wallpapers

PLASTIC

Smile Plastics Ltd
Mansion House
Ford
Shrewsbury SY5 9LZ
Tel. +44 (0)1704 509888
www.smile-plastics.co.uk
Recycled plastic sheets for furniture, work surfaces and panelling

Yemm & Hart
1417 Madison, Suite 308
Marquand
MO 63655
Tel. +1 573 783 5434
www.yemmhart.com
Recycled plastic sheets and panels

RAMMED EARTH

Adobe Factory
PO Box 510
Alcade
New Mexico 87511
Tel. +1 505 852 4131

Centre for Earthen Architecture
University of Plymouth
School of Architecture and Design
Roland Levinsky Building
Plymouth PL4 8AA
Tel. +44 (0) 1752 600600

RUBBER

US Rubber Recycling Inc
1231 South Lincoln Street
Colton
CA 92324
Tel. +1 9098251200
www.usrubber.com

Dalsouple
PO Box 140, Showground Road
Bridgwater
Somerset TA5 1HT
Tel. +44 (0)1278 727777
www.dalsouple.com

STONE

Bath and Portland Stone
Moor Park House
Moor Green
Corsham
Wiltshire SN13 9PH
Tel. +44 (0)1225 810390

Delabole Slate
Pengelly, Delabole
Cornwall PL33 9AZ
Tel. +44 (0)1840 212242
www.delaboleslate.co.uk

Paris Ceramics
583 Kings Road
London SW6 9DU
Tel. +44 (0)20 7371 7778
www.parisceramics.com

Quartzitec
15 Turner Court
Sussex, New Brunswick
Canada E4E 2S1
Tel. +1 506 433 9600
Stone tile made of quartz fragments bonded with Portland cement

Stonell Ltd
521–525 Battersea Park Road
London SW11 3BN
Tel. +44 (0)20 7738 0606
www.stonell.com

TIMBER

Associated Timber Services Ltd
Honey Pot Lane
Colsterworth
Grantham NG33 5LT
Tel. +44 (0)1476 860117
www.associatedtimber.co.uk
Supplier of certified timber

Benchmark
Bath Road, Kintbury
Hungerford, Berkshire RG17 9SA
Tel. +44 (0)1488 608020
www.benchmark-furniture.com
Handmade furniture from certified timbers and locally sourced materials

Centre Mills Antique Floors
PO Box 16, Aspers
PA 17304
Tel. +1 717 677 9698
www.centremillsantiquefloors.com
Salvaged and remilled wood products, including flooring

Forest Stewardship Council (UK)
11–13 Great Oak Street
llanidoes, Powys SY18 6BU
Tel. +44 (0)1686 431916
www.fsc-uk.org
Organization that sets standards for timber management and products worldwide; provides information on suppliers of FSC-certified timber

Forest Stewardship Council (US)
212 Third Avenue North, Suite 280
Minneapolis
MN 55401
Tel. +1 612 353 4511
Freephone 877 372 5646
www.fscus.org

Timbmet
Tel. +44 (0)1865 862223
www.timbmet.com
*Use of timber to cut energy
consumption in passive houses*

UK Timber Frame Association
www.timber-frame.org
*Useful guide to using timber in
construction*

WOOD FLOORING

**The Hardwood Flooring
Company Ltd**
31–35 Fortune Green Road
London NW6 1DU
Tel. +44 (0)20 7431 7000

**The Hardwood Flooring
Company Inc**
237 Center Street
Healdsburg,
CA 95448
Tel. +1 707 431 9124
www.hardwoodflooringcompany.com
Hardwood flooring and worktops

Junckers Ltd
Unit A, 1 Wheaton Road
Witham,
Essex CM8 3UJ
Tel. +44 (0)1376 534700
www.junckers.co.uk

Junckers Hardwood Inc.
95 Grand Street, Unit 3
New York, NY 10013
Tel. +1 800 878 9663
www.junckershardwood.com

LASSCo Ropewalk
Millstream Road
London SE1 3PA
Tel. +44 (0)20 7394 8061
www.lassco.co.uk
Reclaimed timber flooring

Solid Floor
69 New King's Road
London SW6 4SQ
Tel. +44 (0)20 7371 9551
www.solidfloor.co.uk

SALVAGE

American Salvage
7001 NW 27th Avenue
Miami
FL 33147
Tel. +1 305 691 7001
www.americansalvage.com

Au Temps Perdu
28–30 Midland Road
St Philips
Bristol BS2 0JY
Tel. +44 (0)117 929 9143
www.autempsperdu.co.uk

Edinburg Architectural Salvage Yard
31 West Bowling Green Street
Leith
Edinburgh EH6 5NX
Tel. +44 (0)131 554 7077
www.easy-arch-salv.co.uk

LASSco
30 Wandsworth Road
London SW8 2LG
Tel. +44 (0)20 7394 2100
www.lassco.co.uk
*Long established and comprehensive
salvage company*

Nostalgia
Hollands Mill,
Shaw Heath, Stockport
Cheshire, SK3 8BH
Tel. +44 (0)161 477 7706
www.nostalgia-uk.com
Large collection of reclaimed fireplaces

SALVO
www.salvoweb.com
Directory of salvage dealers

Walcot
The Yard
108 Walcot Street,
Bath BA1 5BG
Tel. +44 (0)1225 444404
www.walcot.com

Whole House Building Supply
1955 Pulgas Road
East Palo Alto
CA 94303
Tel. +1 650 856 0634
www.driftwoodsalvage.com

GREEN ROOFS

Bauder Ltd
Broughton House
Broughton Road
Ipswitch
Suffolk IP1 3QR
Tel. +44 (0)1473 257671
www.bauder.co.uk

ICB
Unit 1, Dominion Centre
Elliott Road
Bournemouth BH11 8JR
Tel. +44 (0)1202 579208
www.icb.uk.com
Sustainable roofing systems

Index Building Products Limited
17 Wigmore Street
London, W1U 1PQ
Tel. +44 (0)20 7409 7151
www.indexbp.co.uk
Green roof systems

Roofscapes Inc
7114 McCallum Street
Philadelphia
PA 19119
Tel. +1 215 247 8784
www.roofmeadow.com

ZinCo Premium Green Roof
Systems from Alumasc
White House Works, Bold Road,
Sutton, St. Helens
Merseyside WA9 4JG
Tel. +44 (0)1744 648400
www.alumasc-exteriors.co.uk
Green roof systems

GARDENING &
LANDSCAPE DESIGN

Aqua Landscape Design
c/o Castle Gardens
New Road
Sherborne
Dorset DT9 5NR
Tel. +44 (0)8458 123 222
www.aqualandscapedesign.co.uk
Natural pools

BBS Green Roofing
www.green-roofing.co.uk
Green roofs

British Wild Flower Plants
Burlingham Gardens
31 Main Road
North Burlingham NR13 4TA
Tel. +44 (0)1603 716615
www.wildflowers.co.uk

Ernst Conservation Seeds
9006 Mercer Pike
Meadville
PA 16335
Tel. +1 814 336 2404
www.ernstseed.com

Mobilane
P.O. Box 44
Stoke-on-Trent ST6 9AE
Tel. +44 (0)1870 2427710
www.mobilane.co.uk
*Green screens for your garden and
home*

The Reveg Edge
PO Box 361 Redwood City
CA 94064
Tel. +1 650 325 7333
www.ecoseeds.com

Wiggly Wigglers
Lower Blakemere Farm
Blakemere
Herefordshire HR2 9PX
Tel. +44 (0)1981 500391
www.wigglywigglers.co.uk
Compost bins and wormeries

INDEX

ACKNOWLEDGEMENTS

The publisher would like to thank the following photographers, agencies and designers for their kind permission to reproduce the following photographs:

3 Obie Bowman; 4 Tim Pyne Creative Director m-house; 8–9 Paul Warchol/Steven Holl Architects; 10 PA Photos/Riccardo de Luca; 12–13 Arcaid/Alan Weintraub/Backen Gillam Architects; 14 Photozest/Inside/Eric Saillet/Architect Bruno Pantz; 17 Jefferson Smith/Bere Architects; 18 Micheal Winter/Bill Dunster/Zedfactory; 21 Ake E:son Lindman/Architect Claesson Koivisto Rune; 22 View Pictures/Hufton and Crow/Sheppard Robson Architects; 24 Alamy/Chris Batson; 25 Reiner Blunck/Stuchbury & Pape; 26 Science Photo Library/David Nunuk; 27 Edifice/Gillian Darley; 28 Laurent Rouvrais; 29 left Laurent Rouvrais; 29 right IPC/Living etc/Dan Duchars; 30 Simon Kenny/architect John Cockings 31 View Pictures/ Hufton and Crow/Stephen Robson Architects; 34 Camera Press/MCM/Philippe Garcia; 35 Narratives/Jan Baldwin; 36 Alamy/Jan Sandvik; 37 view Pictures/Hufton and Crow/Stephen Robson Architects; 39–41 Michael Franke/Architect Bill Dunster/zedfactory; 43 Camera Press/Coté Sud/Bernard Touillon; 44 Alamy/Pearlimages; 45 Photozest/C Fiorentini; 46 Alamy/Mark Bolton; 47 Lluis Casals/Architect Victor Lopez Cotelo; 48 Photozest/Inside/D Vorillon/Archeo Architects & Putnam Pritchard; 49 Contactsphotography/Jared Fowler/Architect Donovan Hill; 51 Richard Davies/Seth Stein Architects; 52 Elizabeth Felicelli/Pulltab Design; 54 left Reiner Blunck/Bischof-Partner; 54 Right Solatube; 55 left Simon Kenny/Architect Bruce Rickard; 55 Right Michaelis Boyd

Architect/Richard Lewisohn; 56 Zapaimages.com/Conrad White; 57 Reiner Blunck/Bischof-Partner; 58 left Camera Press/MCM/Alexandre Weinberger; 58 Right Richard Davies/Architects Seth Stein; 60 Simon Kenny/ Architect John Cockings; 61 Laurent Rouvrais; 62 Simon Kenny/Architect Bruce Rickard; 63 GAP Photos/Elke Borkowski; 64–65 Richard Powers/Bark Design Architects; 66 Mainstream Images/Ray Main/architect Jonathan Manser; 68 Camera Press/MCM/Marie Kalt/Daniel Rozenstroch; 69 Simon Kenny/artist Jo Bertini; 70 left Alamy/ Andrew Butterton; 70 right Michael Franke; 71 above Narratives/Architect Annalie Riches; 71 below IPC + Syndication/Living Etc/Paul Massey; 72 left Eco Space/Andy Spain; 72 right Mainstreamimages /Ray Main/ Baileyshome andgarden.com; 73 above Mainstreamimages/Arch Mole Architects; 73 below Richard Barnes/Fougeron Architecture; 74–75 Simon Kenny/designer Genevieve Furzer; 76 left IPC + Syndication/Homes & Gardens/Tom Leighton; 76 right Camera Press/Coté Ouest/ Guillaume de Laubier; 77 left Taverne Agency/Prue Ruscoe/ Producer Tami Christiansen; 77 right Redcover.com/Winifried Heinze; 78 Michael Franke; 79 IPC + Syndication/Living Etc/Paul Raesdie; 80 Amy Eckert; 81 left Arcaid/Martine Hamilton-Knight; 81 right Jake Fitzjones/ www.burdhaward.com; 82 Interieurs/ChiChi Ubina; 83 above Narratives/Jan Baldwin/architect Derick de Bruyn; 83 below Michaelis Boyd Architect/Richard Lewisohn; 84 Camera Press/ MCM/Jerome Galland/architects Anne Lacaton and Jean-Pierre Vassal; 85 above Narratives/Jan Baldwin; 85 below Michaelis Boyd Architect/Richard Lewisohn; 86 left IPC +

Syndication/Living Etc/Thomas Stewart; 86 right Simon Kenny/architect Clinton Murray; 87 IPC + Syndication/ Homes & Gardens/Paul Raeside; 88 Mainstreamimages/Ray Main; 89 Paul Warchol/Seven Holl Architects; 90 left Richard Powers/Harvey Langston-Jones Architect; 90 right Simon Kenny/Architect Clinton Murray; 91 Richard Powers/Architect Harvey Langston-Jones; 92 Richard Powers/Lindsey Claire Architectus; 92–93 Taverme Agency/Nathalie Krag/Producer Tami Christiansen; 93 above Simon Kenny/Morgan Dickson Architects; 93 below Simon Kenny/Architects: Response Group/Perry ; 94–95 Degelo Architects/Rudi Walti; 97 Narratives/Alejandro Mezza & Escalante/Diego Montero; 98 Camera Press/MCM/Catherine Ardouin; 99 The Interior Archive/Mark Luscombe-White/design Lindi Trost; 100 Linnea Press/Heidi Lerkenfeldt/ styling Pernille Vest; 101 Richard Powers/Jenny Kee; 102 Tim Pyne Creative Director m-house; 105 above Jean-Baptiste Barache, Architect DPLG; 105 Centre and below Marcus Lee of FLACQ Architects; 107 Paul Smoothy/ Shariar Nasser/Belsize Architects; 108 above Paul Smoothly/Shahriar Nasser/ Belsize Architects; 108 below Camera Press/MCM/Gaelle le Boulicaut; 109 above Camera Press/MCM/V Leroux/Catherine Ardouin/Jacques Ferrier Architects; 109 below Richard Powers/MXA Development; 110–111 Michael Franke/FLACQ Architects; 112 left Camera Press/Maison Française/ Gaelle le Boulicaut; 112 Right Narratives/Jan Baldwin; 113 IPC + Syndication/Marie Claire/Rebecca Duke; 114 left Narratives/ Quickimage; 114 Right Obie Bowman/Tom Rider; 115 left Mainstreamimages/Ray Main; 115 Right Richard Powers;

116 Arcaid/Alan Weintraub/ Architect Howard Backen; 116 below Media 10 Images/Edina van der Wyck; 117 Reiner Blunck/Stutchbury & Pape; 118–119 Camera Press/MCM/ Gilles de Chabaneix; 121 Baufritz; 122 left Mainstream/Ray Main/ lasdun.com; 122 Right Narratives/Alejandro Mezza and Ezequiel Escalante. Architect Antonio Ledesma; 123 above Redcover.com/Warren Smith; 123 below Left IPC + Syndicatin/ Living Etc/Mikkel Vang; 123 below Right Narratives/A. Mezza & E. Escalante; 124 above Auro Paints; 124 below Holly Joliffe; 125 redcover.com/Paul Ryan/Goff; 127 Narratives/Jan Baldwin/Home of Alastair Hendy; 128 IPC + Syndication/Living Etc/Jennifer Cawley; 129 Camera Press/Home/ Anel van der Merwe; 131 Camera Press/ACP/Ute Wegmann; 132 Camera Press/MCM/Mai-Linh; 134 left Fab Pictures/ Thomas Ott; 134 Right View Pictures/Sue Barr/Robert Dye Associates; 135 Redcover.com/Dan Duchars; 136 Robert Dye Associates; 137 Robert Dye Associates/Julian Cornish Trestrail; 138 Above Left Richard Davies/Architects Seth Stein: 138 above Right Timothy Soar/RDA; 138 below Marcus Lee of FLACQ Architects; 139 left Ake E:son Lindman/ Architect Claesson Koivisto Rune; 139 Right Paul Smoothy/Shariar Nasser/Belsize Architects; 140 Camera Press/ Maison Française/Francis Amiand; 141 Arcaid designed by Paxton Locher Architects/Contact Alex Fergusson; 142 Arcaid/Backen Gillam Architects; 143 Marcus Lee of FLACQ Architects; 144 Simon Kenny/Architects Lindsay and Kerry Clare; 145 above Taverne Agency/Nathalie Krag/Producer: Tami Christiansen; 145 below Michael Lee of FLACQ; 146 Simon Kenny/Architects Lindsay and Kerry Clare; 147 Arcaid/Associated Architects; 148 Architect Kevin

Fellingham; 150 fabpics/Jésus Granada; 151 Ecoscene/Bruce Harber; 152 left Rex Features/ Geoffrey M Blackman; 152 Right Mainstream/Ray Main/ MichaelisBoyd.com; 153 Harpur Garden Images/Steve Putnam RHS Chelsea 2007; 154 Harpur Garden Library/Jeff Dutt and Philippa O'Brien RHS Chelsea 2003; 155 Camera Press/MCM/Gilles de Chabaneix; 156–157 Harrison Architects/Contractor: CJR Associates/Photo Rob Harrison; 158/MMGI/Marianne Majerus; 159 Arcaid/Associated Architects; 160 Gap Photos/Suzie Gibbons; 161 above Left MMGI/Bennet Smith, Holiday Inn Green Room, RHS Hampton Court Flower Show 2008, design: Sarah Eberle; 161 above Right Gap Photos/ Photos/Pernilla Bergdahi; 161 below Left Derek St Romaine/ design: Claire whitehouse, RHS Chelsea 2005; 161 below Right Derek St Romaine/design: Scenic Blue, RHS Chelsea 2007; 162 left Derek St Romaine/design Michael Gallais, Chaumont-sur-Loire 2001; 162 Right IPC + Syndication/ Country Homes & Interiors/Tim Young ; 163 left Gap Photos//Elke Borkowski; 163 Right Derek St Romaine/design Cleve West; 164 Gap Photos/Leigh Clapp; 165 above Eric Gizard Associé; 165 below Simon Kenny/designer Genevieve Furzer; 166 Derek St Romaine; 167 MMGI/Marianne Majerus, design: Stephen Hall; 168 Gap Photos/ Leigh Clapp; 169 Harpur Garden;Library; 170 Simon Kenny/designer Genevieve Furzer; 172 IPC + Syndication/ Beautiful Kitchens/Kristen Chamley; 173 IPC + Syndication/ Carolyn Barber; 175 IPC + Syndication/ Living Etc/Nick Keane; 176–177 Marianne Majerus; 178 Camera Press/ MCM/Mai-Linh; 180–181 Camera Press/MCM/Gaëlle Le Boulicaut; 182 Ed Reeve/Adjaye & Associates/ Eurban; 184–187 Reiner Blunck/

Glen Murcutt; 188–191 Espen Grønli/Henrik E Nielson Arkitektur; 192–195 Richard Halbe/Zoka Zola; 196–199 Ed Reeve/Adjaye & Associates/ Eurban; 200–203 Camera Press/MCM/ Philippe Garcia/Catherine Ardouin/ architecte Jean-Baptiste Barache; 204–207 Doug Fogelson/DRFP/ Wilkinson Blender Architects; 208–211 Simon Kenny/Roth Architects Pty; 212–215 View Pictures/Artur/Frank A Rummele/Frieder Gros ; 216–219 View Pictures/ESTO/ Peter Aaron/Joel Sanders Architects and Andrea Steele AND Architects; 220–223 Ake E:son Lindman/ Architect Claesson Koivisto Rune; 224–227 Simon Kenny/Sandberg Schoffel Architects; 228–231 Whitney Sander Catherine Holliss, Sander Architects; 232–235; Camera Press/Avantages/Paul Kozlowski; 236–239 View Pictures/ Peter Cook/Bere Architects; 237 Bere Architects/Jefferson Smith; 238 View Pictures/Peter Cook/Bere Architects ; 240–243 Photozest/ Inside/Eric Saillet/ architect Bertrand Bonnier; 244–247 Richard Barnes/Anne Fougeron Architects; 248 Marsh:Grochowski Architects; 249 Michael Franke/ Marsh: Grochowski Architects; 250 Marsh:Grochowski Architects 251 left Marsh:Grochowski Architects; 251 right Michael Franke/Marsh: Grochowski Architects; 253 Reiner Blunck/Bischof-Partner; 272 Taverne agency/Nathalie Krag.

Every effort has been made to trace the copyright holders. We apologize in advance for any unintentional omissions and would be pleased to insert the appropriate acknowledgement in any subsequent publication.